LIFE

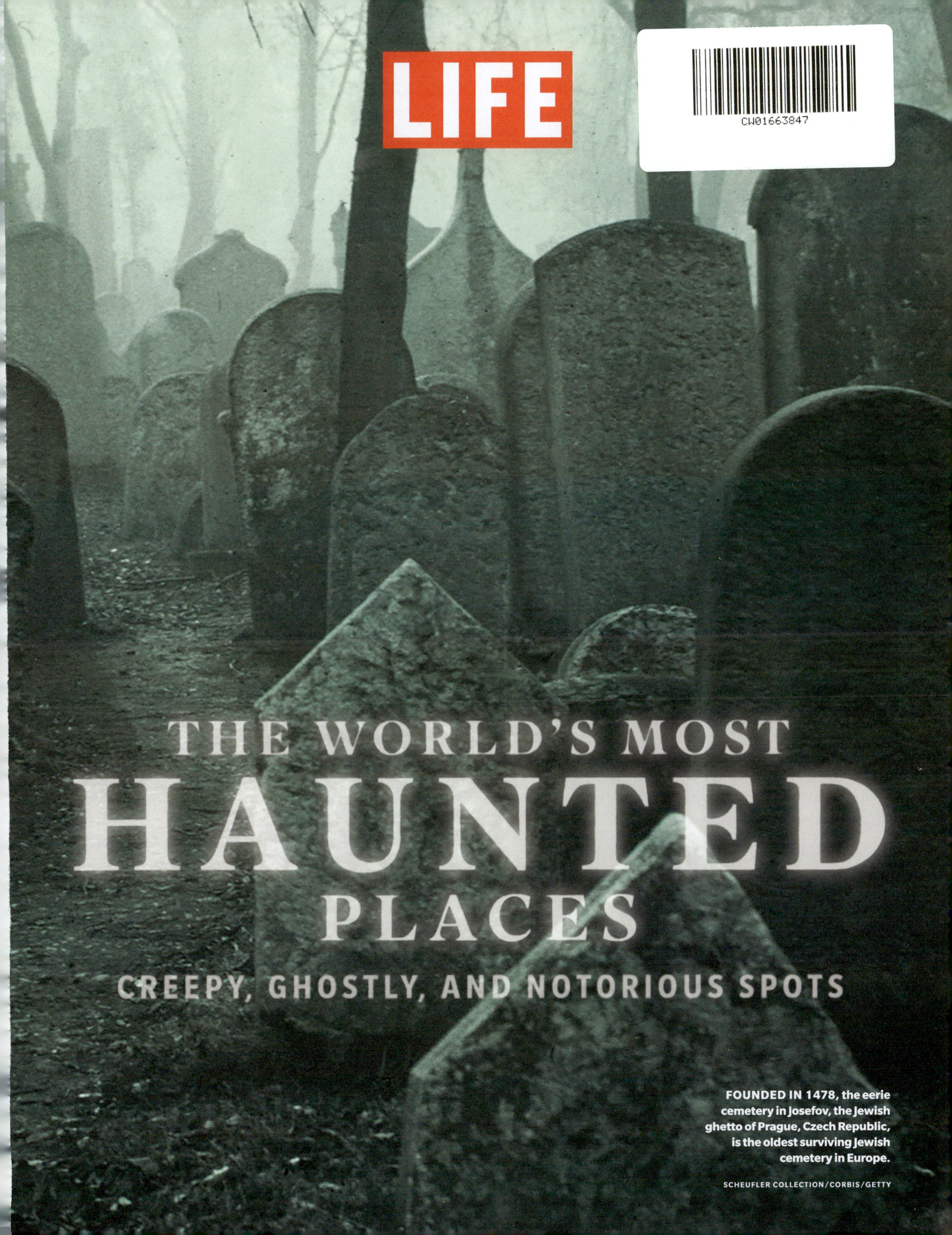

THE WORLD'S MOST HAUNTED PLACES

CREEPY, GHOSTLY, AND NOTORIOUS SPOTS

FOUNDED IN 1478, the eerie cemetery in Josefov, the Jewish ghetto of Prague, Czech Republic, is the oldest surviving Jewish cemetery in Europe.

SCHEUFLER COLLECTION/CORBIS/GETTY

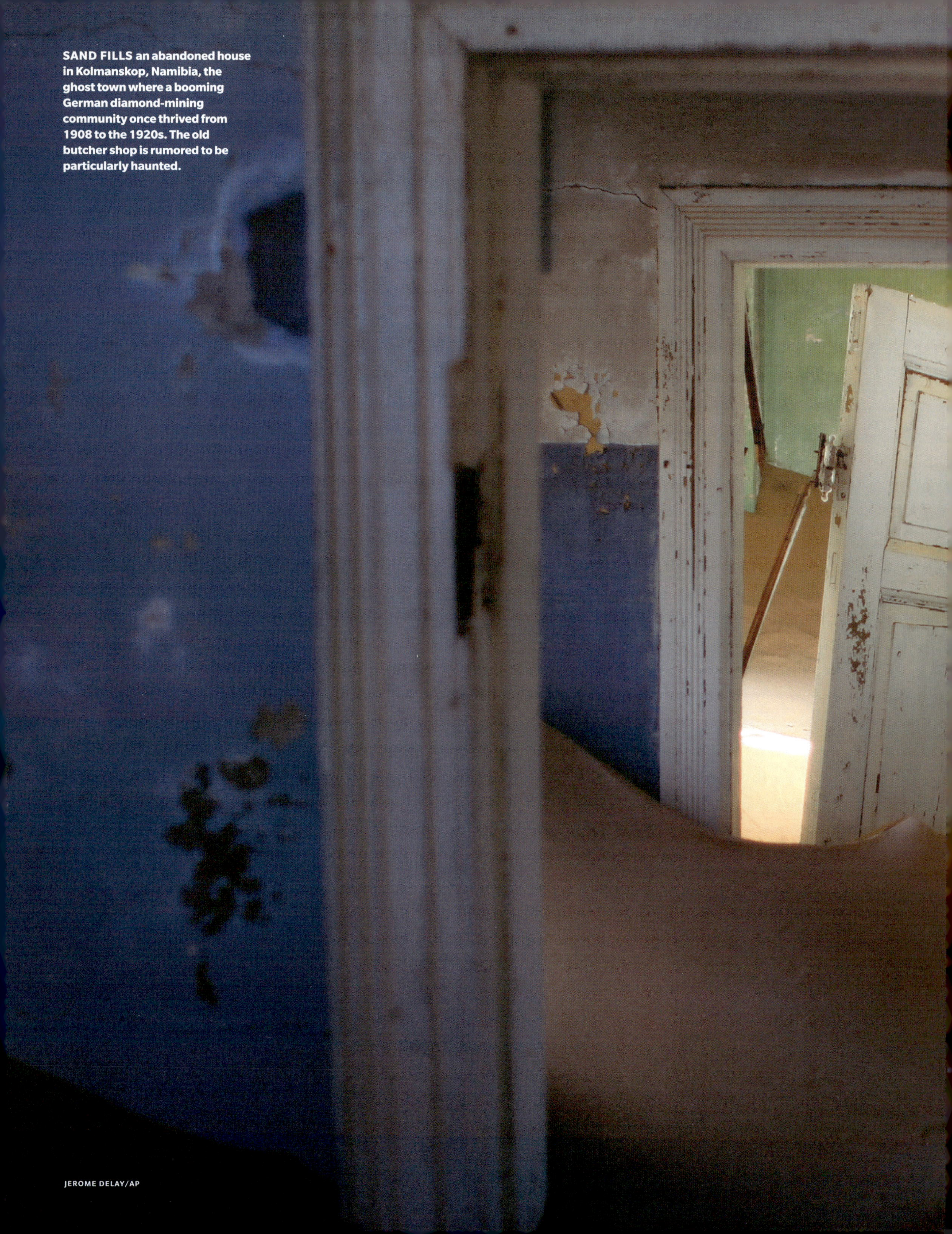

SAND FILLS an abandoned house in Kolmanskop, Namibia, the ghost town where a booming German diamond-mining community once thrived from 1908 to the 1920s. The old butcher shop is rumored to be particularly haunted.

JEROME DELAY/AP

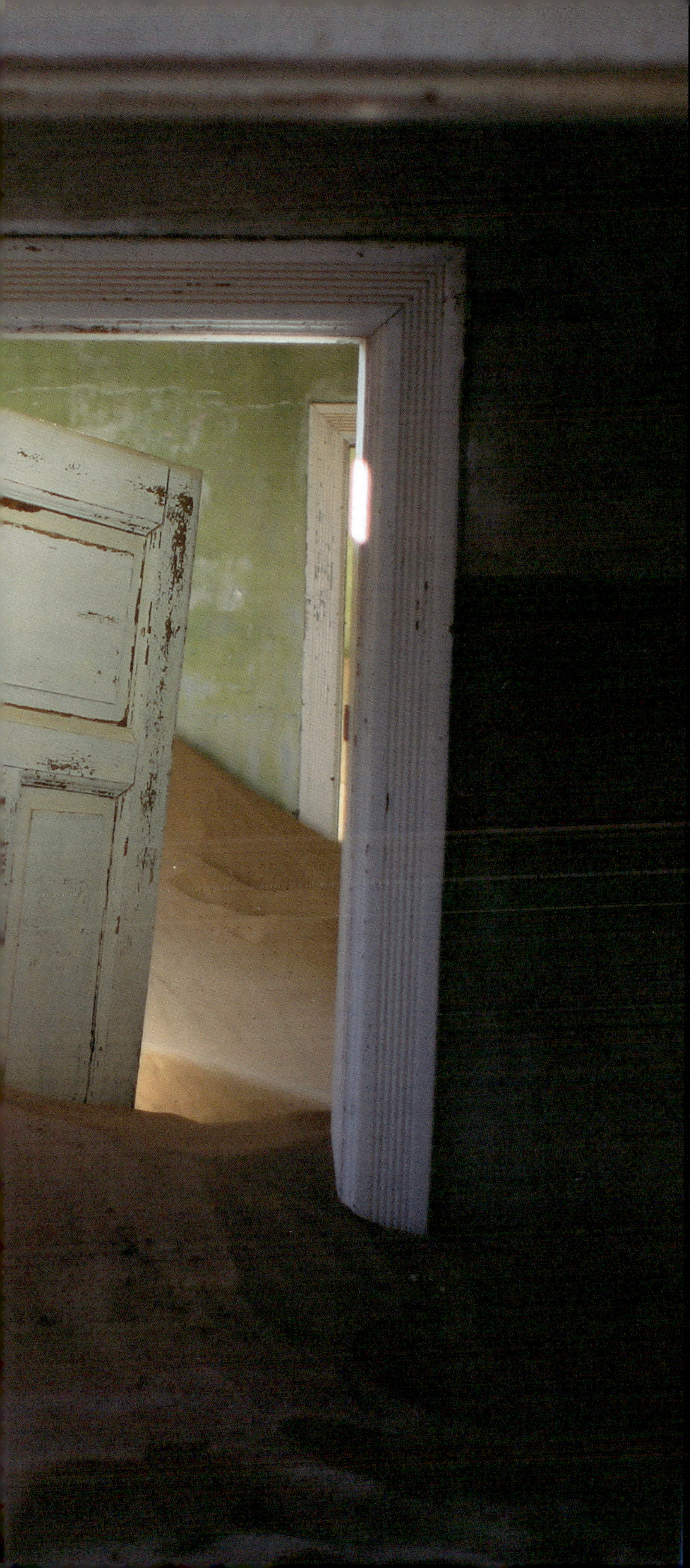

LIFE

The World's Most Haunted Places

Creepy, Ghostly, and Notorious Spots

EDITOR/WRITER J.I. Baker
DIRECTOR OF PHOTOGRAPHY Christina Lieberman
CREATIVE DIRECTOR Mimi Park/Design Park Inc.
COPY CHIEF Parlan McGaw
COPY EDITOR Joel Van Liew
PICTURE EDITOR Rachel Hatch
WRITER-REPORTERS
Amy Lennard Goehner, Daniel S. Levy
PHOTO ASSISTANTS Steph Durante (2018 Edition), Caitlin Powers

TIME INC. BOOKS, A DIVISION OF MEREDITH CORPORATION
SENIOR VICE PRESIDENT, FINANCE Anthony Palumbo
VICE PRESIDENT, MARKETING Jeremy Biloon
DIRECTOR, BRAND MARKETING Jean Kennedy
SALES DIRECTOR Christi Crowley
ASSOCIATE DIRECTOR, BRAND MARKETING
Bryan Christian
ASSOCIATE DIRECTOR, FINANCE Jill Earyes
SENIOR MANAGER, FINANCE Ashley Petrasovic
SENIOR BRAND MANAGER Katherine Barnet

EDITORIAL DIRECTOR Kostya Kennedy
CREATIVE DIRECTOR Gary Stewart
DIRECTOR OF PHOTOGRAPHY Christina Lieberman
EDITORIAL OPERATIONS DIRECTOR Jamie Roth Major
MANAGER, EDITORIAL OPERATIONS Gina Scauzillo

TIME INC. PREMEDIA
Richard K. Prue (Director), Richard Shaffer (Production), Keith Aurelio, Kevin Hart, Rosalie Khan, Patricia Koh, Marco Lau, Brian Mai, Rudi Papiri, Clara Renauro

SPECIAL THANKS Brad Beatson, Melissa Frankenberry, Kristina Jutzi, Kate Roncinske

Published by LIFE BOOKS, an imprint of Time Inc. Books
225 Liberty Street • New York, NY 10281

Vol. 18, No. 19 • September 28, 2018

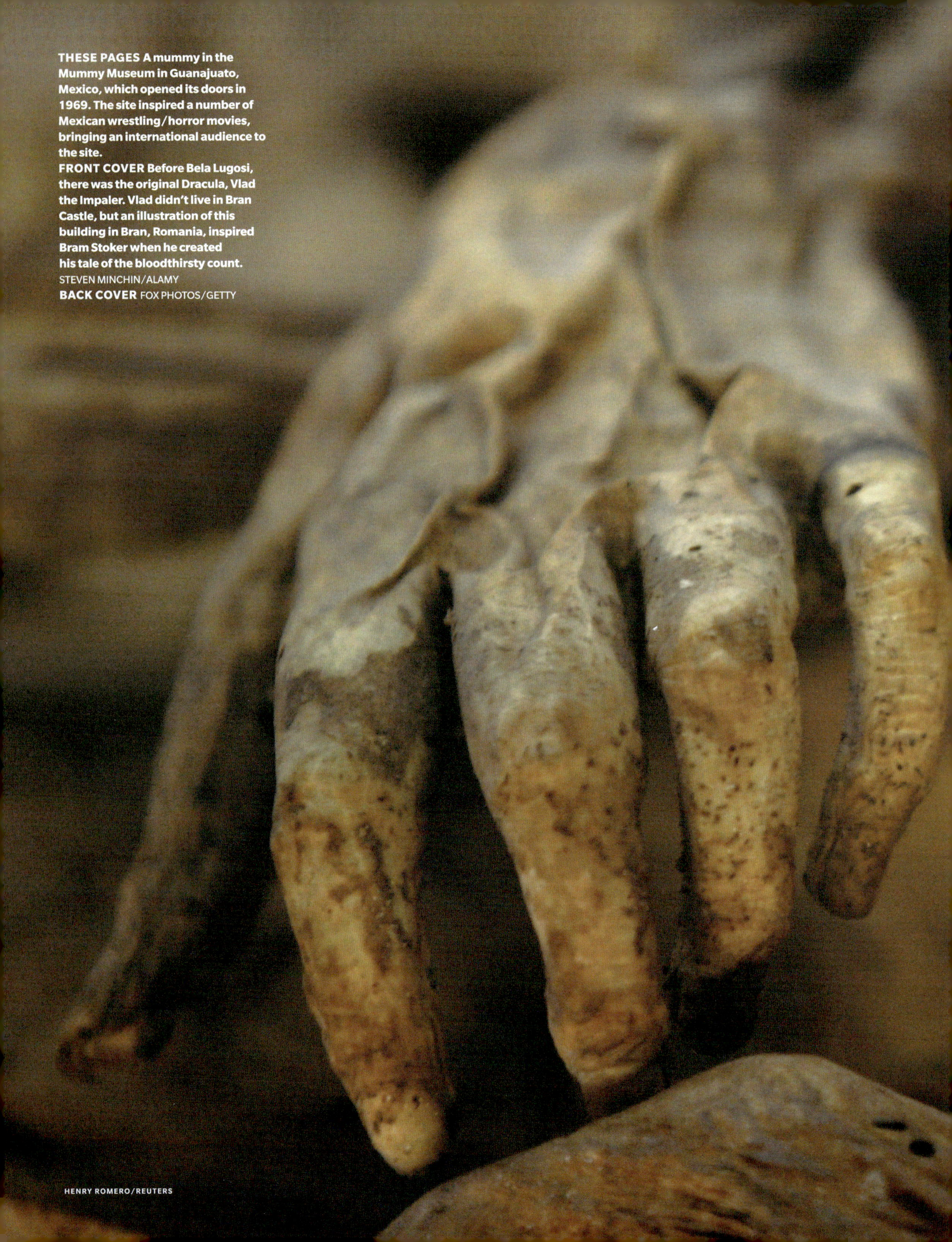

THESE PAGES A mummy in the Mummy Museum in Guanajuato, Mexico, which opened its doors in 1969. The site inspired a number of Mexican wrestling/horror movies, bringing an international audience to the site.

FRONT COVER Before Bela Lugosi, there was the original Dracula, Vlad the Impaler. Vlad didn't live in Bran Castle, but an illustration of this building in Bran, Romania, inspired Bram Stoker when he created his tale of the bloodthirsty count.
STEVEN MINCHIN/ALAMY

BACK COVER FOX PHOTOS/GETTY

HENRY ROMERO/REUTERS

CONTENTS

INTRODUCTION 6

GHOSTLY, GHASTLY U.S. & CANADA 8

SCARY, SPECTRAL LATIN AMERICA 36

BLOODY, BONE-CHILLING ASIA & AUSTRALIA 48

HAIR-RAISING, HAUNTED EUROPE 64

UNCANNY, UNEARTHLY AFRICA 88

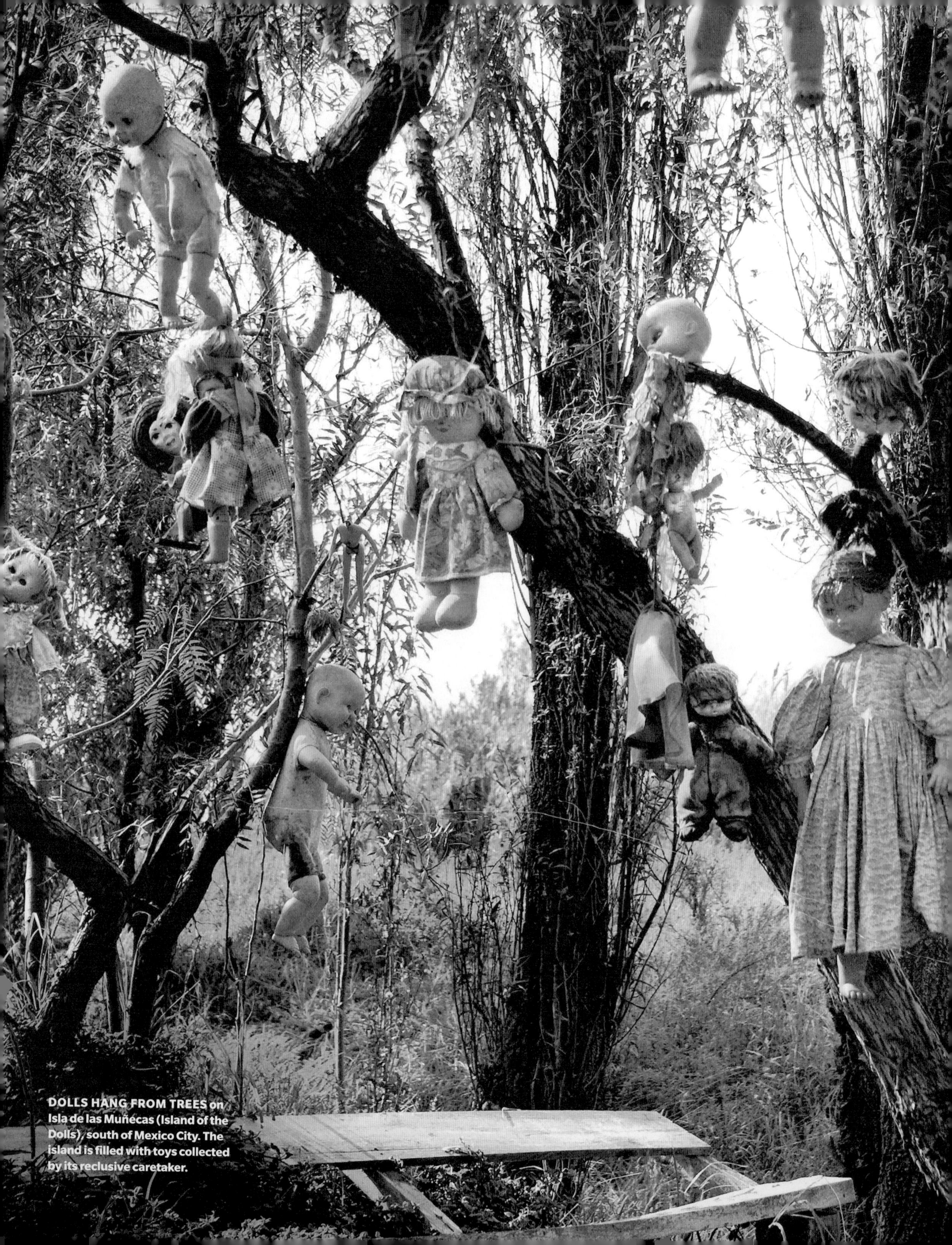

DOLLS HANG FROM TREES on Isla de las Muñecas (Island of the Dolls), south of Mexico City. The island is filled with toys collected by its reclusive caretaker.

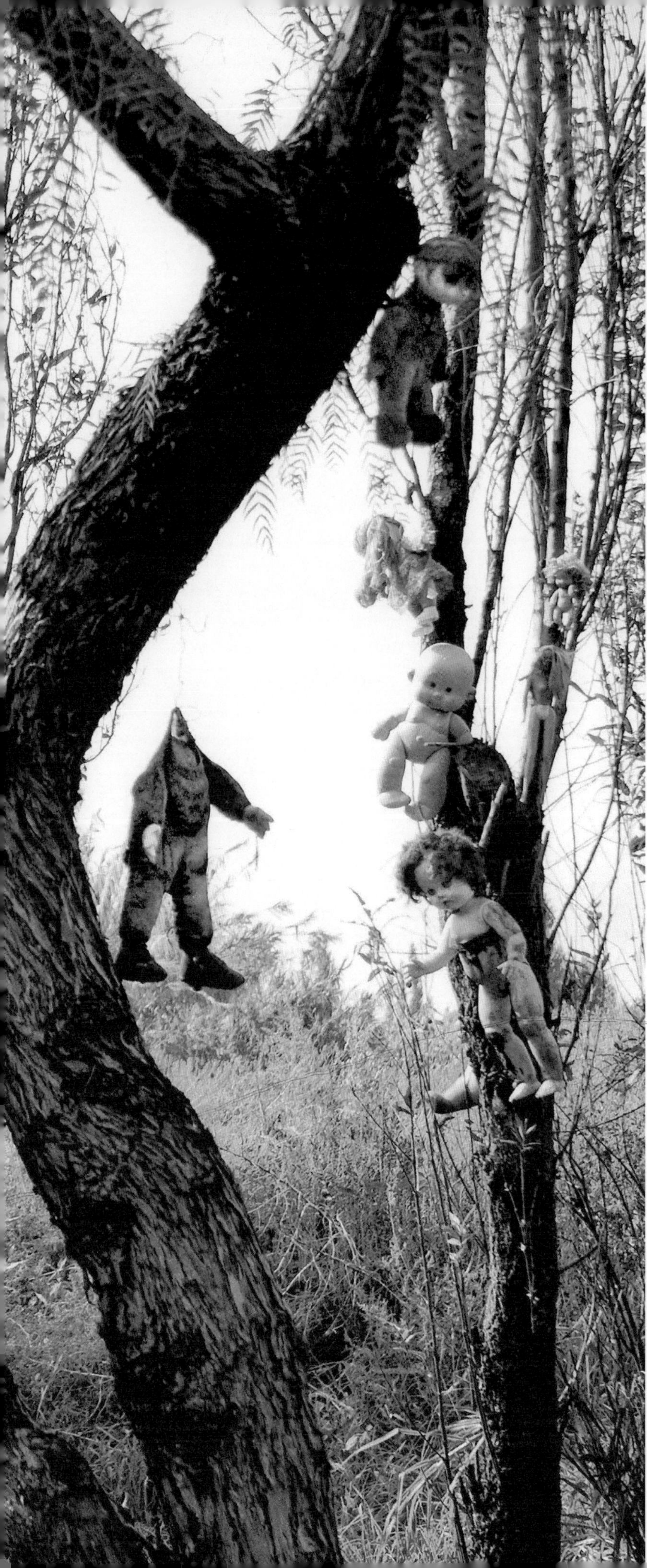

DAVID MAURICE SMITH/OCULI/REDUX

INTRODUCTION

BY J.I. BAKER

"THERE IS NO END to the old houses, with resounding galleries, and dismal state-bedchambers, and haunted wings shut up for many years, through which we may ramble . . . and encounter any number of ghosts," Charles Dickens once wrote.

The great English writer might as well have added Polish caves, Babylonian ruins, and Mexican mummy museums to his list of ghostly places—as we here at LIFE have done, bringing you a book filled with blood-curdling photos and eerie stories about the world's creepiest spots. Think the hotel that inspired *The Shining,* the *Amityville Horror* house, and the dilapidated farm that was home-sweet-home to the serial killer who inspired *The Texas Chainsaw Massacre, The Silence of the Lambs,* and *Psycho.*

No, not all these spots are strictly haunted. Some—like Australia's Uluru (a.k.a. Ayers Rock) or the ancient ruins submerged under South America's Lake Titicaca—are deeply mysterious, maybe even spiritual. Others—like Kolmanskop, Africa's sand-covered ghost town—are downright unnerving. But they all have one thing in common: They seem to exist partly in the known world, and partly in a shadowy realm we can't completely comprehend.

So get ready, if you dare, to encounter any number of ghosts, ghouls, yetis, haunted dolls—and other things that go bump in the night. ■

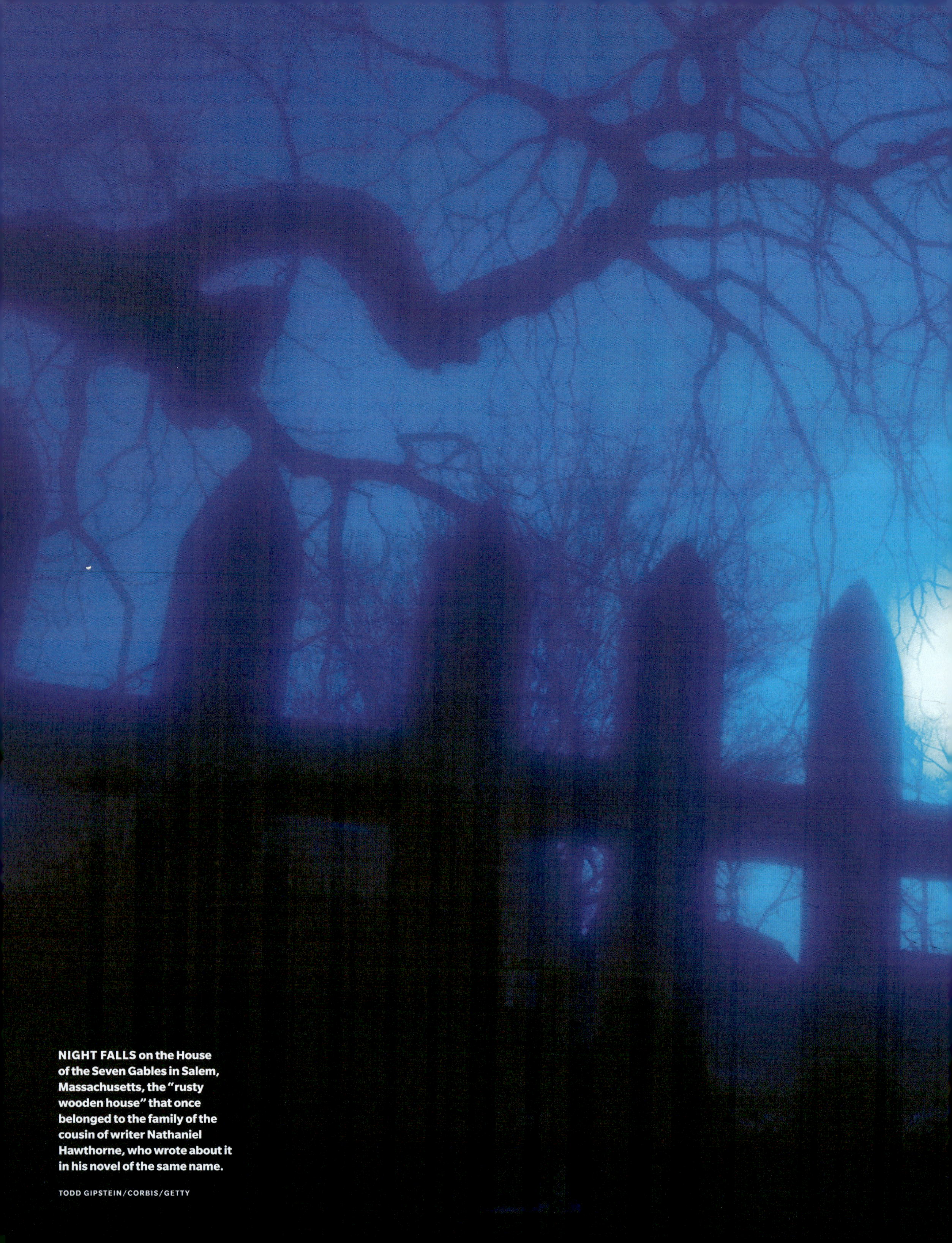

NIGHT FALLS on the House of the Seven Gables in Salem, Massachusetts, the "rusty wooden house" that once belonged to the family of the cousin of writer Nathaniel Hawthorne, who wrote about it in his novel of the same name.

TODD GIPSTEIN/CORBIS/GETTY

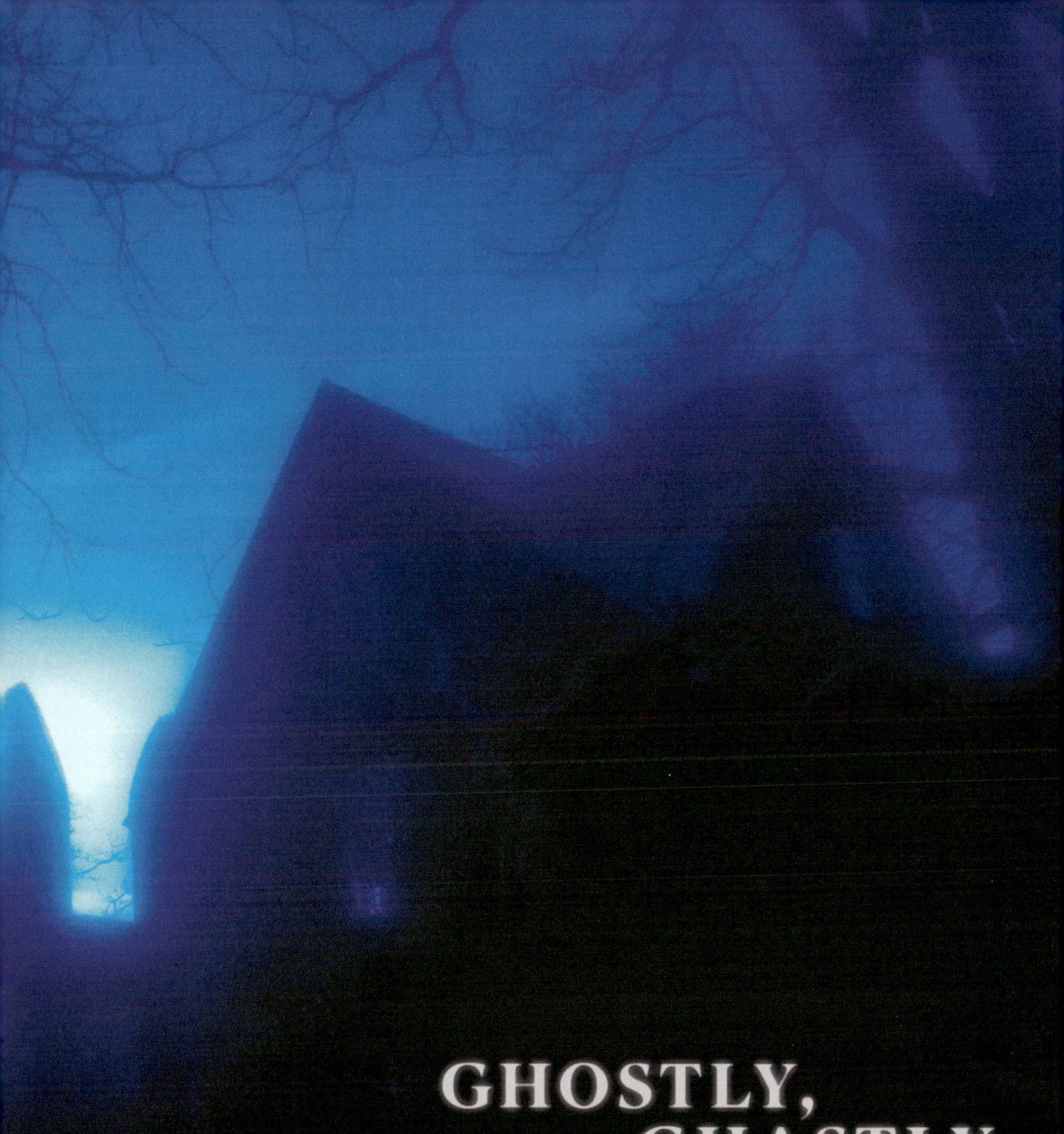

GHOSTLY, GHASTLY U.S. & CANADA

Here in the New World there are plenty of old ghosts—from steamy spirits Down South to the wintry wraiths of the Great White North

THE PARANORMAL PRISON

ALCATRAZ

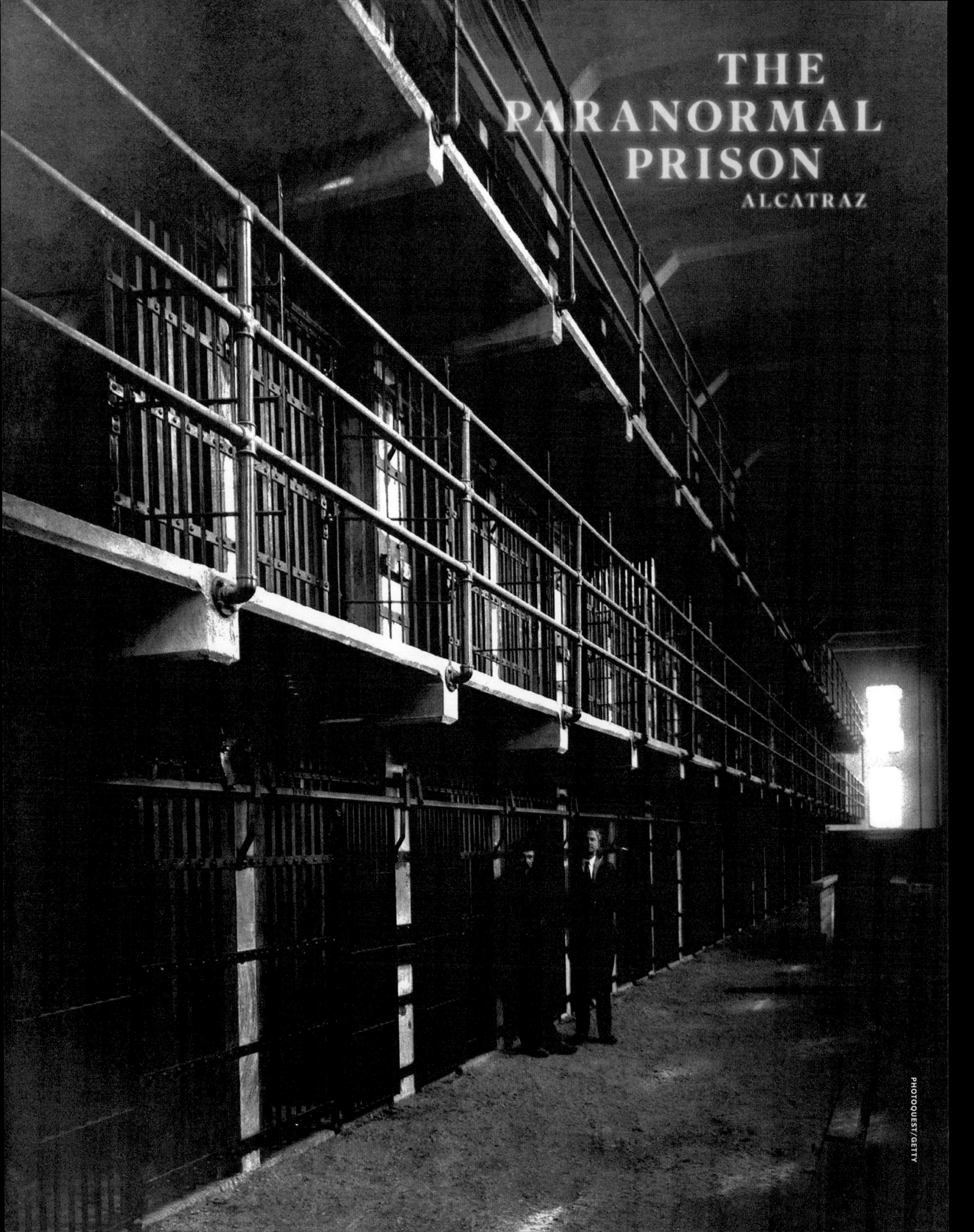

PHOTOQUEST/GETTY

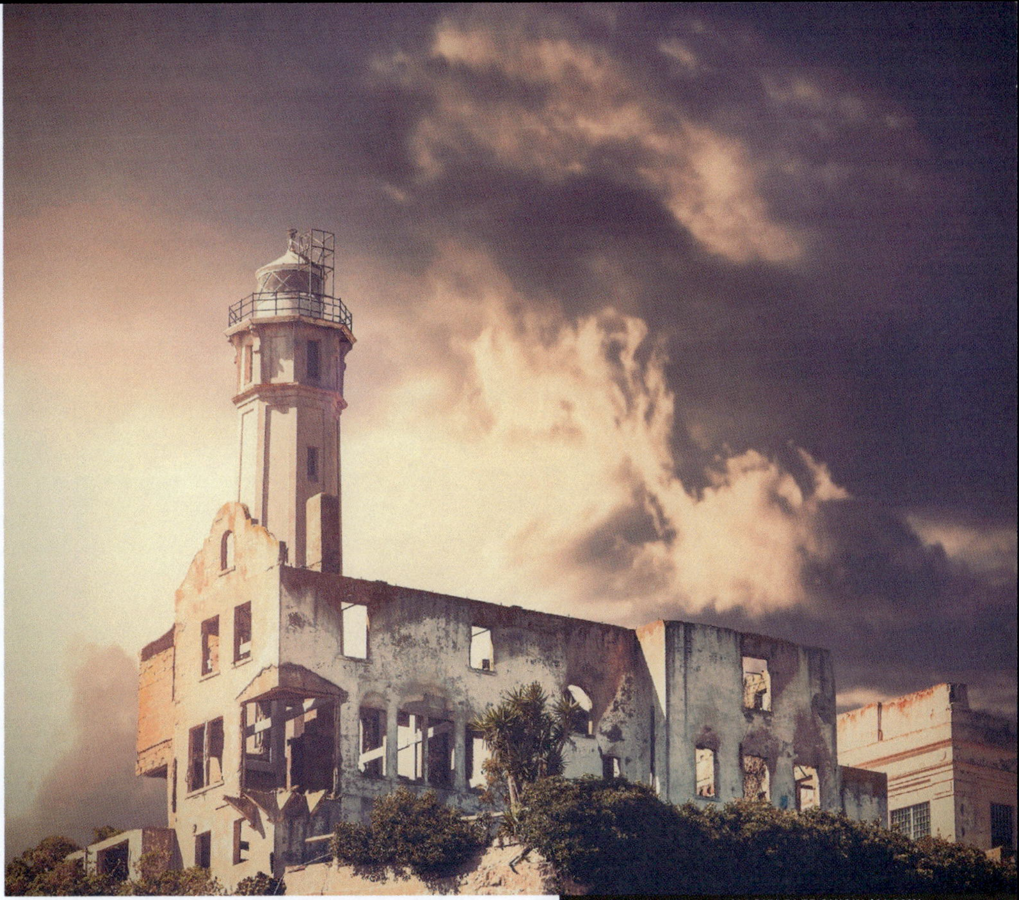

MACIEJ BLEDOWSKI/ALAMY

ON MAY 2, 1946, in what became known as the Battle of Alcatraz, six prisoners overpowered guards, stole their weapons, and tried to escape from the prison on this isolated island in San Francisco Bay. But when they realized they were missing the key they needed to flee into the recreation yard, they grew desperate, took captives, and started shooting.

Over the next 48 hours, two prison officers were killed and 18 injured. Three would-be escapees were shot to death in the utility corridor between cell blocks—the very spot that, 36 years later, San Francisco radio anchor Ted Wygant was exploring with a psychic when he was overcome by a feeling of violence and evil. "I got this tremendous feeling of anger," he told the Travel Channel. "I felt this presence beneath us in the dirt where these three men had died."

This is only one of many supernatural stories involving the so-called Rock, which has been a Civil War fortress, a bird sanctuary, and the birthplace of the American Indian Red Power movement—in addition to the brutal home for thousands of hardened convicts. Rejected as unmanageable by other prisons, these men were called the Incorrigibles, according to former inmate Leon "Whitey" Thompson. "You step on a toe, it's gonna wind up in a death."

Many of these long-departed inmates are now said to be unruly spirits. A spectral Al Capone has been heard practicing his banjo in the shower room. (He was a member of the prison band the Rock Islanders.) Mobster Alvin "Creepy" Karpis calls the bakery and kitchen home, while George "Machine Gun" Kelly has reportedly materialized in the chapel.

But the most haunted spot in the prison, according to many paranormal investigators, is D Block, the site of the infamous 1946 escape attempt—and of the island's best spook story. Though the tale seems apocryphal, it's too good not to mention: A prisoner locked in cell 14-D—one of the "Hole" cells—supposedly screamed that someone else was in the dark, cramped space with him. When guards finally opened the door, they found him dead, strangulation marks from a spectral attacker on his neck. This little setback did not, however, prevent the late prisoner's ghost from showing up for roll call that night.

Unlike so many haunted places, Alcatraz doesn't commercially capitalize on its reputation. In fact, the National Park Service calls the spook stories "flights of fancy," as does the island's official tour website: "There are no authenticated cases of ghost sightings by any of Alcatraz's residents over the years, whether they were soldiers, prisoners, correctional officers, family members or park rangers," the site reads.

But how would you "authenticate" a ghost sighting, anyway? And former prisoner Thompson, for his part, believes the hype. "This island is haunted," he said. "It is the island of the damned." ■

ABOVE: ALCATRAZ Island in San Francisco Bay. Opposite: The view along the notorious D Block. In 2014, a British tourist saw the dark specter of a woman in a picture she took of the former visitation room. A trick of the light? A hoax? Possibly.

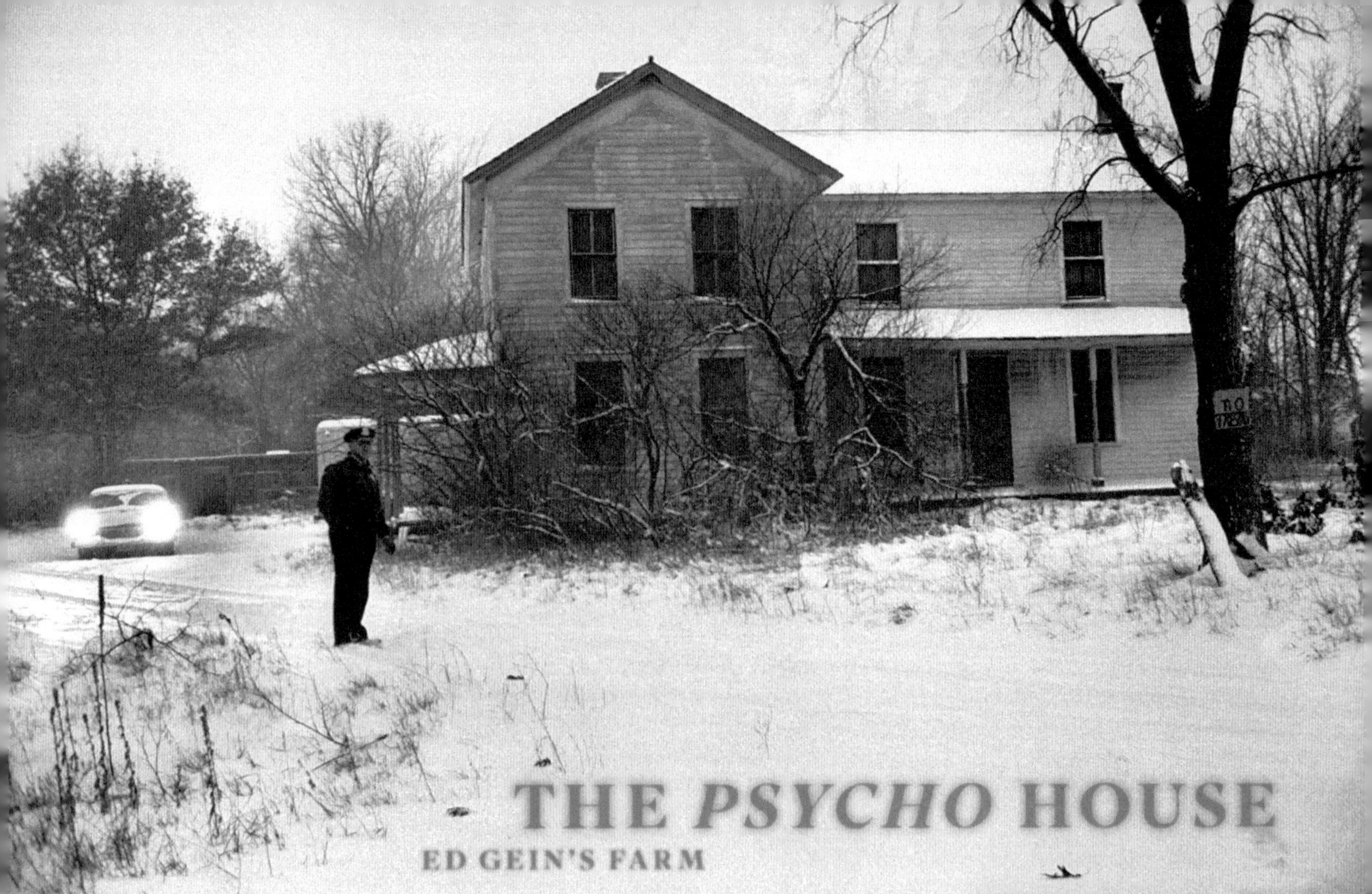

THE *PSYCHO* HOUSE

ED GEIN'S FARM

FRANK SCHERSCHEL/LIFE/THE PICTURE COLLECTION

SOMEWHERE in the Plainfield, Wisconsin, cemetery lies an unmarked grave belonging to the man who—thanks to his Hollywood influence—may be America's most infamous serial killer. In the same burial ground lies what remains of the women he dug up in the 1950s—and turned into a perverse variety of handicrafts. Not surprisingly, the place is said to be haunted by the restless soul of one of the fiend's victims—unnamed in death as in life—prowling the lonely graves.

In November 1957, Plainfield was shaken to its core after 58-year-old Bernice Worden, owner of the local hardware store, disappeared. Her son told the local sheriff that he'd found blood in the store—and that a 51-year-old local handyman named Ed Gein had recently come in looking for antifreeze.

Tracing Gein down to the ramshackle, isolated farmhouse where the odd man had lived alone since the death of his mother, the sheriff found Worden hanging by her feet, decapitated and eviscerated, in the shed.

But that was only the beginning of the horror.

In the garbage-strewn house, law enforcement officers found chairs reupholstered with fatty human skin; a soup bowl made from a human skull; a shade-pull made of lips; masks made from human faces; a belt made of female nipples; a vest made from a female torso; embalming supplies; and anatomy books and detective magazines that Gein read by kerosene lamps. There were also human heads—one belonging to Mary Hogan, who had run a Plainfield tavern and had mysteriously disappeared in 1954.

In the end, the remains of 11 women were discovered in the house.

Continued on page 15

ABOVE: On November 20, 1957, a deputy sheriff stands outside of the Plainfield, Wisconsin, farmhouse belonging to mass murderer Ed Gein (opposite), following the discovery of bodies and body parts inside. "Edward Gein had two faces," wrote the *Stevens Point Journal*. "One he showed to the neighbors. The other he showed only to the dead."

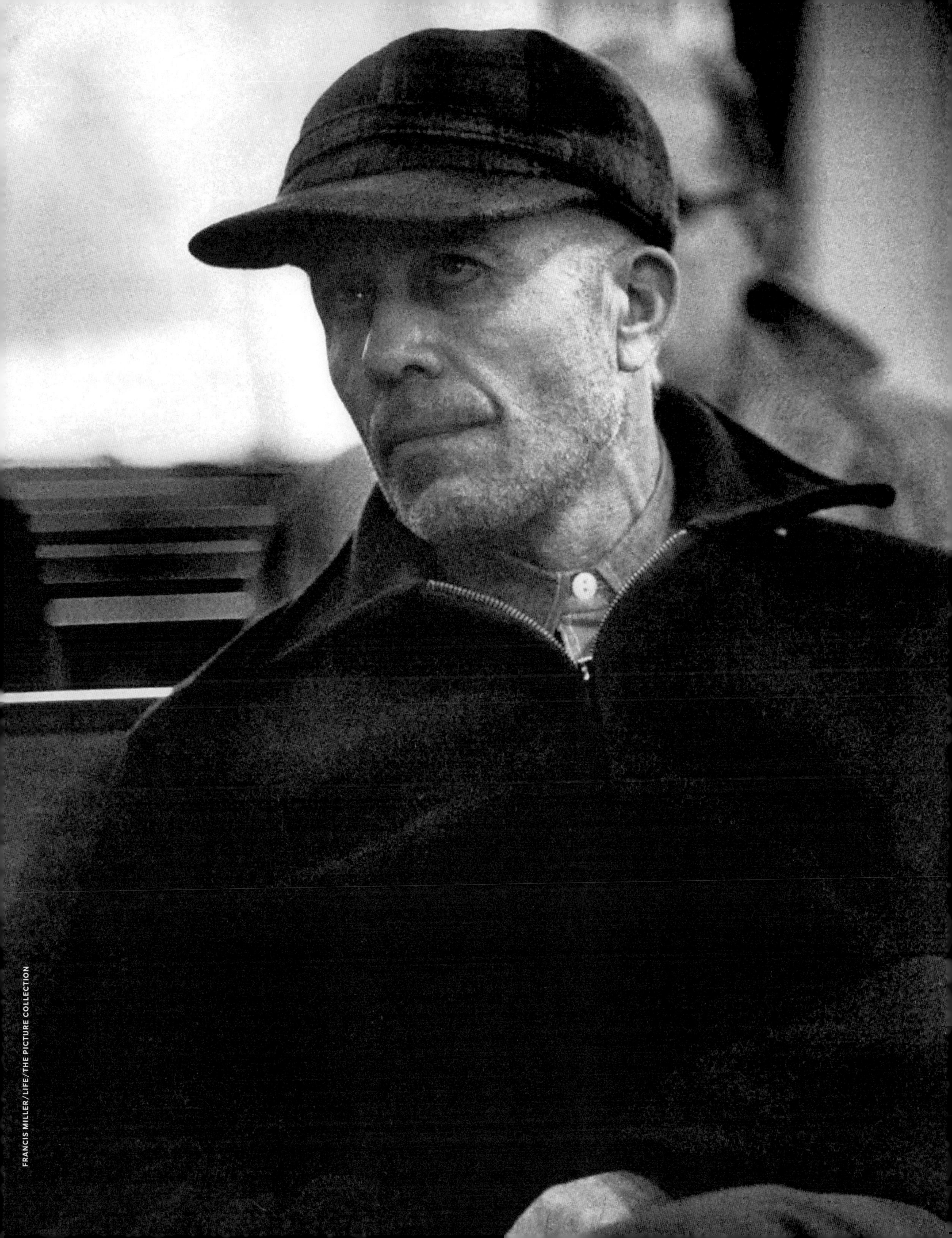

FRANCIS MILLER/LIFE/THE PICTURE COLLECTION

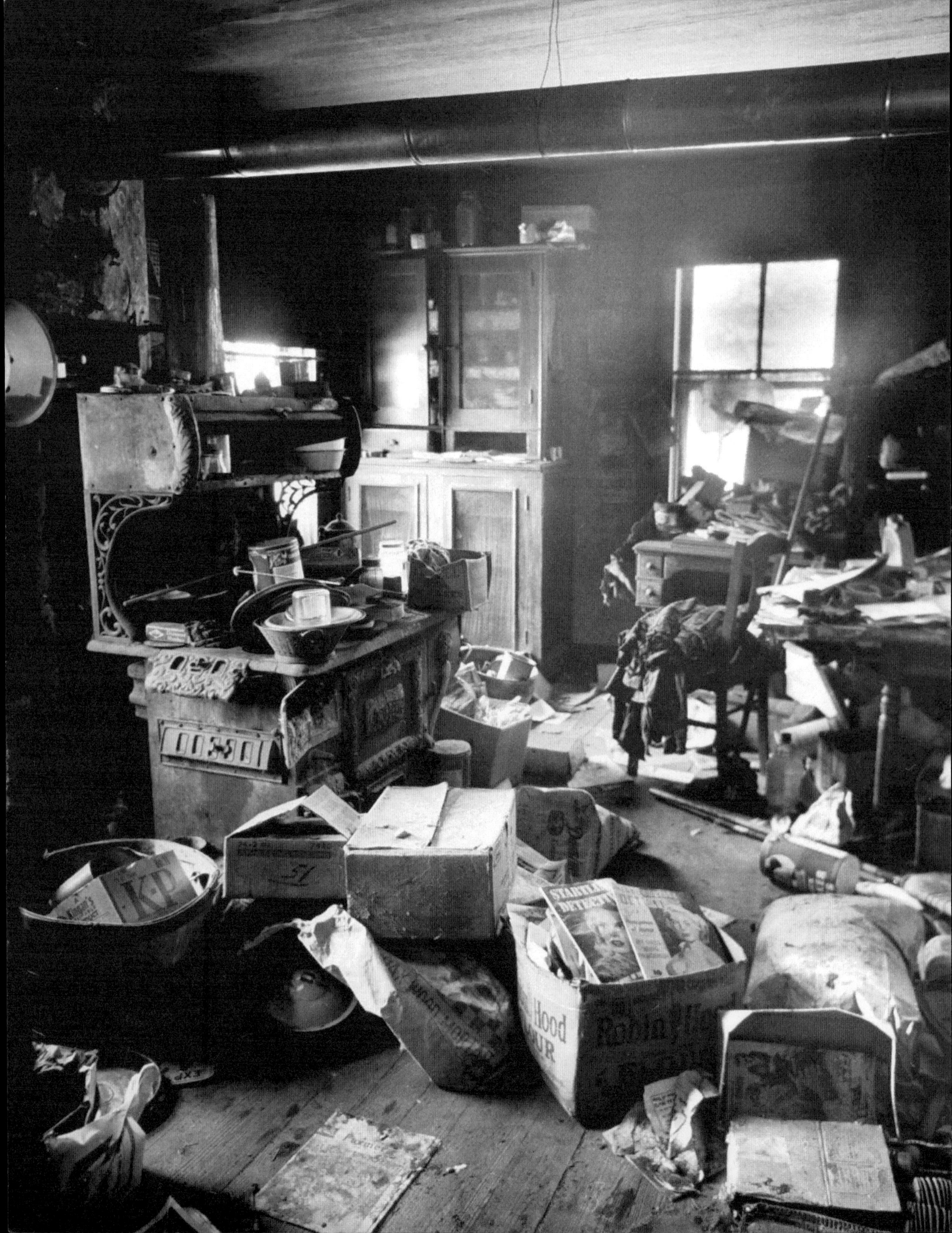
K-P
Hood

Two of them (Hogan and Worden) Gein claimed to have shot to death; nine had been, he said, unearthed from local graves. Many of them had been "tanned," as with taxidermy, their flesh used by Gein as garments.

The only immaculate part of the dwelling was the nailed-shut room that had belonged to Gein's mother, Augusta. The fanatically religious woman had subjected her unstable son to ceaseless rants about the evils of women. Her alcoholic husband, George, died in 1940, followed by Gein's brother, Henry, under mysterious circumstances in 1944, leaving Gein to share the house with his mommy, the love of his life. But when Augusta, too, died in 1945, Gein found himself alone.

Well, *almost.* The necrophiliac bachelor started digging up graves, using the remains of female bodies for company. He dressed in woman's clothes, some fashioned from corpses, wishing that he had been born a woman (his mother had prayed for a daughter).

Gein's oblivious neighbors found him mostly harmless. "Ed Gein baby-sat for me once for about an hour," local resident Mrs. George Foster told LIFE. "Just sat there, ate peaches, and watched TV." Locals did, however, acknowledge that he was odd. He talked obsessively, for instance, about crime and women. Former girlfriend (imagine!) Adeline Watkins said, "We discussed every murder we heard about. Eddie explained the mistakes the murderer made."

Declared insane in 1958, Gein died of cancer at age 77 in Mendota Mental Health Institute. But his perverse legacy endures, having inspired some of the greatest horror films ever made, among them *The Texas Chainsaw Massacre, The Silence of the Lambs,* and a little-known classic called *Deranged.*

But the most enduring product of the Gein legend began in 1959 when writer Robert Bloch published a potboiler called *Psycho,* which Alfred Hitchcock turned into the classic 1960 film. In it, Norman Bates, the character based on Gein, says, "A boy's best friend is his mother."

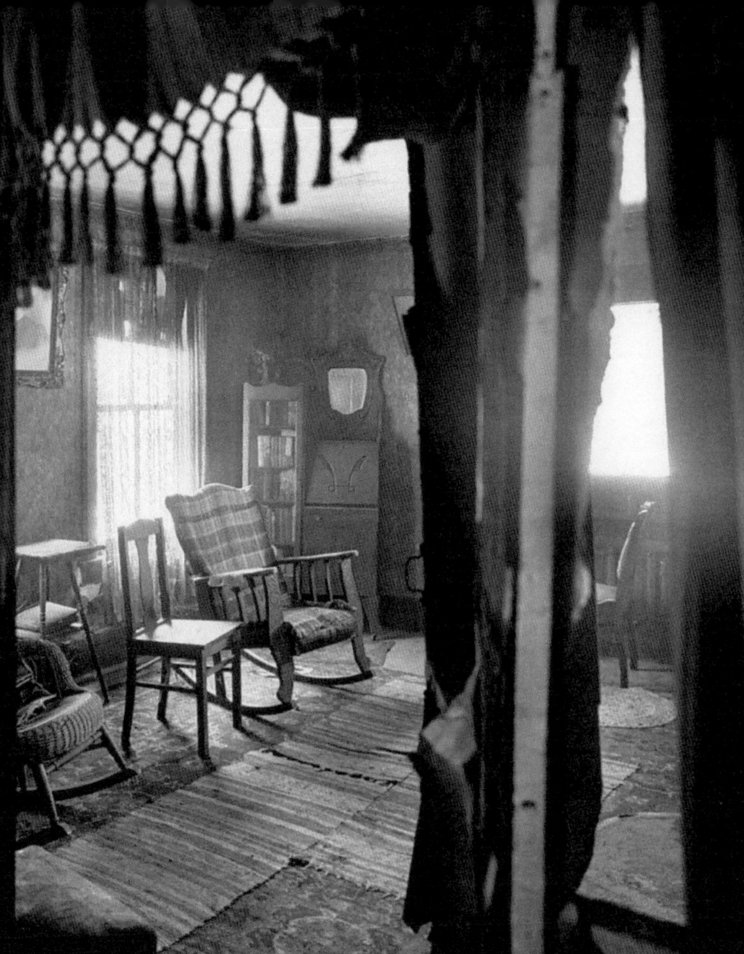

FRANK SCHERSCHEL/LIFE/THE PICTURE COLLECTION (2)

SUNSET BOULEVARD/CORBIS/GETTY

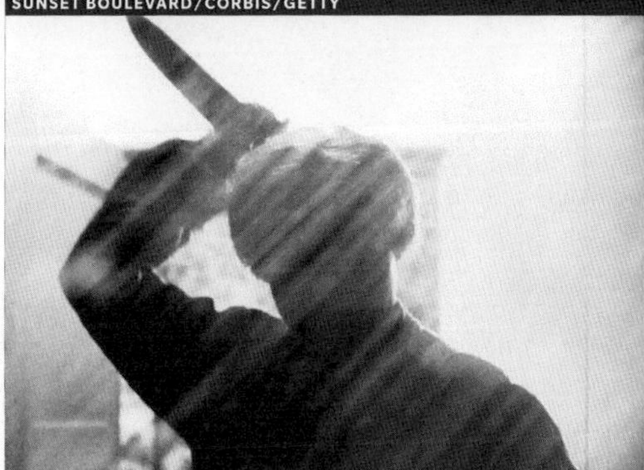

VORTEX-HENKEL-HOOPER/BRYANSTON/KOBAL/REX/SHUTTERSTOCK

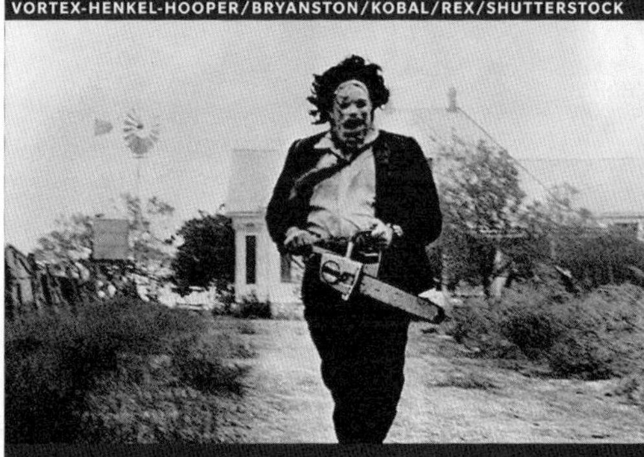

ORION/COURTESY EVERETT

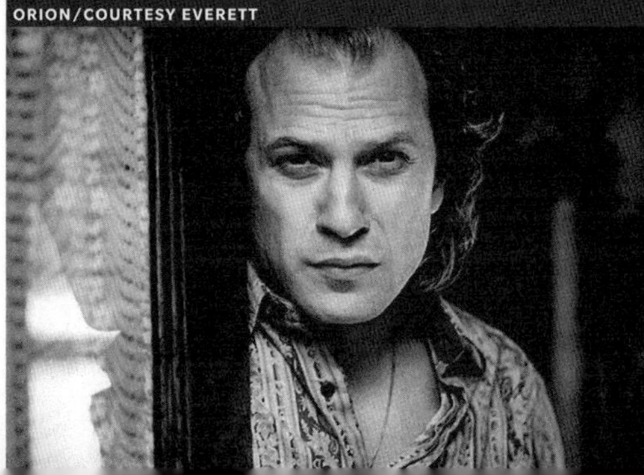

OPPOSITE PAGE: Ed Gein's filthy kitchen, where (among other horrors) a chair was found that had been "reupholstered" in human skin. (Three more were eventually discovered.) A study in contrast: Above, the tidy room that belonged to the ghoul's beloved mother. After Mommy Dearest's death in 1945, her room was locked and never entered. At left, some of the classic films and characters inspired by the Gein story: From top, Norman/Norma Bates in *Psycho;* Leatherface in the first version of *The Texas Chainsaw Massacre;* and Jame Gumb (a.k.a. Buffalo Bill) in *The Silence of the Lambs.*

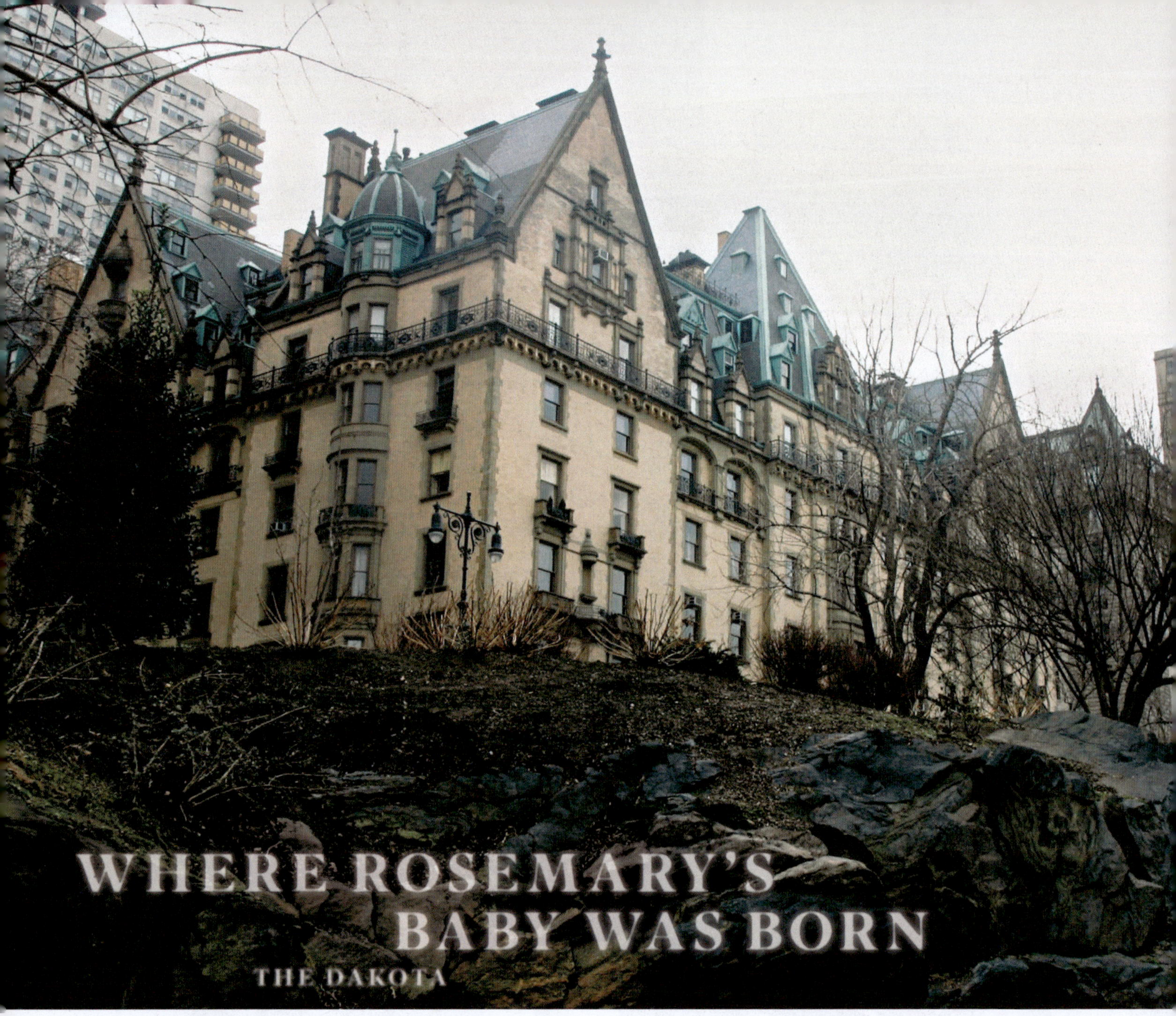

WHERE ROSEMARY'S BABY WAS BORN

THE DAKOTA

WHEN JOHN LENNON and Yoko Ono moved into the Dakota on 72nd Street and Central Park West in 1973, they were well aware the building was rumored to be haunted. So they hired a medium to conduct a séance in their seventh-floor apartment—and reached Jessie Ryan, the recently departed wife of *Dirty Dozen* actor Robert Ryan, who'd sold them the unit.

No blithe spirit, Jessie promptly announced that she intended to stay in the couple's digs, which did not make the Ryans' daughter Lisa happy. "If my mother's ghost belongs anywhere," she told Ono, "it's here with me."

Most of the Dakota's spirits don't belong here, of course, but they seem to have been in residence since the building was completed in 1884. Built for Singer Sewing Machine president Edward S. Clark in Manhattan's then-rural Upper West Side, the German Renaissance Revival structure was reportedly called the Dakota because its location was "as remote as Dakota Territory."

Over time, the Dakota's sinister reputation has grown along with its environs. This was, after all, where Lennon was murdered in 1980. And

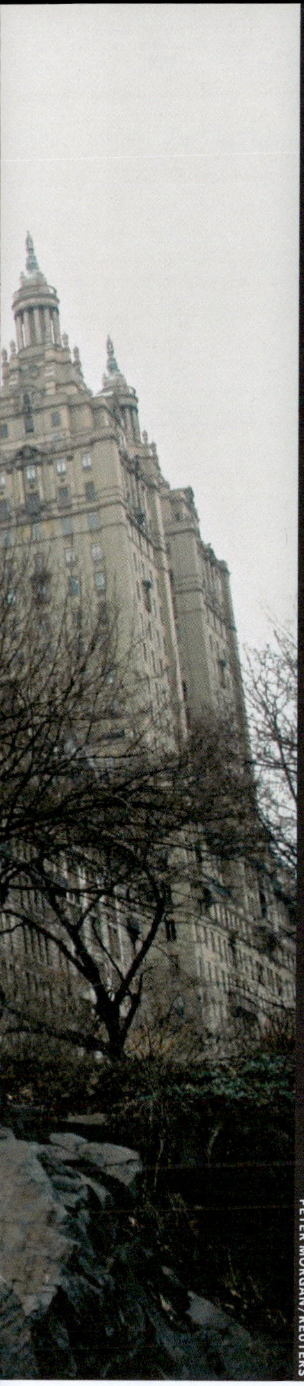

PETER MORGAN/REUTERS

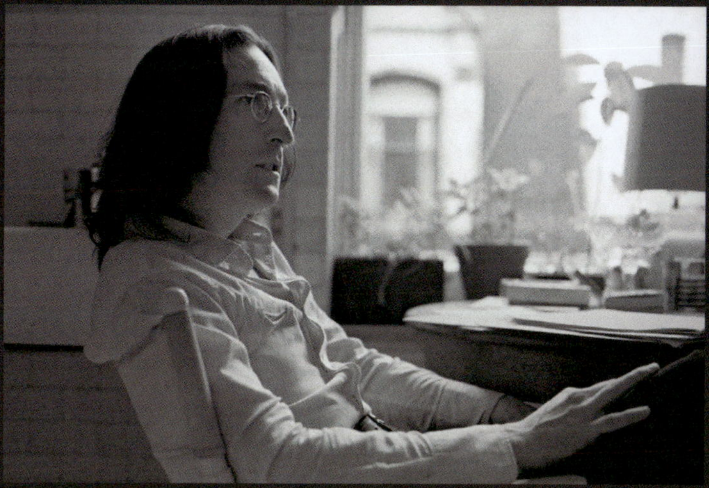

BRIAN HAMILL/GETTY

FAR LEFT: Melanie Griffith, Antonio Banderas, Cher, and Billy Joel are among the rich and famous who have been denied membership to one of Manhattan's most exclusive clubs: residents of the Dakota apartment building. But plenty of ghosts—including one who insisted on living with John Lennon and Yoko Ono—never had to gain the co-op board's approval. At left: Lennon sits in the kitchen of his Dakota apartment in 1975. Below: The building's entrance, where Lennon was shot on December 8, 1980, seen on the 23rd anniversary of his death.

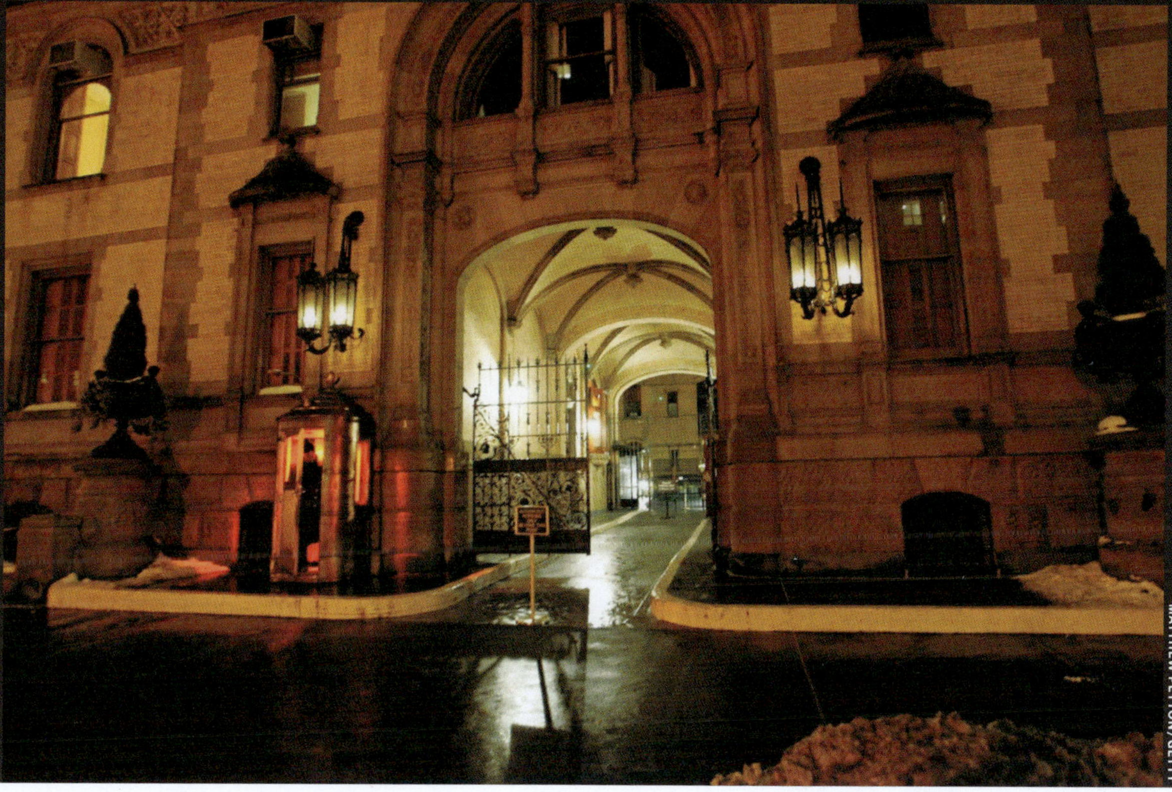

MATTHEW PEYTON/GETTY

Ira Levin used it as the setting for his classic 1967 novel, *Rosemary's Baby.* Though the novelist called it the "Black Bramford," he drew on the Dakota's dark mojo for inspiration. "Over the years," one character said, "the Bramford has had far more than its share of ugly and unsavory happenings."

In Levin's world, these include cannibalism, witchcraft, satanism, and murder. But he may well have added the "real-life" spirit of a beautiful blonde girl in a yellow dress. Some have called her the "house ghost," others a bad omen. "It's my birthday," she allegedly said to a painter who later fell to his death. Others have seen the ghost of a man with the face of a small boy. And a mysterious fire started inside writer Rex Reed's apartment. "I thought, 'Welcome to the Dakota!'" he later told Stephen Birmingham in *Life at the Dakota.*

Here, elevators move on their own. Footsteps are heard where no mortal walks. Rumblings sound through the walls, and the past seems to coexist with the present. A chandelier was seen through the window of one resident's apartment as he walked to the building—despite the fact that he had no chandelier, only the remains of one.

Many phenomena seem to emanate from the basement—including the so-called Man with a Wig, who is known for taking off his wig and shaking it angrily. In Levin's novel, Rosemary calls the basement "kind of creepy." So does singer Roberta Flack, a longtime resident who refuses to enter it. "This building has been occupied by a lot of strong people," she told Birmingham. "They stay, they have memories. They come back." ■

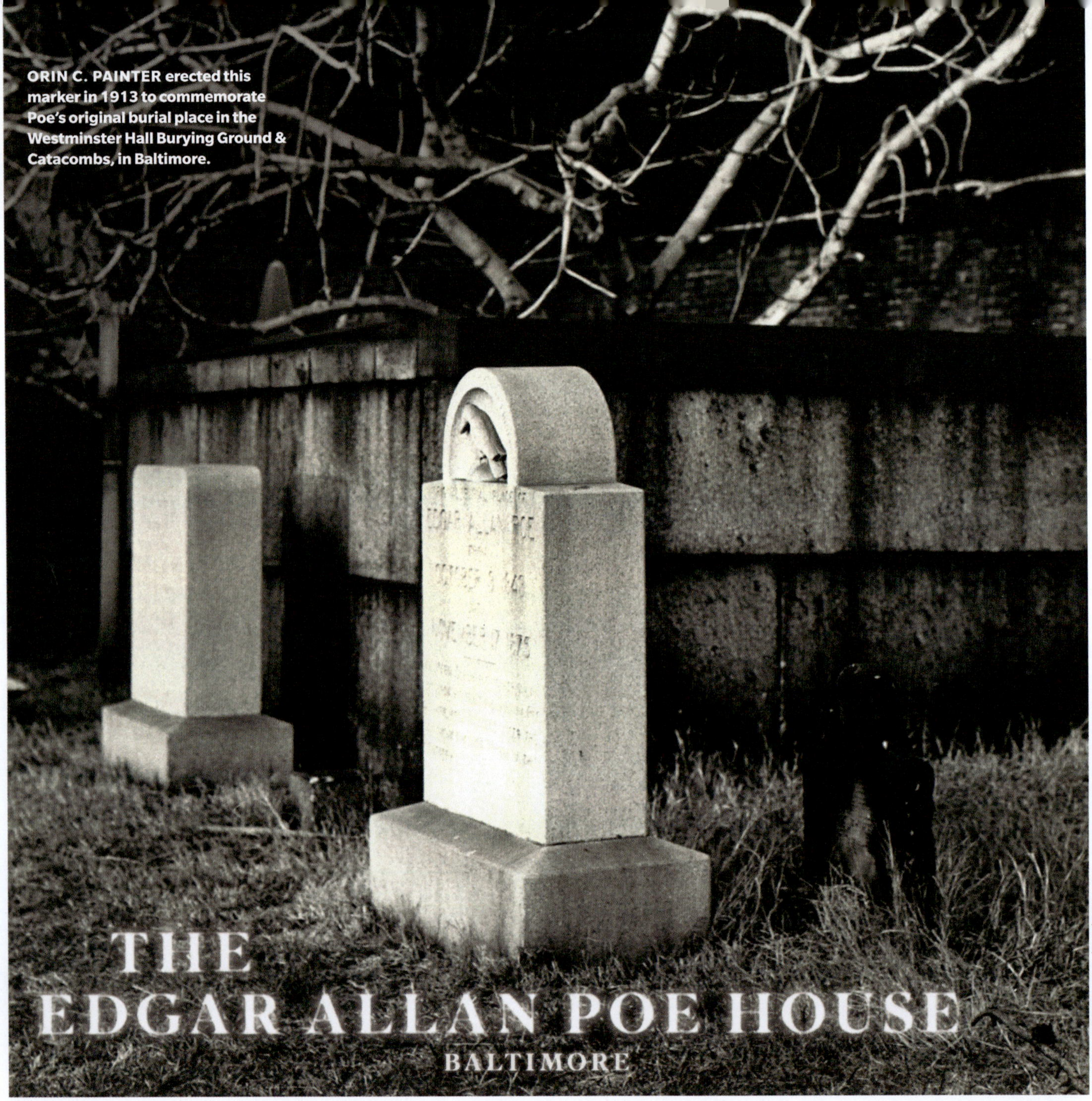

ORIN C. PAINTER erected this marker in 1913 to commemorate Poe's original burial place in the Westminster Hall Burying Ground & Catacombs, in Baltimore.

NINA LEEN/LIFE/THE PICTURE COLLECTION

THE EDGAR ALLAN POE HOUSE

BALTIMORE

IN THE EARLY MORNING hours of September 27, 1849, Edgar Allan Poe left Richmond, Virginia, on a steamer heading to Baltimore. He wasn't seen again until nearly a week later, when he was found—delirious, probably drunk, and wearing someone else's clothes—in a Baltimore tavern. Hospitalized, the great writer raved, repeatedly shouting someone's name—until, on October 7, he muttered "Lord help my poor soul," and died.

Now a museum, the Edgar Allan Poe House on Baltimore's Amity Street is where the writer lived in the early 1830s. It is, locals say, haunted—but not by Poe's "poor soul." Some have seen the spirit of a stout old woman dressed in clothing of the early 1800s. Others have reported visitations of a specter known as "Mr. Eddie." Doors and windows open and shut when no one is there; visitors sometimes feel persistent tapping on their shoulders; and a neighbor has seen candle-like lights bobbing in the museum after closing time.

Poe's ghost *has* been seen in the town's port area, Fell's Point, where the writer seems to have wandered during his final days in the city. A spirit affectionately named "Edgar" is said to prowl The Horse You Came In On Saloon, Baltimore's oldest pub. And beginning in 1949, a mysterious person known as the "Phantom Toaster" toasted the great writer with a glass of cognac at his grave every January 19 (Poe's birthday), leaving behind the unfinished brandy bottle and three red roses. Since 2009, however, the Toaster has been—quoth the Raven—"Nevermore." ■

THE WINCHESTER MYSTERY HOUSE

SAN JOSE, CALIFORNIA

"THERE IS SOMETHING of the awful 'House of Usher' about it," one journalist wrote of the Winchester Mystery House after it first opened to the public in San Jose, California, in 1923. "I, for one, would tremendously like to give a Hallowe'en party in this old home."

The rumors about the mazelike Victorian mansion started soon after its eccentric owner, Sarah Winchester, began her elaborately idiosyncratic construction. And they continue to this day, fueled in part by the guides who lead tourists through the bizarre structure's odd nooks and crannies, past doors that open into walls, and up staircases that go nowhere. There are now 160 rooms, 2,000 doors, 10,000 windows, 47 stairways, 47 fireplaces, 13 bathrooms, and six kitchens. (Tourists are warned against wandering off—they could be lost for hours.)

This is how the story goes: After losing both her only child and her husband in New England, Winchester (the heiress to the Winchester Repeating Arms Company fortune) consulted a Boston psychic. He told her that her family was cursed by the souls—American Indians and Civil War soldiers among them—who had been killed by Winchester rifles, "The Gun That Won the West." The only way to placate those restless spirits was to build a rambling house for them to inhabit.

Dutifully, Winchester moved to California, where she bought an unfinished farmhouse in 1886. For the next 38 years, she renovated and rebuilt her home, reportedly hiring construction workers to work around the clock; as long as the hammering continued, the rumor went, she could stay alive.

The truth, however, is somewhat more complicated. Known in her youth as the Belle of New Haven, Winchester was later crippled with rheumatoid arthritis and, having lost her fabled looks, rarely ventured outside. Her obsessive need for privacy and refusal to speak publicly allowed yellow journalists and nosy neighbors to say anything they wanted about her with impunity—and, of course, they did.

But the fact remains that visitors and staff alike claim to hear footsteps and breathing, see apparitions from other eras, find locked doors suddenly open—and even smell chicken soup. In the end, the 1920s journalist was not far off when she compared the eerie structure to the House of Usher. Like Poe's melancholy domicile, the Winchester place remains "a mystery all insoluble." ■

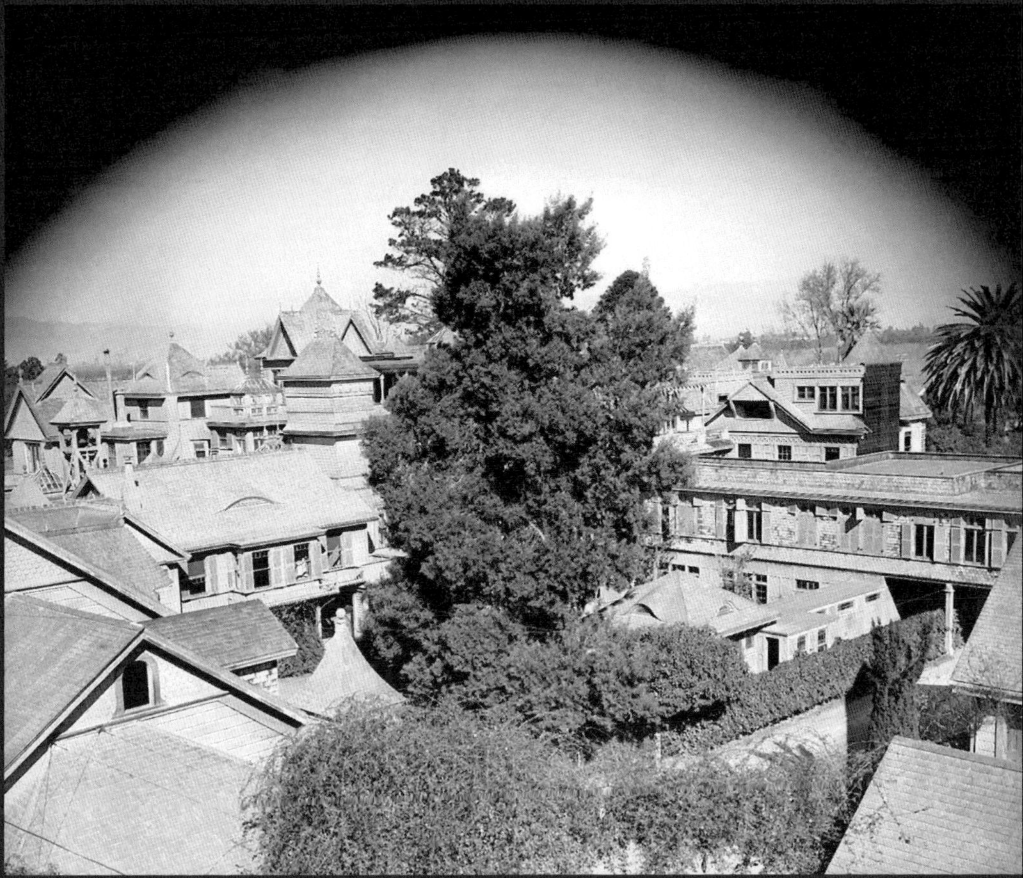

BETTMANN/GETTY

ABOVE: The Winchester Mystery House as it stood in the late 1930s. Much of this place's outré reputation was fueled by the era's version of tabloid journalism. But the house's eccentric, ailing owner, Sarah Winchester, may well have been a spiritualist (not uncommon at the time), holding séances in the house's so-called Blue Room.

JUST BELOW: A ghostly figure walks Pirate's Alley, formerly home to the likes of William Faulkner, who wrote his first novel there. Bottom: The interior of the New Orleans Historic Voodoo Museum. Right: St. Louis Cemetery No. 1, where the Voodoo Queen, Marie Laveau, is interred.

OTHERWORLDLY NEW ORLEANS

LOUISIANA

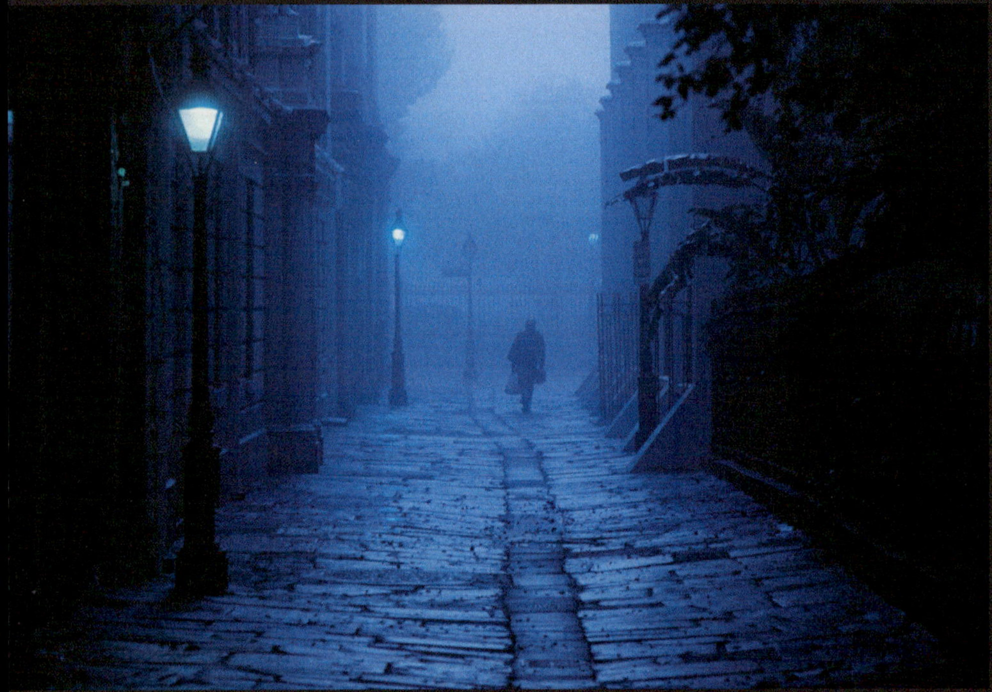

BOB KRIST/CORBIS/GETTY

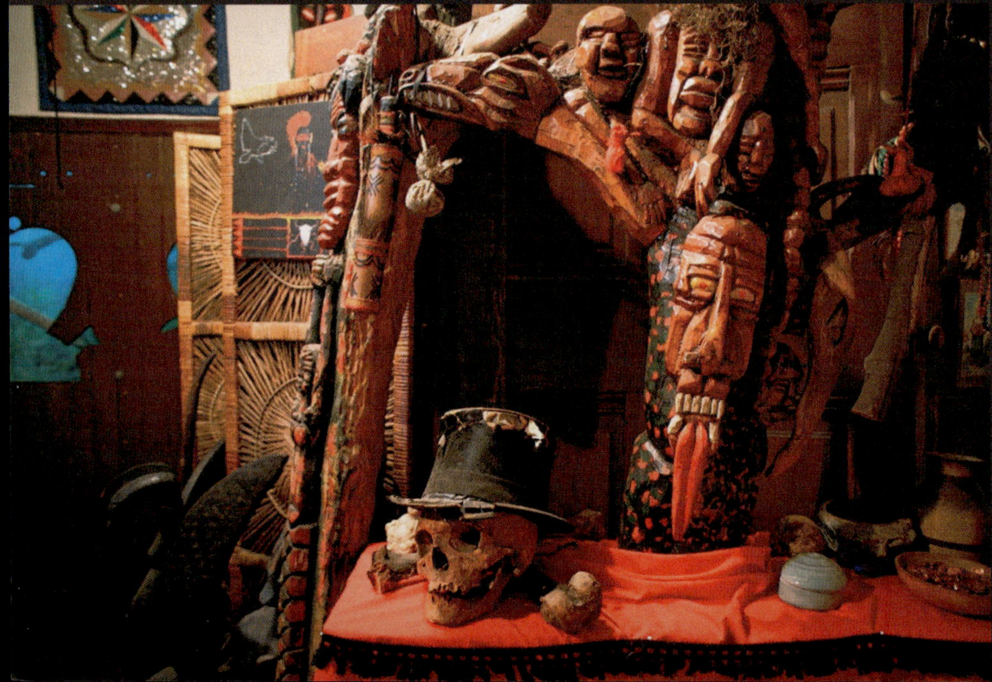

ROBERT HOLMES/CORBIS/VCG/GETTY

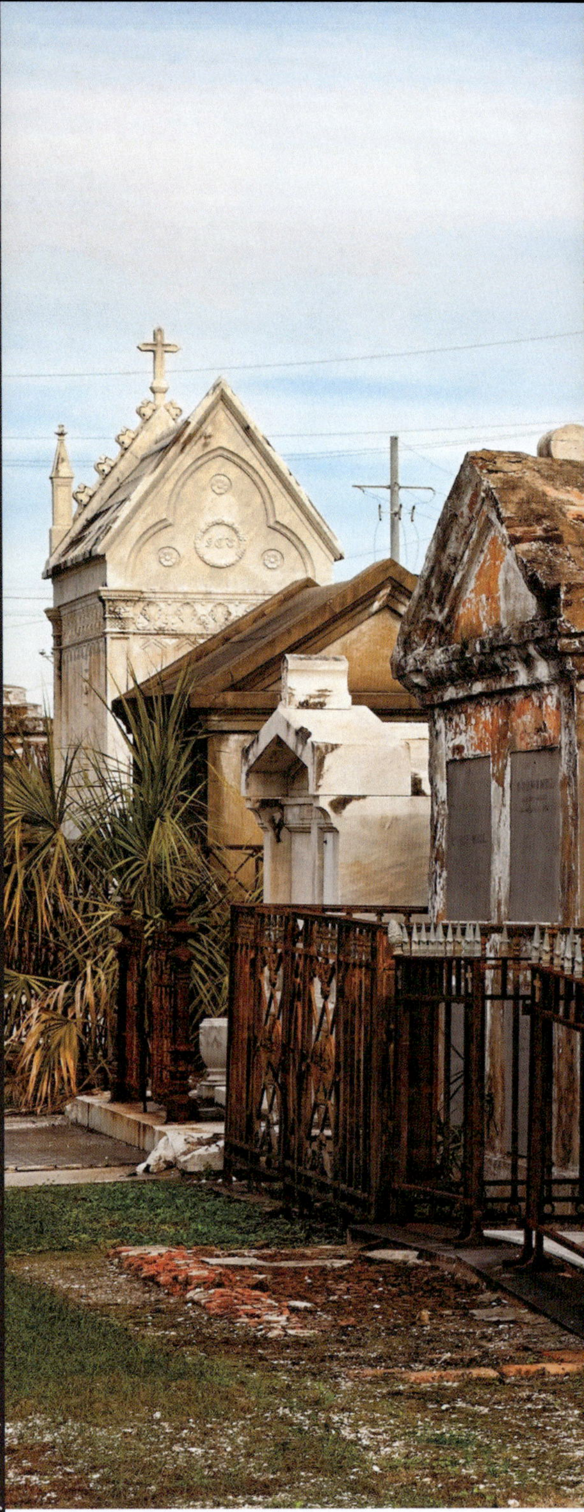

JOHN WANG/PHOTOGRAPHER'S CHOICE RF/GETTY

WHAT MAJOR U.S. city advertises rental apartments as "Haunted" or "Not Haunted," as if ghosts were amenities like air-conditioning or a 24-hour doorman? If you guessed Boston, you're wrong. We're talking, of course, about New Orleans, Louisiana, where spirited real estate sales are among the many reasons why the port city between the Mississippi River and

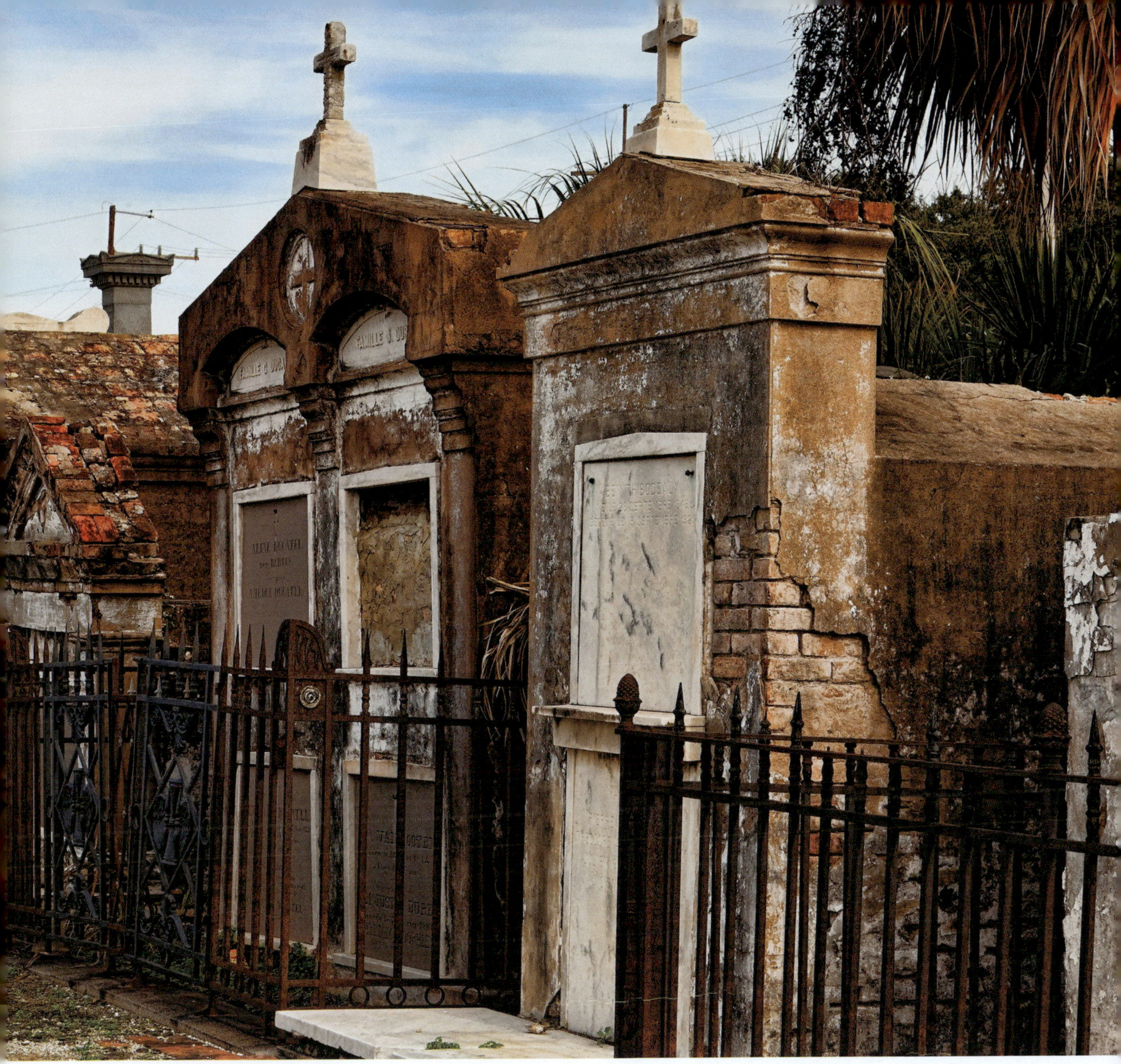

Lake Pontchartrain is considered the most unearthly urban enclave in the United States.

How did the Crescent City become a ghost town—literally? Maybe it has something to do with its multicultural mix of spiritual traditions: Native American, French, Spanish, Creole, Cajun, and—not least—voodoo, an amalgam of African religions and Catholicism. Or maybe it's the fact that, because the water table is so high, tombs (called "Cities of the Dead") are all built aboveground, leaving restless spirits to roam the steamy streets.

There's a ghost story (or a library of them) on virtually every corner here—from the spirit of a suicide that haunts the Louisiana National Guard armory to the legend of the Voodoo Queen, Marie Laveau, interred in St. Louis Cemetery No. 1. Not long ago, a New York magazine editor, in the city for a convention, crawled into her hotel bed one night—and immediately felt the presence of a man beside her. When he wrapped his arms around her, she was too terrified to scream—and stayed awake in his "arms" until sunrise, when he vanished.

Maybe hotels here should take a cue from rentals, advertising haunted and unhaunted rooms along with continental breakfast. ■

THE WITCH HUNT VILLAGE

SALEM, MASSACHUSETTS

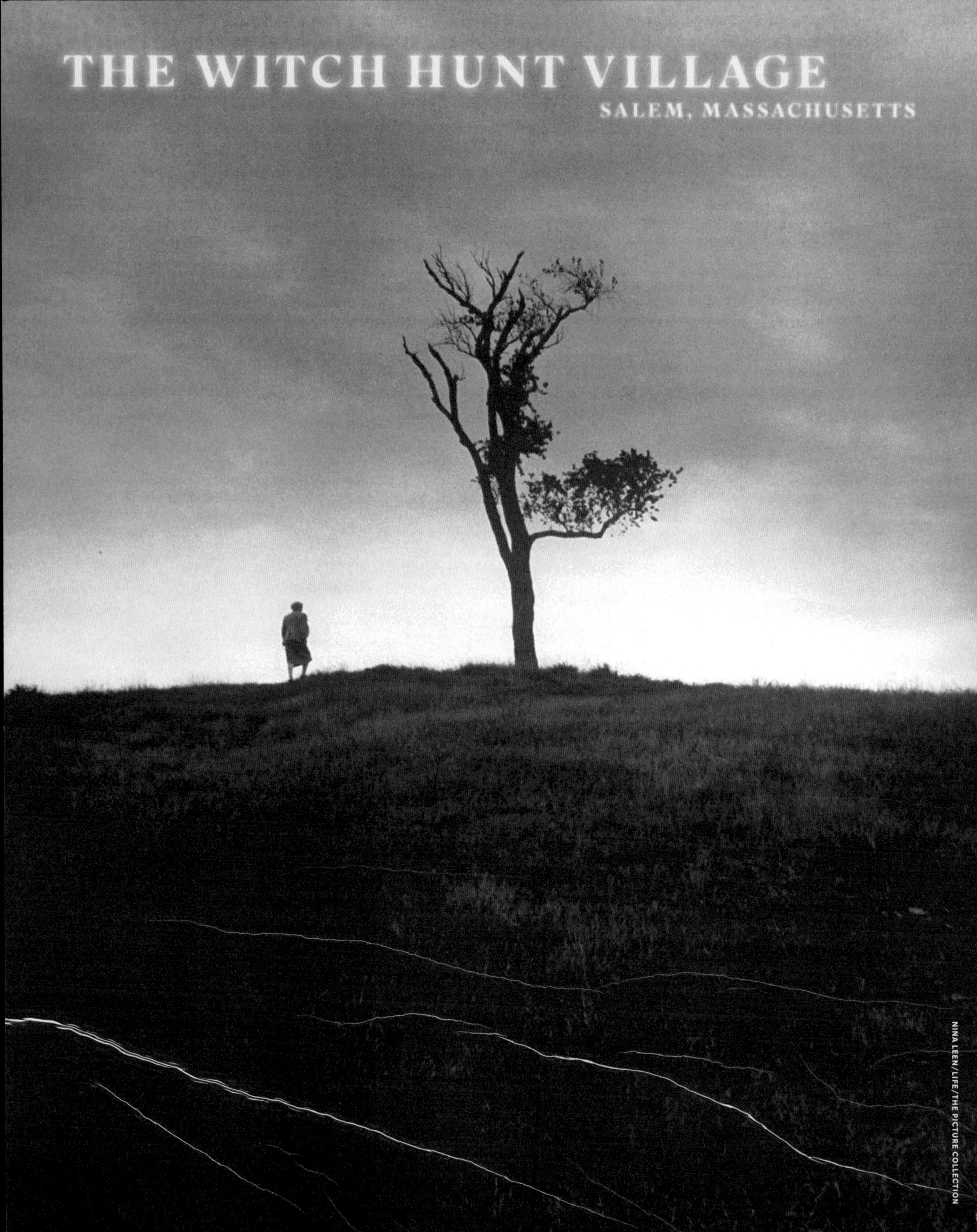

NINA LEEN/LIFE/THE PICTURE COLLECTION

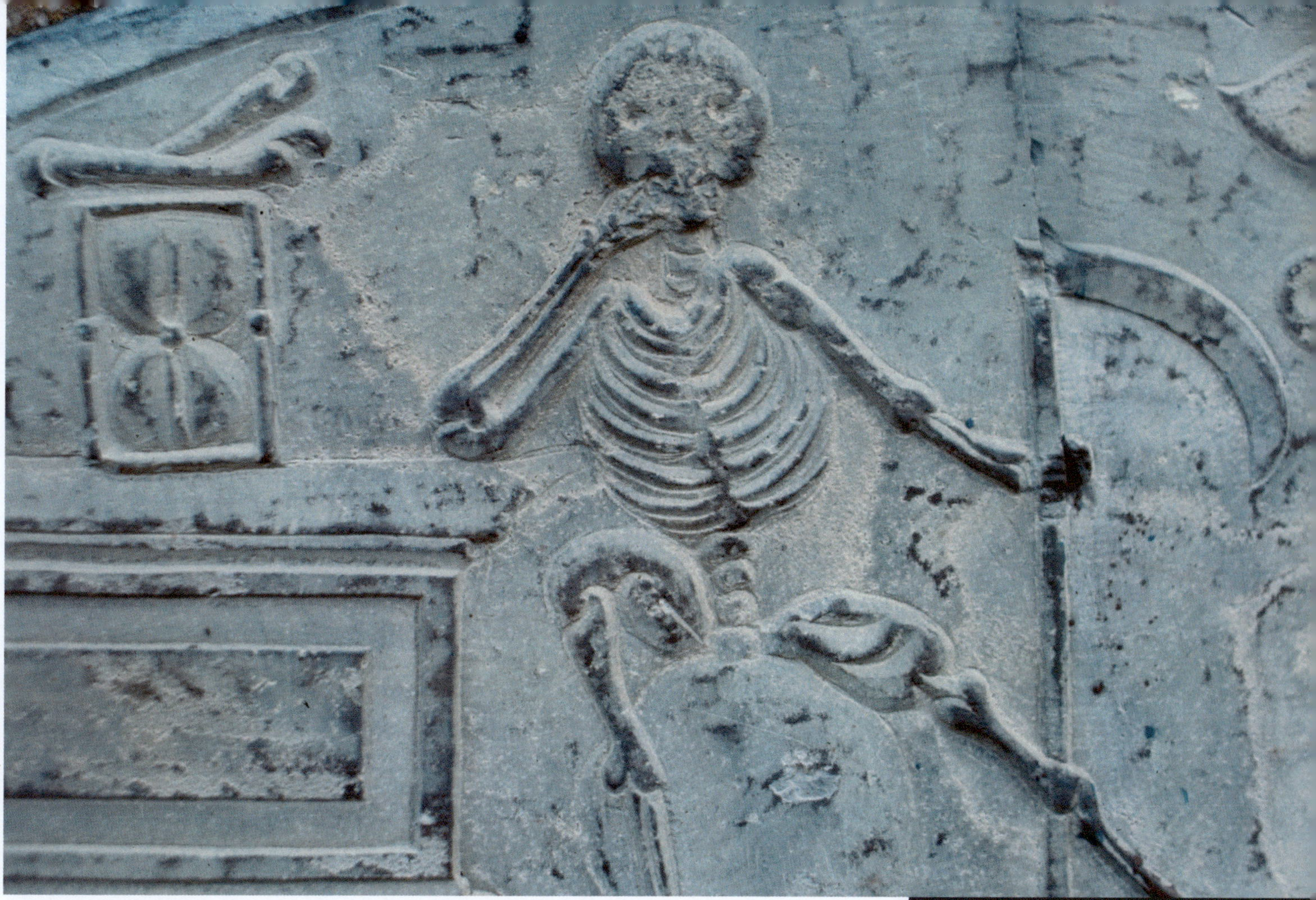

PHILLIP HARRINGTON/ALAMY

"THE DEVIL CAME TO ME and bid me serve him," said Tituba, the Caribbean slave who was working for Salem Village's minister, Samuel Parris, when his young daughter and niece began to suffer fits in the winter of 1692. Supposedly influenced by the Bajan woman's fortune-telling, the girls (and their friends) were soon called victims of witchcraft.

Thus the town's notorious witch hysteria began.

Driven by ever-increasing accusations from the coterie of "possessed" girls, the Salem court convicted and hanged 19 townspeople found guilty of witchcraft in 1692. But not all these souls went placidly to their unhallowed graves. In fact, three of them uttered hellish curses that some believe afflict Salem to this day.

A beggar named Sarah Good, having lost her unborn child in jail after being convicted of witchcraft in June 1692, was brought to Gallows Hill with four other "witches" in July. When Reverend Nicholas Noyes tried to elicit a confession, a furious Good shouted, "I am no more a witch than you are a wizard, and if you take away my life, God will give you blood to drink!"

In 1717—so tradition holds—Noyes suffered an internal hemorrhage and choked to death on his own blood.

More than 100 years later, Nathaniel Hawthorne, a descendant of the witch-hunting judge John Hathorne [*sic*], used this curse to fuel the plot of his third novel, *The House of the Seven Gables*, the name of a Salem house that still stands. (In the introduction to *The Scarlet Letter*, Hawthorne apologized for his ancestors' actions.)

A so-called warlock hurled imprecations too. "Damn you, Sheriff!" the elderly Giles Corey shouted as he was fatally crushed under stones placed on wooden planks in a field near Howard Street,

Continued on page 25

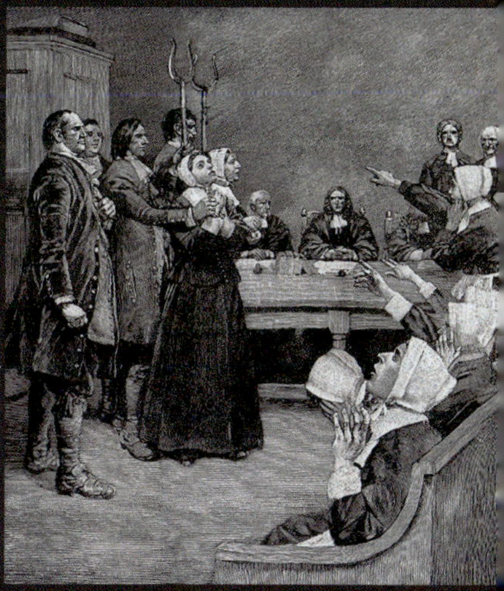

WORLD HISTORY ARCHIVE/ALAMY

OPPOSITE: Marion L. Starkey, author of *The Devil in Massachusetts*, on Gallows Hill in Salem, Massachusetts, in 1949. Top: A tombstone in the old Burying Point, also known as Charter Street Cemetery, the resting place of many involved in the witch hunts. Above: An illustration of the play *Giles Corey, Yeoman*, by Mary E. Wilkins. Corey was an elderly suspected warlock put to death during the Salem Witch Trials by being crushed to death.

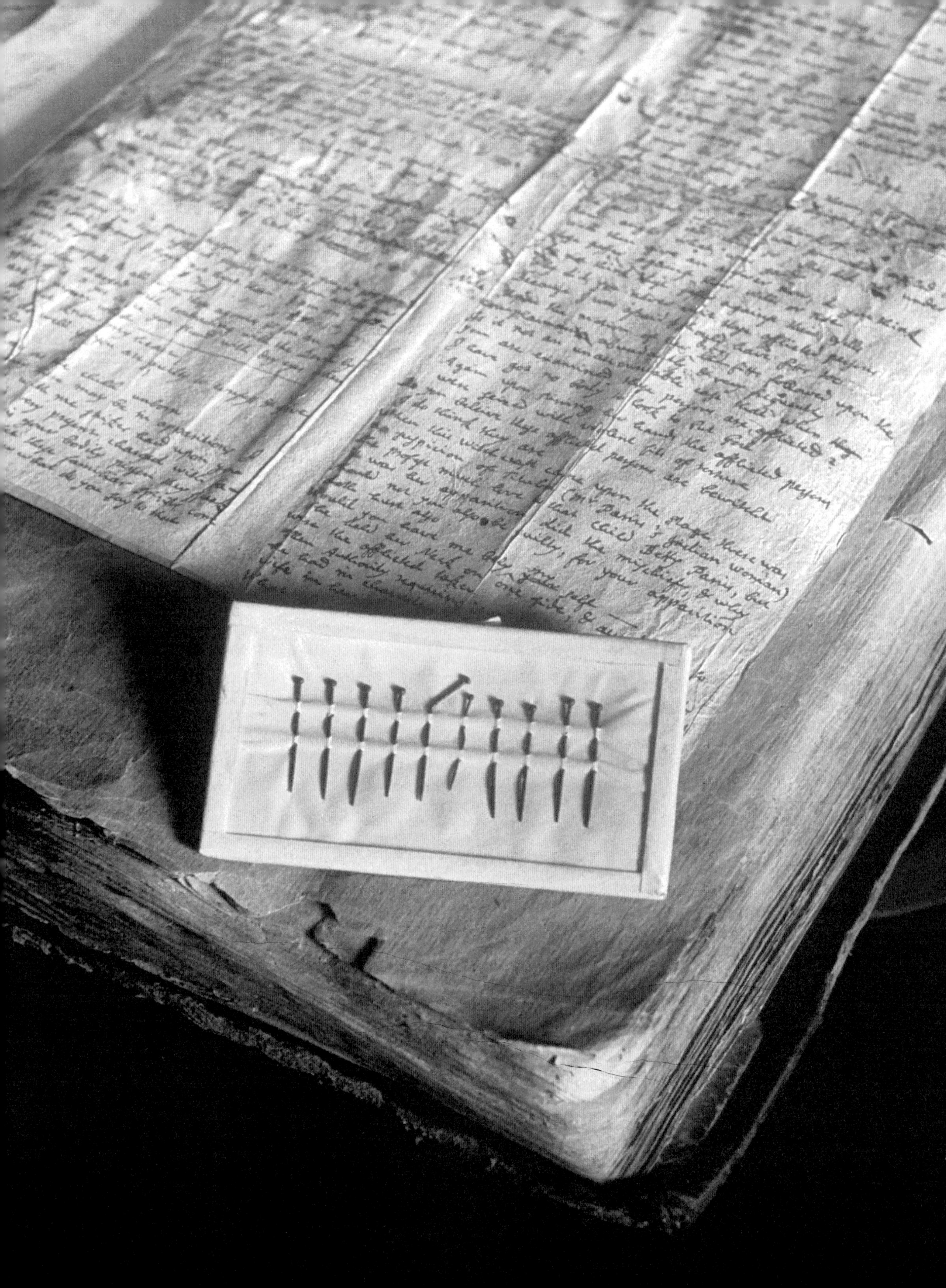

possibly the site of the current Howard Street Cemetery. "I curse you and Salem!"

Hawthorne again: "Tradition was long current that . . . the ghost of Giles Corey, the wizard, appeared on the spot where he had suffered as the precursor of some calamity that was impending over the community." He was reportedly seen, for instance, in the Howard Street Cemetery the night before the Great Salem Fire of July 25, 1914, which left half the town homeless.

Corey was tortured for two or three days by High Sheriff George Corwin, who was ostracized by the town after the trials. When Corwin died of a heart attack in 1696, his family, not wishing to risk a vandalized grave, interred him in his basement—on the same site now occupied by the Joshua Ward House. (Naturally—or should we say, supernaturally?—it's haunted.)

"In the 1970s," according to Rosemary Ellen Guiley, author of *Haunted Salem,* "the last man to serve in the office of sheriff (the office no longer exists), Robert Ellis Cahill, investigated the curse and wrote that all sheriffs as far back as he could trace either died in office of heart problems, or retired with 'an ailment of the blood.'"

In 1978, Cahill's own stint as sheriff was cut short by heart disease.

Another accused witch seemed to predict a future conflagration. "This town shall burn!" shouted Wilmot Redd, who was among the final eight victims to be hanged on Gallows Hill on September 22, 1692. Many years later, of course, Salem did—in the aforementioned fire.

But none of these doomed townsfolk would ever have thought to curse Salem with tourist brochures calling it "bewitching."

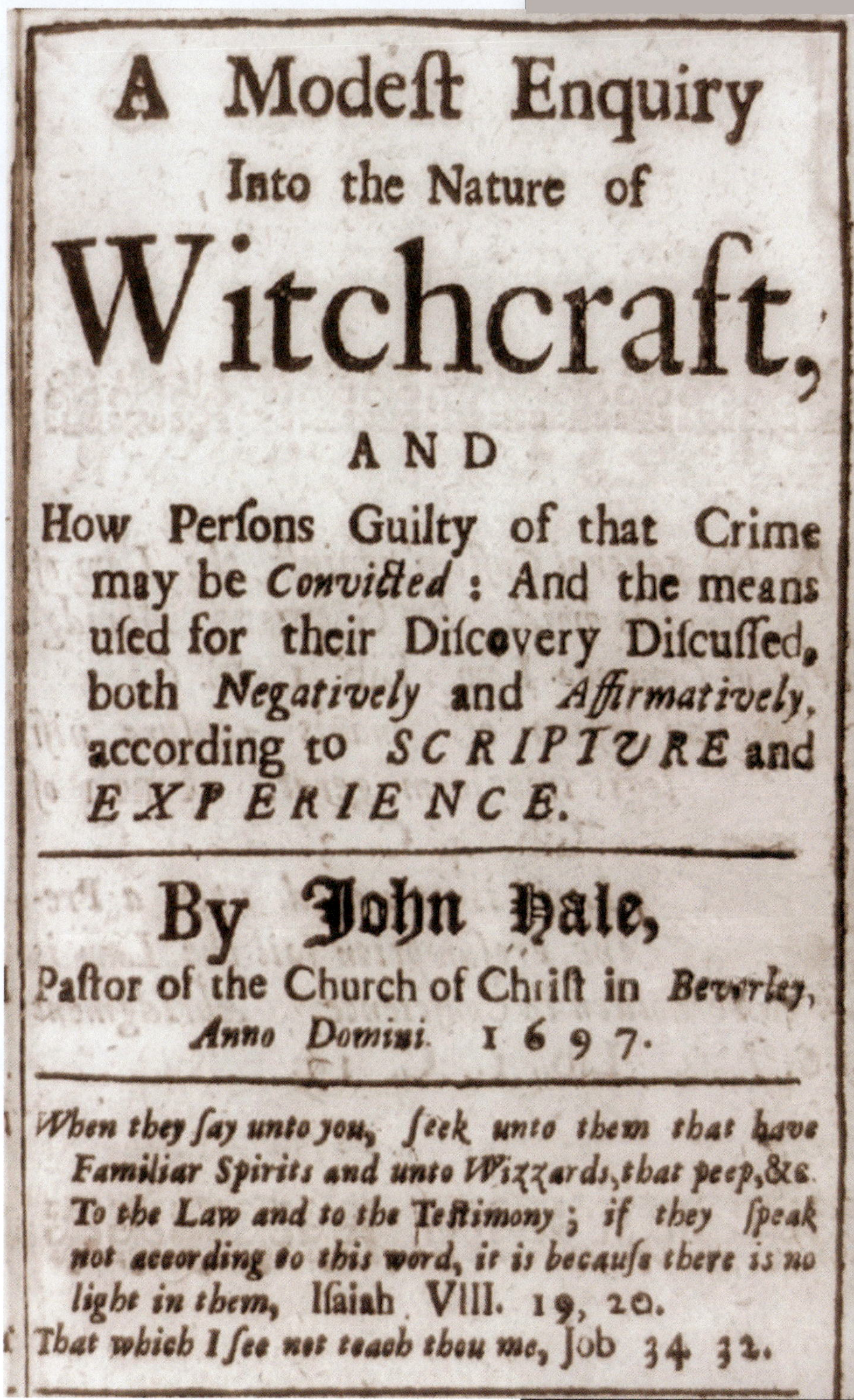

A Modeſt Enquiry Into the Nature of Witchcraft, AND How Perſons Guilty of that Crime may be *Convicted*: And the means uſed for their Diſcovery Diſcuſſed, both *Negatively* and *Affirmatively*, according to *SCRIPTURE* and *EXPERIENCE*.

By John Hale, Paſtor of the Church of Chriſt in *Beverly*, *Anno Domini* 1697.

When they ſay unto you, ſeek unto them that have Familiar Spirits and unto Wizzards, that peep, &c. To the Law and to the Teſtimony; if they ſpeak not according to this word, it is becauſe there is no light in them, Iſaiah VIII. 19, 20.

That which I ſee not teach thou me, Job 34 32.

Not to mention a "3-D Haunted Adventure" or a "terror" house that claims "We're bringing scary back." (One doubts Corey's ghost would agree with that assessment.) There is even—heaven forbid—a statue of Elizabeth Montgomery, star of TV's *Bewitched,* honoring the episodes of the popular show that were shot in the village where all hell broke loose (perhaps literally) in 1692. ■

OPPOSITE: Sewing pins were supposedly used by witches to torture their victims. Above: 1697's *A Modest Enquiry into the Nature of Witchcraft,* by John Hale, a minister who supported the trials—until his second wife was accused of witchery, an event that helped bring an end to the hysteria and deaths. "We walked in the clouds, and could not see our way," Hale later wrote.

"DO YOU SEE the late Joan Dunsmuir?" reads the caption on a photo supposedly showing the ghost of a woman in Craigdarroch Castle, the National Historic Site and museum on Vancouver Island, British Columbia. Though "ghost" photos are taken in supposedly haunted spots all over the world, they often involve tricks of the light—or, say, Photoshop. But in this castle, they may well be spectral selfies.

Built by coal magnate Robert Dunsmuir, the Scottish baronial castle was completed in 1890, but the industrialist died before he could move in. His wife, Joan, took possession but died herself in 1908. When not posing for photos, Joan's ghost has been seen descending the main staircase in a ball gown, and her tallow candles have been smelled on the second floor.

She does not seem to be alone. In the basement, the spirit of a little girl has been seen staring sadly at the floor. And the crying of a child and music from a playerless Steinway piano are sometimes heard echoing among the ornate woodwork and Victorian stained glass in the mansion's 39 rooms.

Plenty of other spots on Vancouver Island are said to be haunted too. Cameron Lake, for one, is the site of a wide range of reported paranormal activity, and the ghost of a Hawaiian ax murderer supposedly haunts the forests of Newcastle Island Park.

Not least, nearby Vancouver's Deadman's Island—once a burial ground for everyone from indigenous Indians to early settlers as well as a quarantine station for smallpox victims—is now home to the haunted HMCS Discovery, a Royal Canadian Navy Reserve division and shore facility. Many reservists have experienced unexplained activity here—including, according to the *Vancouver Courier,* disembodied voices, apparitions, and moving furniture. But at least one witness wanted further proof. "If I have an encounter with ghosts, I want chains," a seaman said. "I want the whole *Ghostbusters* effect." ■

THE FEARSOME FORT

CRAIGDARROCH CASTLE

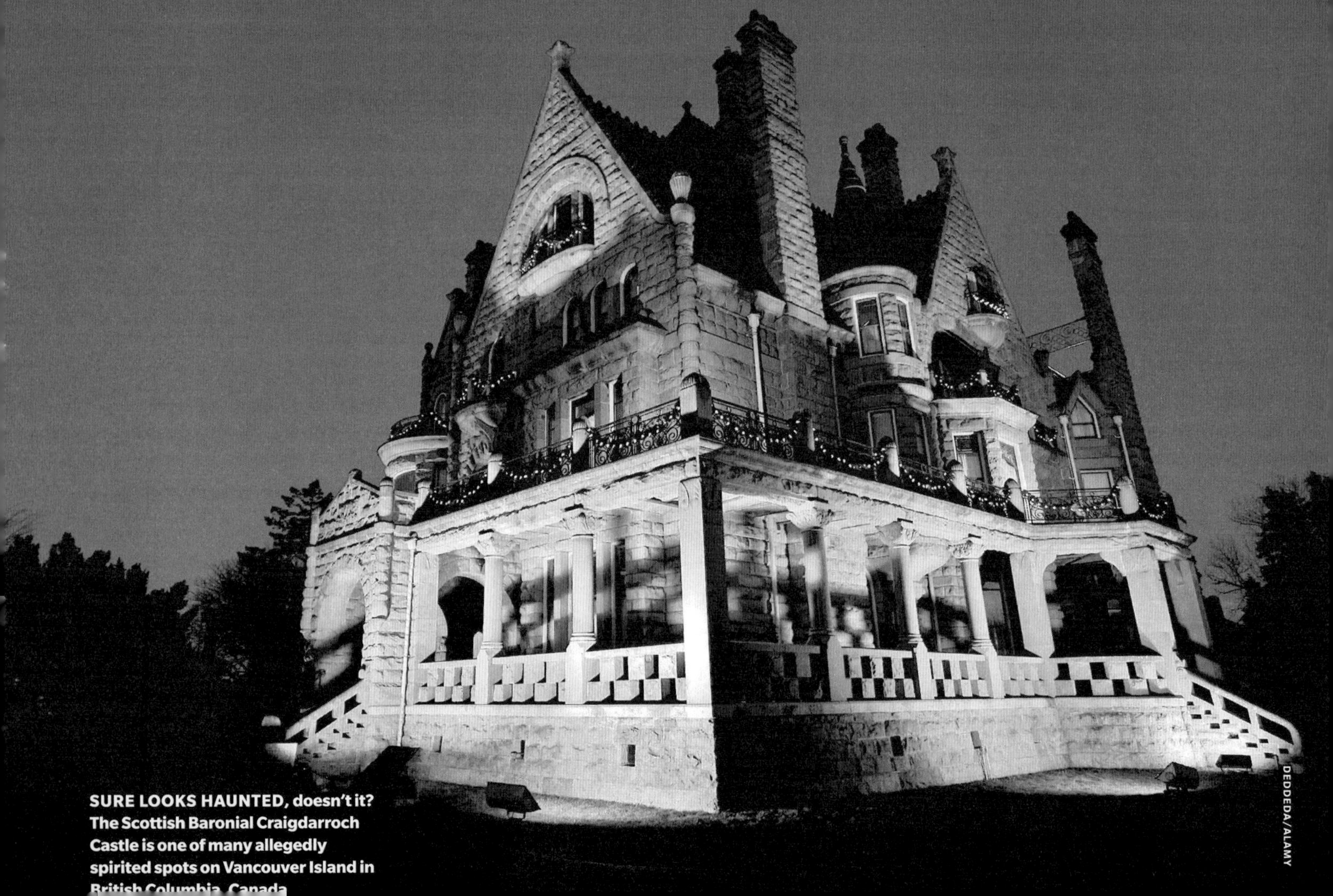

SURE LOOKS HAUNTED, doesn't it? The Scottish Baronial Craigdarroch Castle is one of many allegedly spirited spots on Vancouver Island in British Columbia, Canada

DEDDEDA/ALAMY

THE SHINING'S HOTEL

THE STANLEY

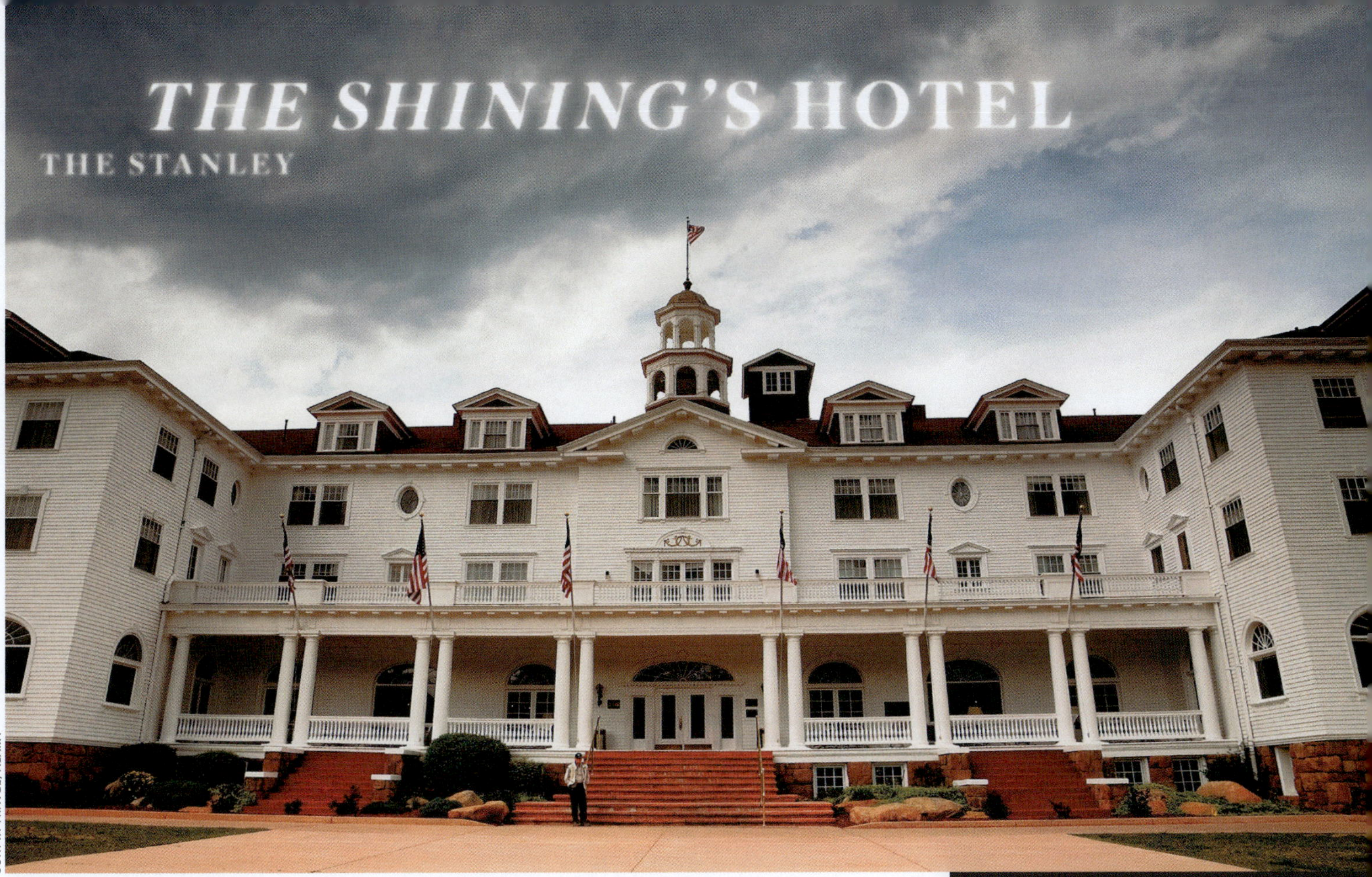

SUNPIX TRAVEL/ALAMY

IT ALL STARTED with a dream. In September 1974, bestselling novelist Stephen King was on vacation with his wife, Tabitha, at the Stanley Hotel in Estes Park, Colorado. "Wandering through its corridors, I thought that it seemed the perfect—maybe the archetypal—setting for a ghost story," King has said. "That night I dreamed of my three-year-old son running through the corridors, looking back over his shoulder, eyes wide, screaming. He was being chased by a fire-hose."

This was, of course, the inspiration for King's classic 1977 novel, *The Shining*, in which the Stanley became the Overlook Hotel of the writer's prodigious imagination. Built in 1909 by the inventor F.O. Stanley, the 140-room hotel is currently on the National Register of Historic Places, but when King visited it had seen better days. Before such TV shows as *Ghost Hunters* made spirit-hunting something of a national sport, the grand hotel was dogged by the rumor that it was haunted. That fact became, paradoxically, a draw after *The Shining* put it on the map. Today, the management plays up the hotel's reputation by offering access to a resident psychic and a five-hour "paranormal investigations tour."

Unlike Jack Torrance, visitors probably won't find a decomposing lady in Room 217's bathtub, but the room is said to be home to the ghost of Elizabeth Wilson, a former maid known to climb into bed between unmarried couples. Other ghosts include Paul, the hotel's former maintenance man, who still enforces the hotel's strict 11 p.m. curfew by telling night owls to "get out!" A humming spirit named Lucy prowls the Concert Hall, and a wraith called Eddie is known as a lothario, stroking female patrons' hair and kissing their cheeks. (Once called the "Stinky Man," he has since presumably found the spectral equivalent of soap.)

More than King's "archetypal place for a ghost story," the Stanley is, according to in-house paranormal investigator Lisa Nyhart, "a Disneyland for spirits." ■

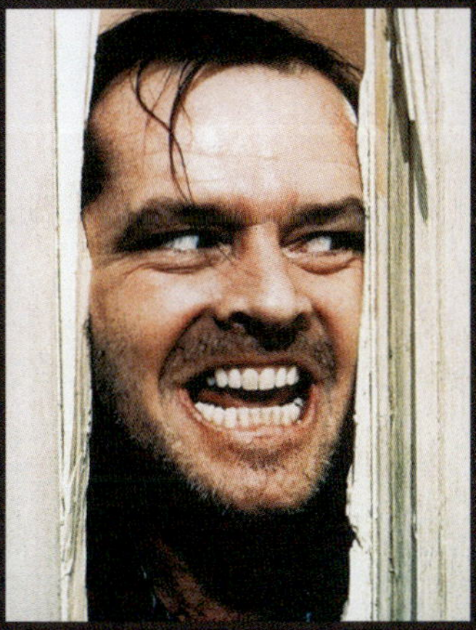

SUNSET BOULEVARD/CORBIS/GETTY

TOP: THE STANLEY HOTEL in Estes Park, Colorado, where a nightmare inspired Stephen King to write *The Shining*. Guests are said to hear spectral children laughing on the fourth floor, along with the sound of merriment from long-vanished parties. Just above: "Heeere's Johnny!" Jack Nicholson leers in Stanley Kubrick's film version.

THE *AMITYVILLE HORROR* HOUSE

LONG ISLAND, NEW YORK

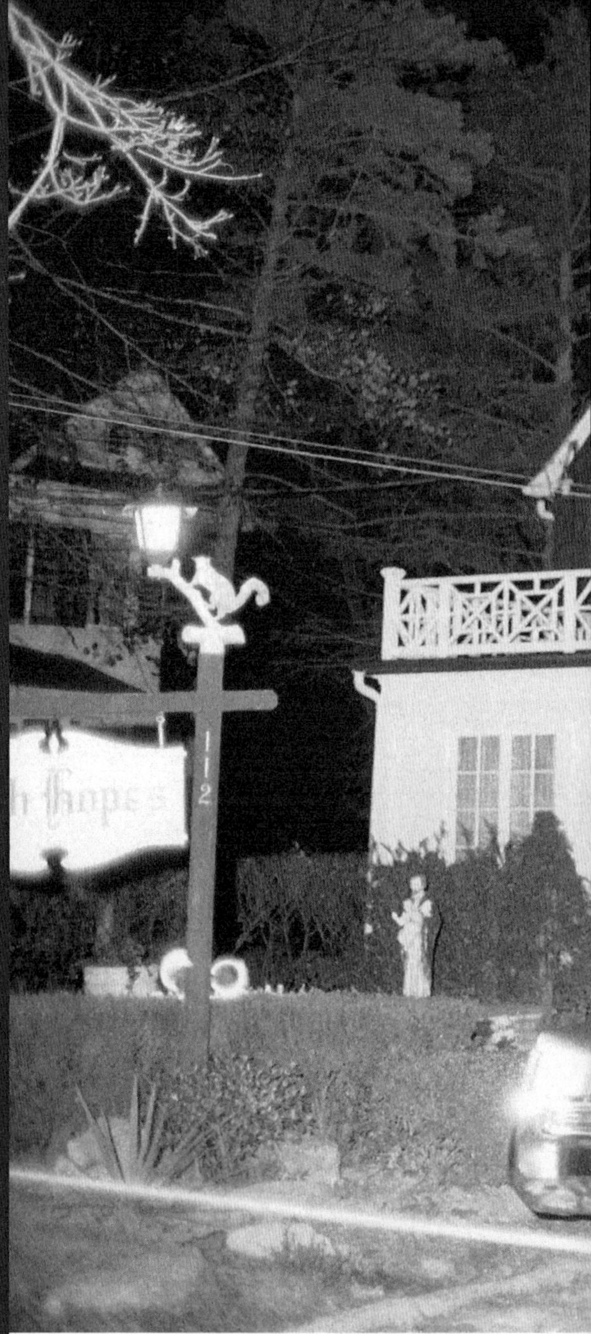

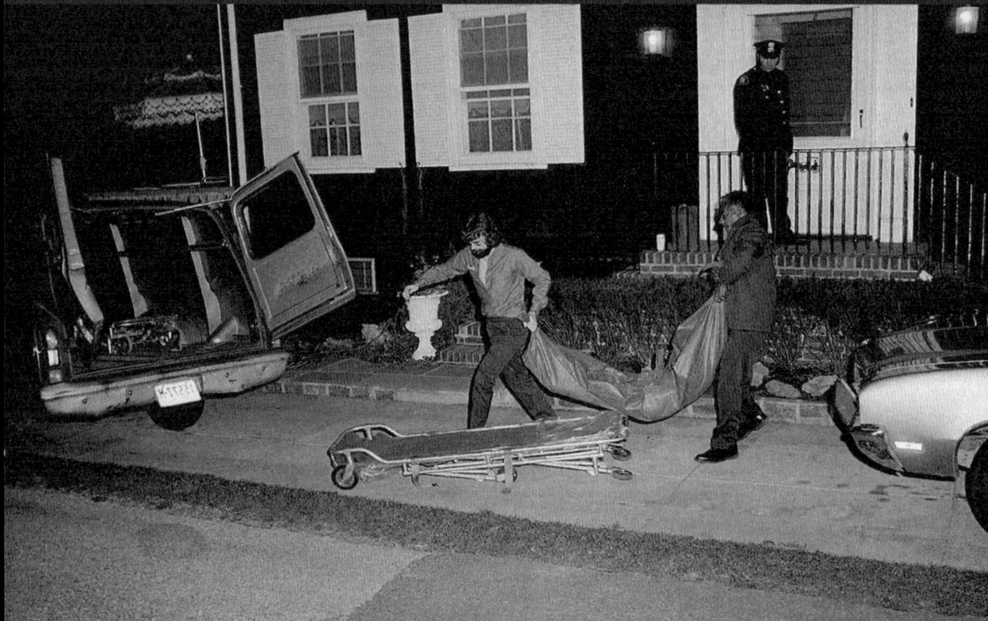

BETTMANN/GETTY (2)

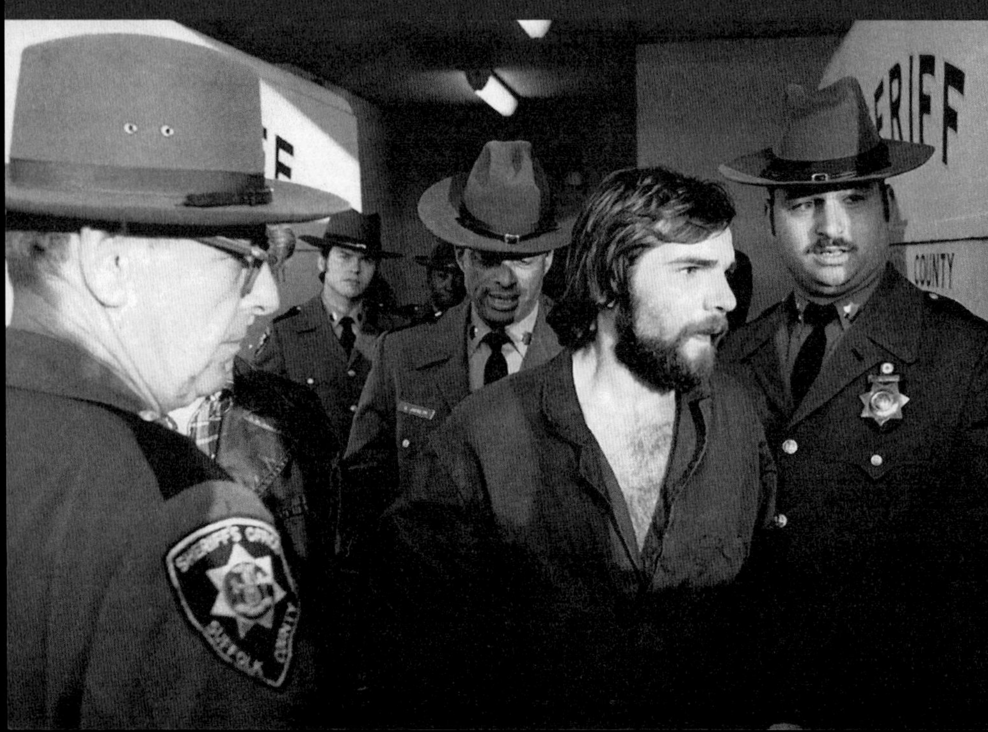

RICHARD DREW/AP

ON NOVEMBER 13, 1974, 23-year-old Ronald DeFeo Jr. slaughtered the other six members of his family at 112 Ocean Avenue in the village of Amityville, New York. One year later, newlyweds George and Kathy Lutz bought the murdered family's stately waterside Dutch Colonial, its bargain-basement price outweighing its gruesome reputation.

Moving in with Kathy's three children from a previous marriage, the Lutzes soon—they later claimed—began experiencing phenomena that had nothing to do with the everyday horrors of home

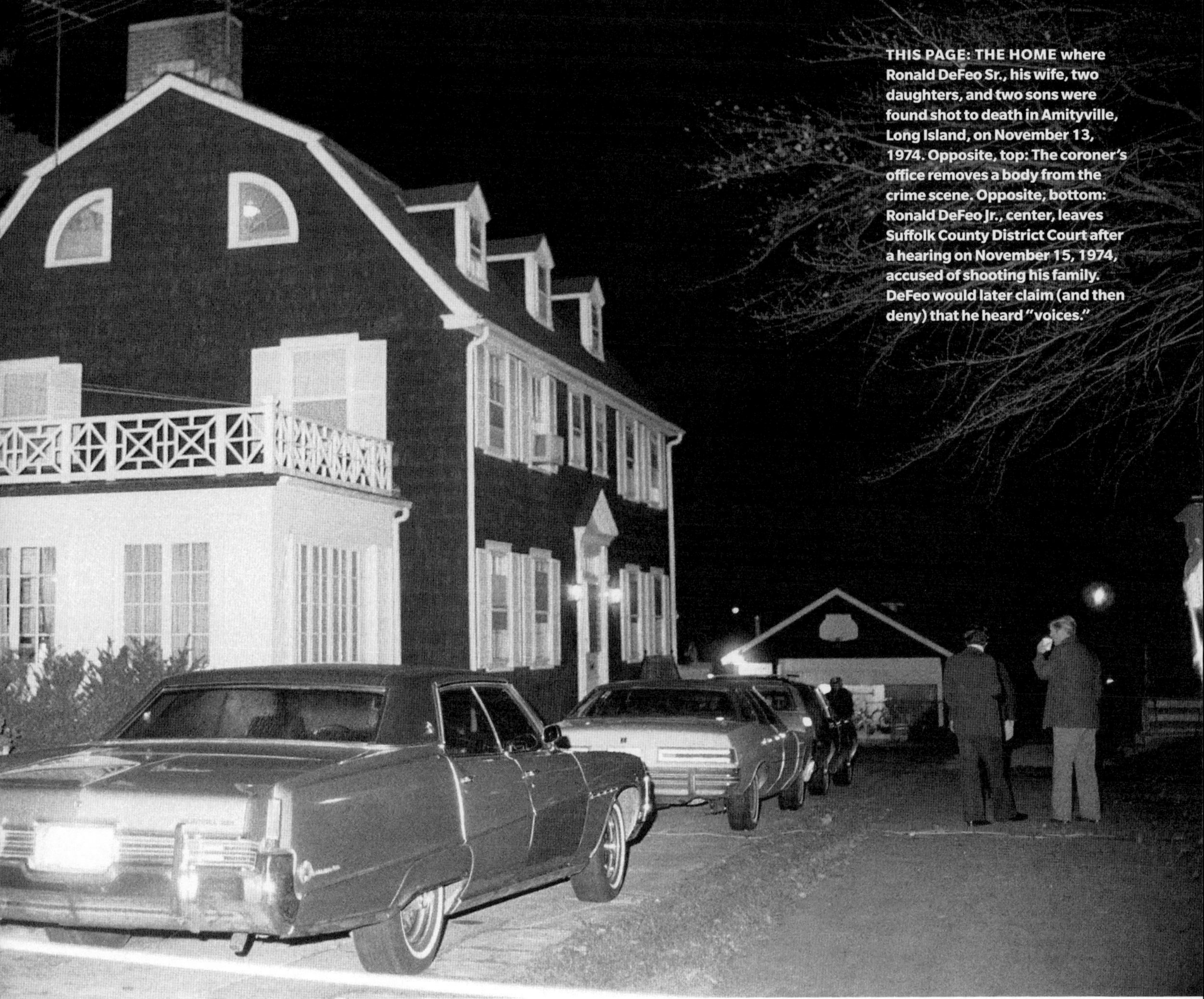

ownership. Some examples? Red eyes at the windows, swarms of flies, ooze seeping though the walls, cloven hoofs in the snow, and a sepulchral voice screaming, "Get out!"

One theory behind the events: Ronald DeFeo Jr. was no mere psychopath but somehow possessed by the house's evil spirits, which may have emanated from the ancient Indian burial ground it was allegedly built on. Pleading insanity, DeFeo said he heard voices that told him to kill his family.

Unwilling to fall victim to the same "forces," the Lutzes fled the house, leaving all their possessions behind—a mere 28 days after they had moved in.

What began as a family tragedy soon morphed into a pop-culture juggernaut. In 1977, the book *The Amityville Horror* became not merely a bestseller but a bona fide phenomenon. In 1979, the movie adaptation became the first entry in a wildly successful horror franchise that continues to this day.

From the beginning, the alleged supernatural events were dogged by controversy, with some calling the whole thing a hoax. (DeFeo, for his part, later disavowed his demon defense.) But it would have been a risk, to say the least, for the Lutzes, who were hardly wealthy, to leave behind a house they had just bought, staking their future on an elaborate lie. This was not, at any rate, your garden-variety "house flipping."

To the end of their days, the Lutzes insisted that their story was true. (Kathy died in 2004, followed by George in 2006.) As to the "horror" house used in the movie: In 2012, it was on the market, its original asking price of $1.45 million reduced to $955K. Demons? No, another sort of domestic disturbance: divorce. ■

THE HEADLESS HORSEMAN'S HAUNTS

SLEEPY HOLLOW, NEW YORK

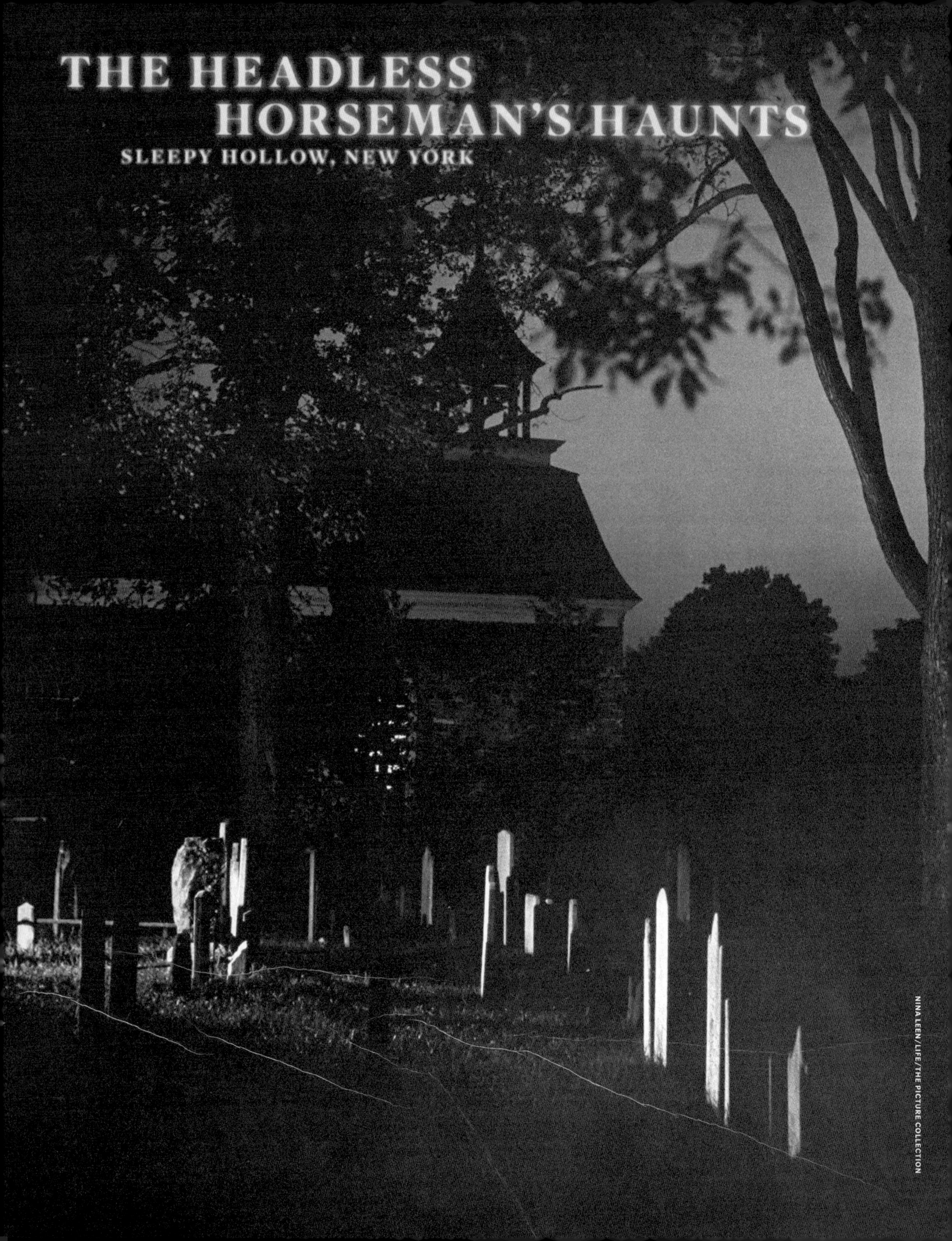

NINA LEEN/LIFE/THE PICTURE COLLECTION

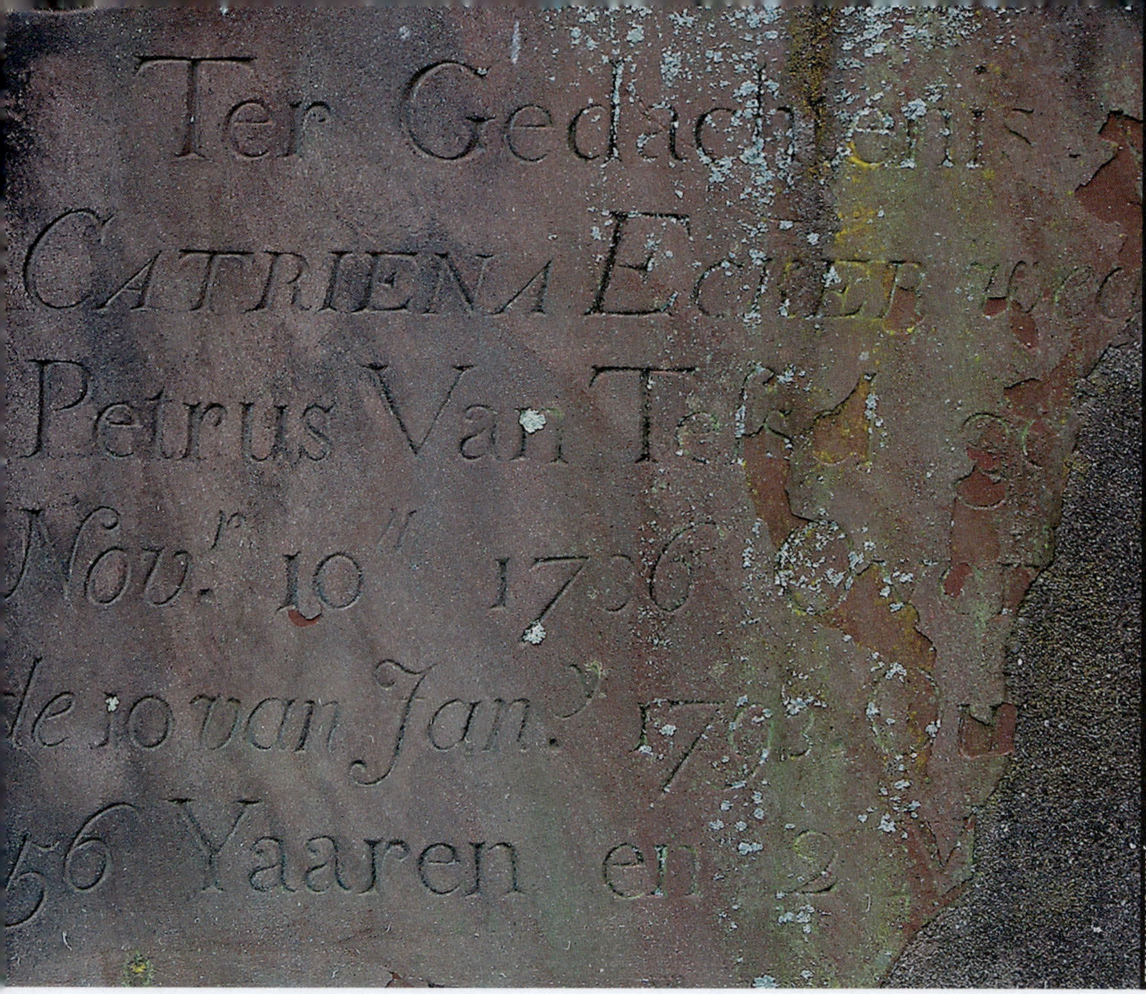

JENNIFER MITCHELL

OPPOSITE PAGE: Sleepy Hollow Cemetery, circa 1944, where author Washington Irving is buried. This page: The gravestone of Catriena Ecker Van Tessel—thought to be the inspiration for Ichabod Crane's love interest—in the burial ground of Sleepy Hollow's Old Dutch Church. This is also where the Headless Horseman was supposedly buried, though the figure was probably derived from German legends.

"A DROWSY, DREAMY influence seems to hang over the land, and to pervade the very atmosphere," wrote Washington Irving of the titular town in "The Legend of Sleepy Hollow," his eerie 1820 story about the lovelorn schoolteacher Ichabod Crane's encounter with the hell-bent Headless Horseman. "The whole neighborhood abounds with local tales, haunted spots and twilight superstitions."

Though Irving invented the name Sleepy Hollow, the village formerly known as North Tarrytown was rechristened after the fictitious enclave in the late 1990s. (Talk about life imitating art.) But what's in a name? Twenty-five miles north of New York City, Sleepy Hollow is now a populous suburb, having long ago lost the bucolic atmosphere that so enchanted Irving. Look closely, though, and you'll see that traces of the old superstitions abound.

Sleepy Hollow's Old Dutch Church and Burying Ground—the oldest church in New York State—is, for instance, rumored to be haunted by Irving's infernal equestrian. (Unlikely, given that the specter was mostly the writer's invention, but what old cemetery doesn't have its ghosts?) This is also the burial place of two women, Catriena Ecker Van Tessel and her niece Eleanor Van Tassel Brush—either of whom may have inspired the character of Katrina Van Tassel, Ichabod's love interest.

Disembodied whispers have been heard in the Sleepy Hollow Cemetery, where Irving himself is buried. The writer's home, Sunnyside, which he designed and where he lived out his last days, is said to be haunted by his ghost (apparently he likes to pinch female visitors). Irving himself claimed to have seen a ghost while he lived there, describing it as "a young lady who wandered through the orchard. She is said to have died of love and green apples." His two spectral nieces have been seen cleaning up after the place is closed.

Nearby towns have their share of spooks, too. Irvington (guess who it's named after?) is home to the Church of St. Barnabas, the "home" of a long-dead former pastor and another former pastor's wife. Unearthly mists and dancing lights have been observed in Scarborough's Sparta Cemetery, the resting place of the so-called Leatherman, an eccentric unidentified man who spent his life wandering around New York and Connecticut wearing nothing but a leather suit.

Though Irving's famous tale has left a sometimes ridiculous legacy in the town that bears its name (you can order Horsemen Bruschetta at the Horseman Restaurant & Pizza, for instance), Ichabod Crane endures—on the library shelves and in our collective imagination, if nowhere else. At the end of "The Legend of Sleepy Hollow," Irving suggests that the lonely schoolteacher's voice can still be heard "at a distance, chanting a melancholy psalm tune among the tranquil solitudes of Sleepy Hollow." ■

FIRST OPENED IN 1888 as a luxury railroad hub, the so-called Castle in the Rockies is one of North America's great mountain getaways, with sweeping views of the Bow Valley in the heart of Banff National Park. Though the lavish resort has 764 guest rooms, one is notoriously missing. There is no room 873 on the eighth floor, even though rooms end in the number 73 elsewhere in the hotel.

Legend has it that a husband murdered his wife and daughter in 873—and the girl's fingerprints simply could not be washed off the mirror. This—along with disembodied screaming and bloody handprints on the walls—caused the hotel to close off the space. "The baseboard is cut where the door [to room 873] would have been," according to EnjoyBanff.com, "and knocking on the wall produces a hollow sound."

Guests have reportedly seen the doomed family's spirits roaming the halls—along with a headless bagpiper and a bartender who tells guests they've had too much to drink. Another well-known ghost is the "Burned Bride," who died when her wedding dress caught fire and who dances in her wedding dress in the Rob Roy dining room and the Cascade Ballroom.

The hotel's friendliest otherworldly occupant is Sam McCauley, a Scottish bellman who died in 1975 and who is said to still operate the elevators. But a hotel security guard cast a little professional doubt on that legend. "The guy works here for decades and what does he do after he dies?" he said to *Canadian Living* magazine. "He comes back and works the elevators? No, I don't believe that." ■

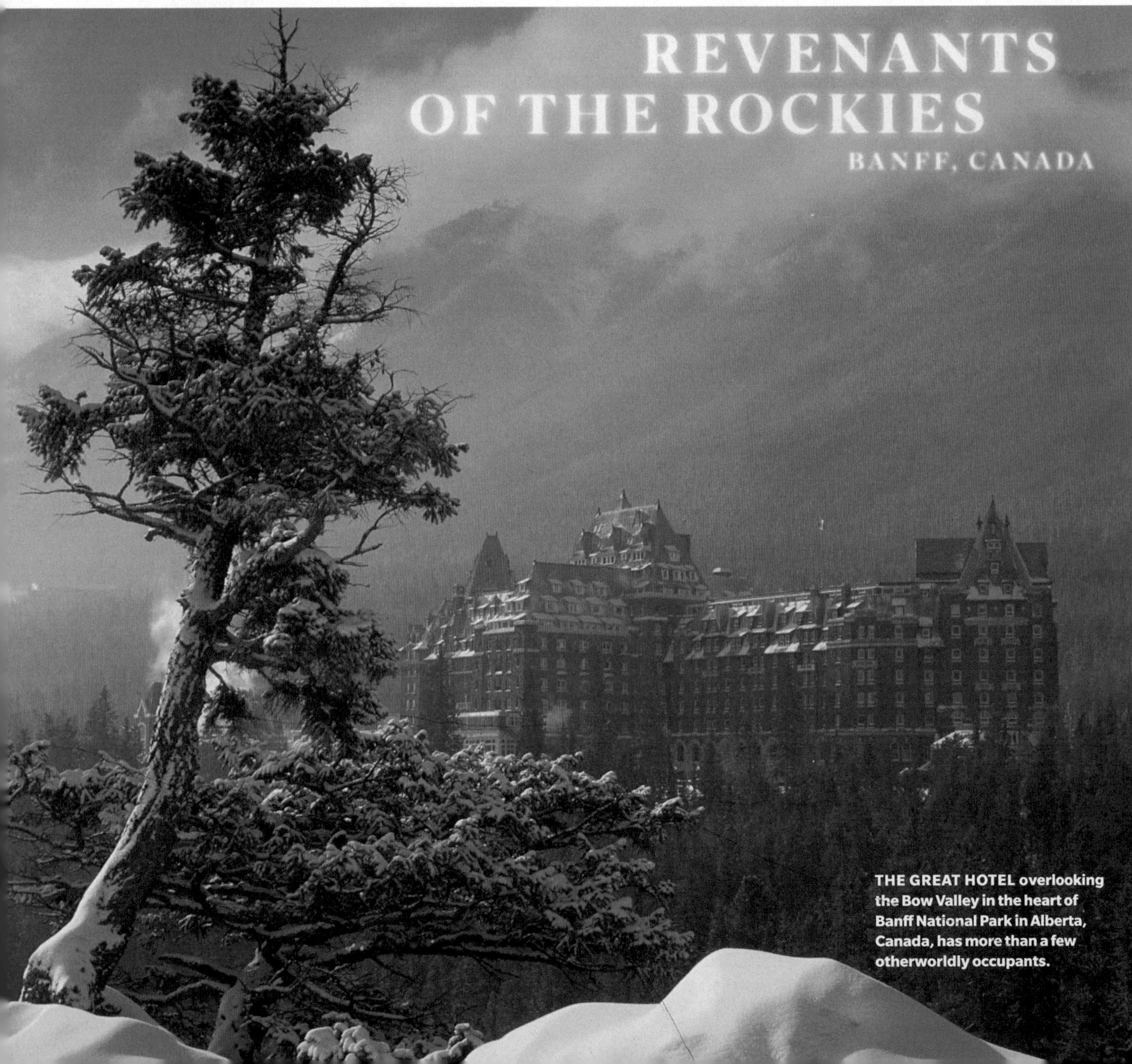

CHRISTIAN HEEB/AURORA

THE GREAT HOTEL overlooking the Bow Valley in the heart of Banff National Park in Alberta, Canada, has more than a few otherworldly occupants.

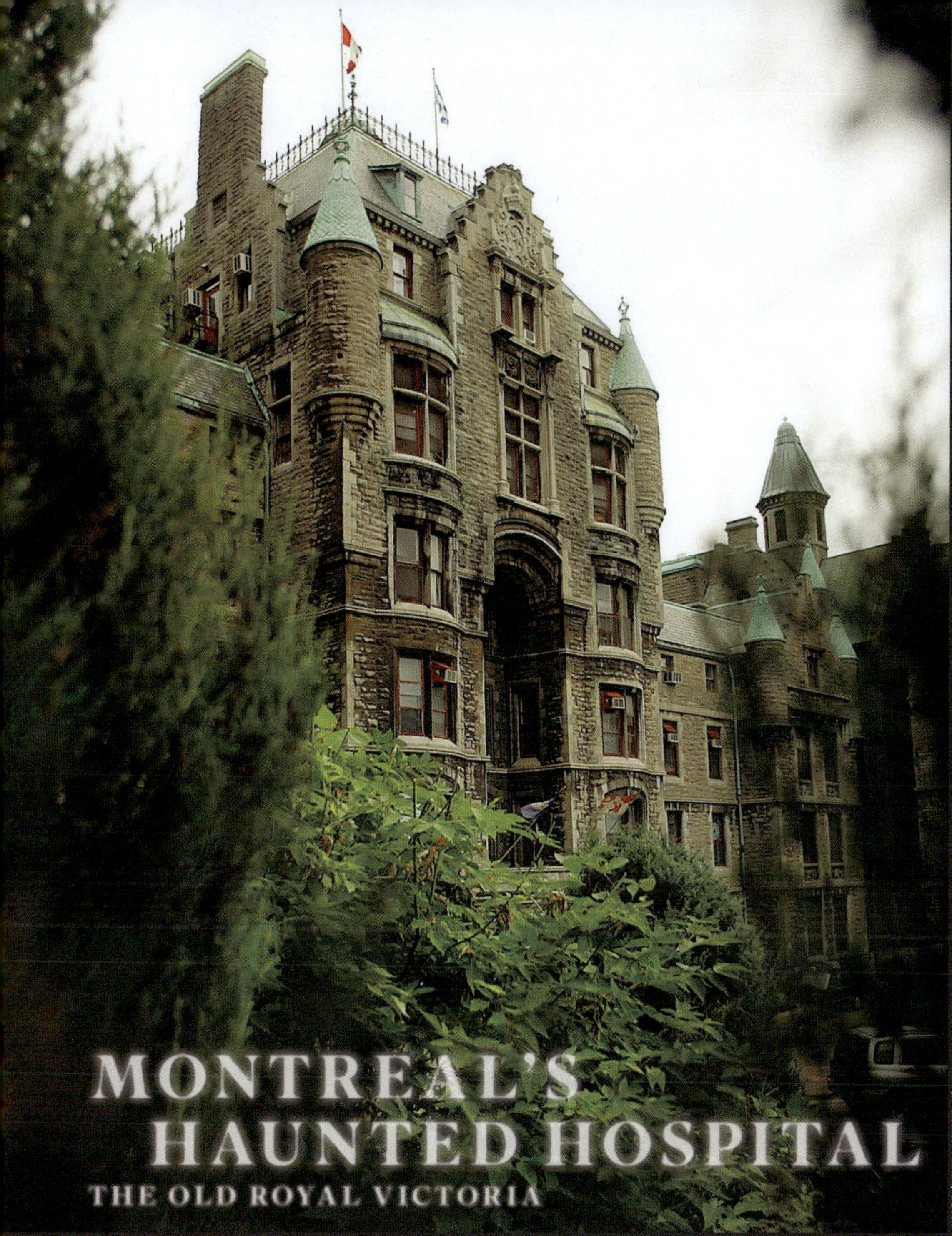

MONTREAL'S Royal Victoria Hospital in Quebec is just one of many supposedly haunted structures in the province's largest city. The Mount Royal Cemetery has the ghost of an Algonquin Indian who supposedly lurks on the cliffs; the Queen Elizabeth Hotel has a wandering woman in white; and 242 William Street is allegedly home to the ghost of a decapitated prostitute, Mary Gallagher, who spends eternity looking for—what else?—her missing head.

CHRISTINNE MUSCHI/TORONTO STAR/GETTY

MONTREAL'S HAUNTED HOSPITAL

THE OLD ROYAL VICTORIA

LOOMING OVER THE CITY on the south slope of Mount Royal, "the Vic" has seen plenty of distressed patients during its 122-year history, but some of them may have never checked out—though presumably not because they liked the food.

After one man died in the cardiac unit, the nurses shut his door—but when they returned with his family, they found the room locked . . . from the inside. A napping nurse once woke to see a "white smoky light" hovering above her, followed by two other apparitions. And one patient claimed that, after speaking to the specter of an old woman, he found himself lying in a pool of blood. (No, he wasn't in the E.R.)

In addition to the usual knockings and flickering lights, the Vic once contained a haunted painting. According to McGill University Health Centre's website, it showed a house in which patients saw a sinister old woman staring from the window. A few times, she even left the house and looked around before going back inside. Not surprisingly, the animated art was removed.

This past April, the operating hospital of the Vic was moved to a new location. Whether the original building becomes a hotel, a condo, or sinks into desuetude, one thing is certain: The hospital's persistent patients may never be discharged. ■

THE MOST HAUNTED SHIP

THE *QUEEN MARY*

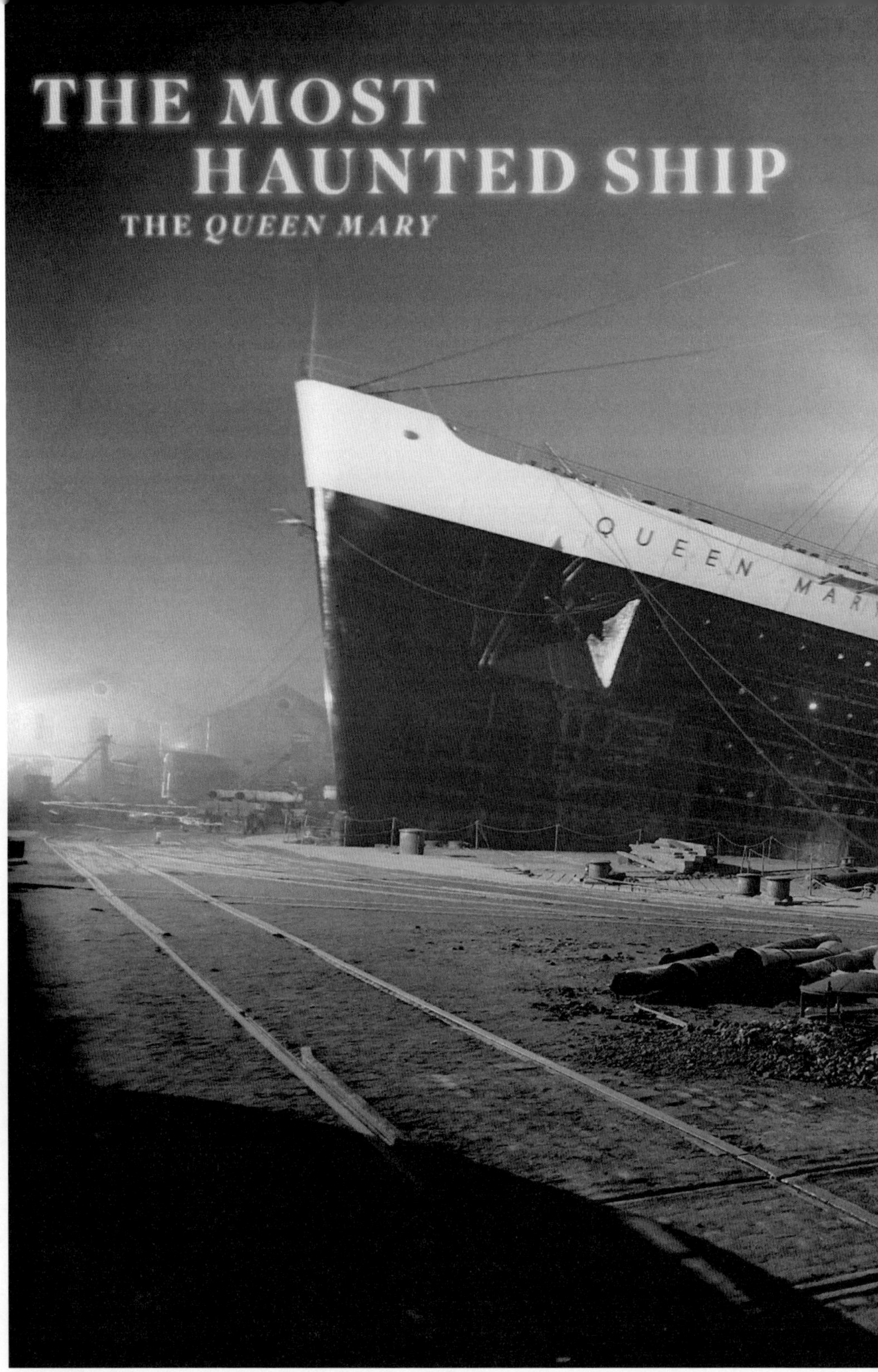

YEARS AFTER the legendary *Queen Mary* luxury liner was permanently docked as a hotel and tourist attraction in Long Beach, California, a marine engineer named John Smith had an unsettling experience while prowling the ship late at night. In a deserted staircase, Smith heard the sound of water rushing and men screaming—but no one was there.

Later, Smith learned that in 1942, when the liner was being used in World War II, it collided with its companion vessel, the HMS *Curacao*, on its way to Gourock, Scotland. The *Curacao* was immediately sheared in two and sunk, killing 338 men. "The very area I heard that mysterious water rushing was the exact same area that was damaged when the ship hit the *Curacao*," Smith told *Unsolved Mysteries*.

It's not surprising that a nearly 80-year-old ship with more than a thousand ocean crossings and a reported 49 deaths behind it would have a reputation for being haunted. Before it was retrofitted, painted gray, and used in the war as the so-called Grey Ghost, the *Queen Mary* began as a luxury liner in 1936, ferrying the likes of Fred Astaire and Bob Hope across the Atlantic.

But during the war, in addition to the collision, many German and Italian POWs carried on the liner may have died, as did soldiers from heat stroke traveling in the Mediterranean and the Indian Ocean. "We know that other deaths from natural causes, suicide and accidents occurred, and there are still others that [the owners] tried to hide for a more dark and sinister reason," wrote Brian Clune in *Ghosts of the Queen Mary*.

Room B-340 is widely believed to be the most haunted on the ship, a site where a family was allegedly murdered. But Clune says this is a fiction created by former owners who wanted to use the unoccupied space as part of a tourist attraction. The *real* site of the murders, Clune says, is room B-474, which is (of course) haunted—as are the B deck (where a morgue and an isolation room were located during World War II), the engine room, the Green Room, and an area known as Shaft Alley.

But the most spirited area on the ship may be the former first-class pool area, home to Little Jackie, a five- or six-year-old girl who is perhaps the ship's most famous ghost. She is playful and talkative, her voice having been allegedly caught many times on tape (you can find examples

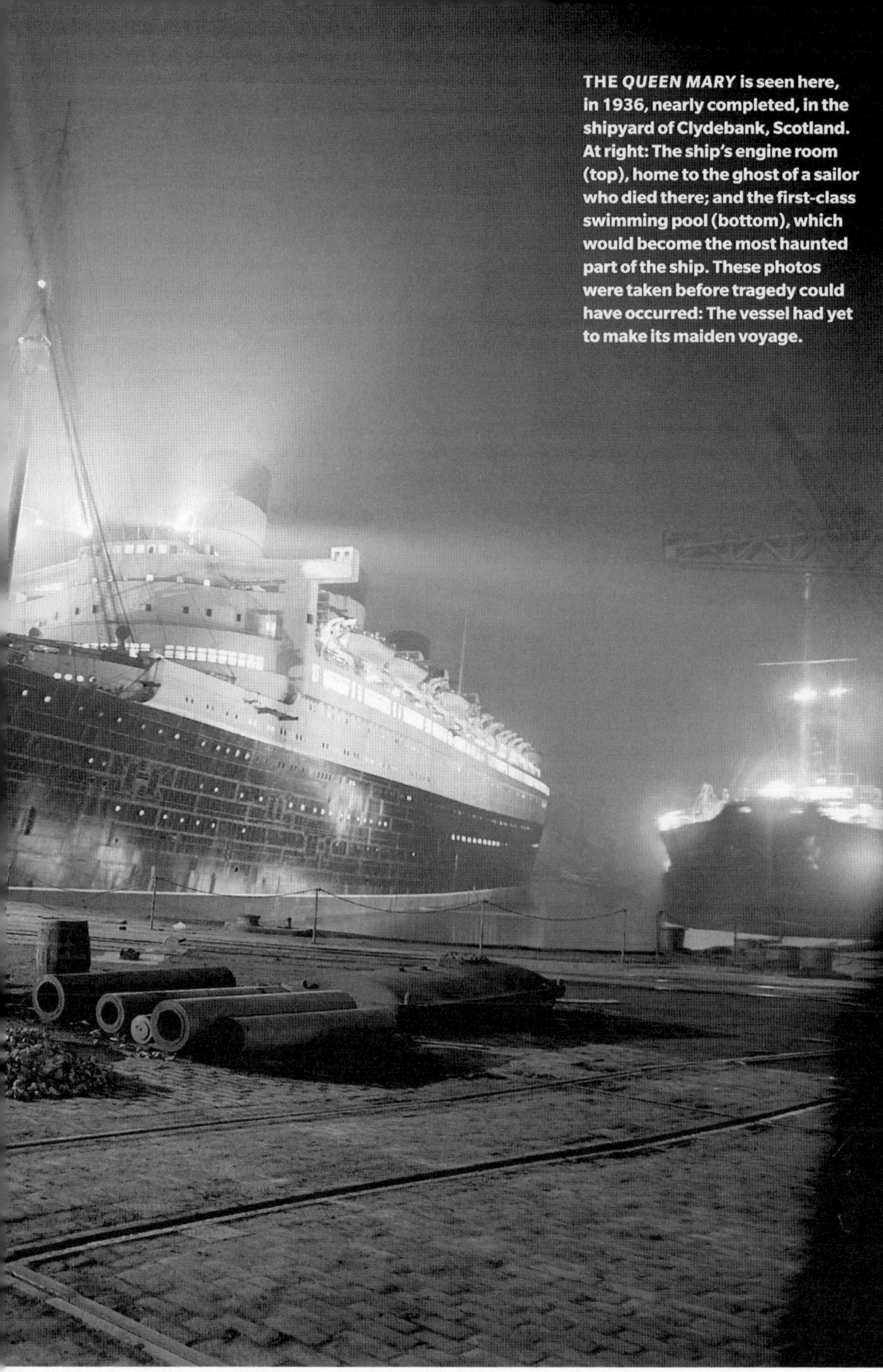

THE *QUEEN MARY* is seen here, in 1936, nearly completed, in the shipyard of Clydebank, Scotland. At right: The ship's engine room (top), home to the ghost of a sailor who died there; and the first-class swimming pool (bottom), which would become the most haunted part of the ship. These photos were taken before tragedy could have occurred: The vessel had yet to make its maiden voyage.

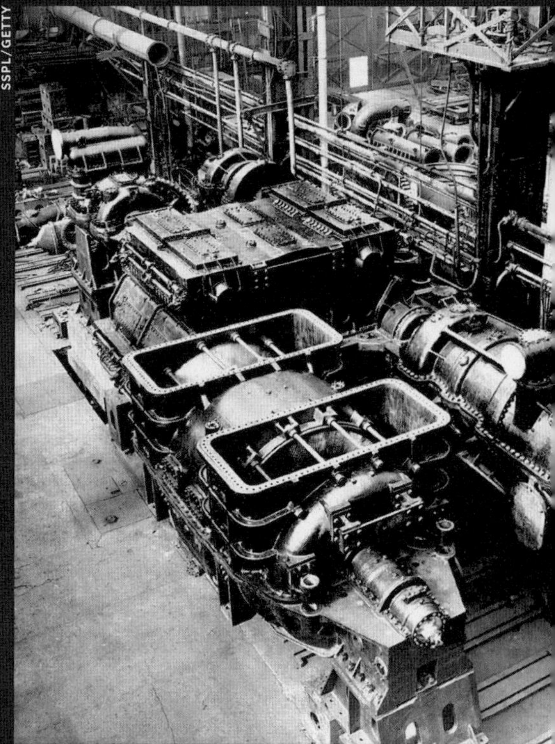

SSPL/GETTY

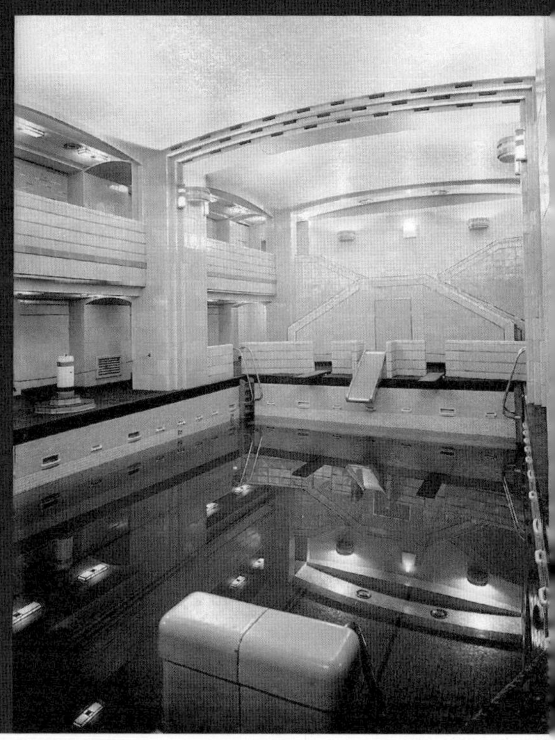

FOX PHOTOS/GETTY (2)

on YouTube). Sadly, she is said to remain on the ship because she is looking for her mother, whom she sometimes cries out for.

Another pool-room ghost is known as Grumpy, a growling, cigarette-smoking spirit said to haunt the storage area beneath the pool. And choking sounds near the old hospital area allegedly emanate from the ghost of an officer who died after drinking poison that he thought was gin.

Still other ghosts include the Lady in White, who is often seen dancing to unheard music in the Queen's Salon, and the spirit of an 18-year-old crewman, John Pedder, who was crushed by airtight door number 13 in Shaft Alley while playing chicken with his co-workers.

These days the grand ship capitalizes on (not to say *exploits*) its spooky reputation by offering haunted tours, interactive attractions, and séances. There's even a dinner special called Dining with the Spirits, which allows you to pair paranormal investigations with more earthbound spirits. Bloody Mary, anyone? ■

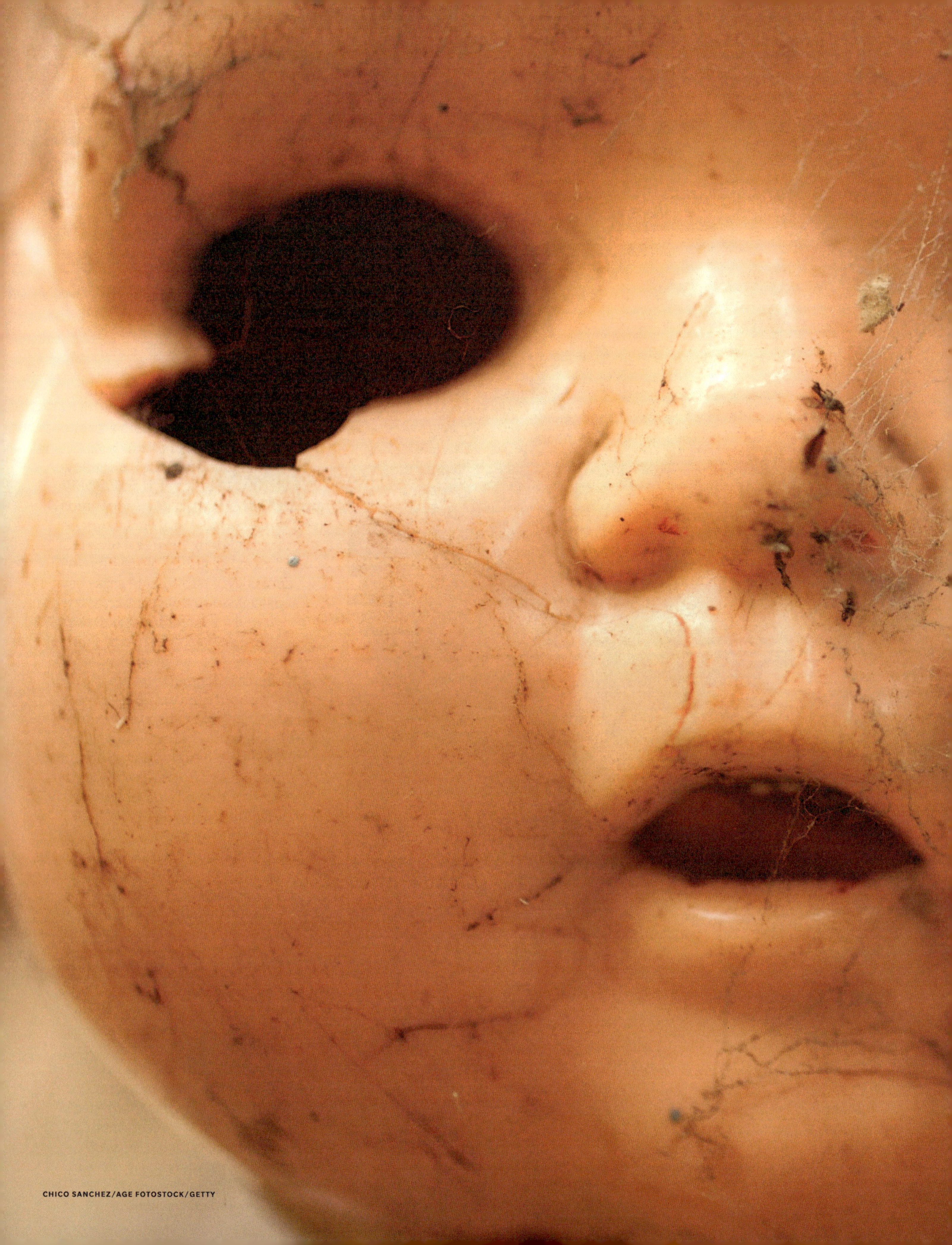

CHICO SANCHEZ/AGE FOTOSTOCK/GETTY

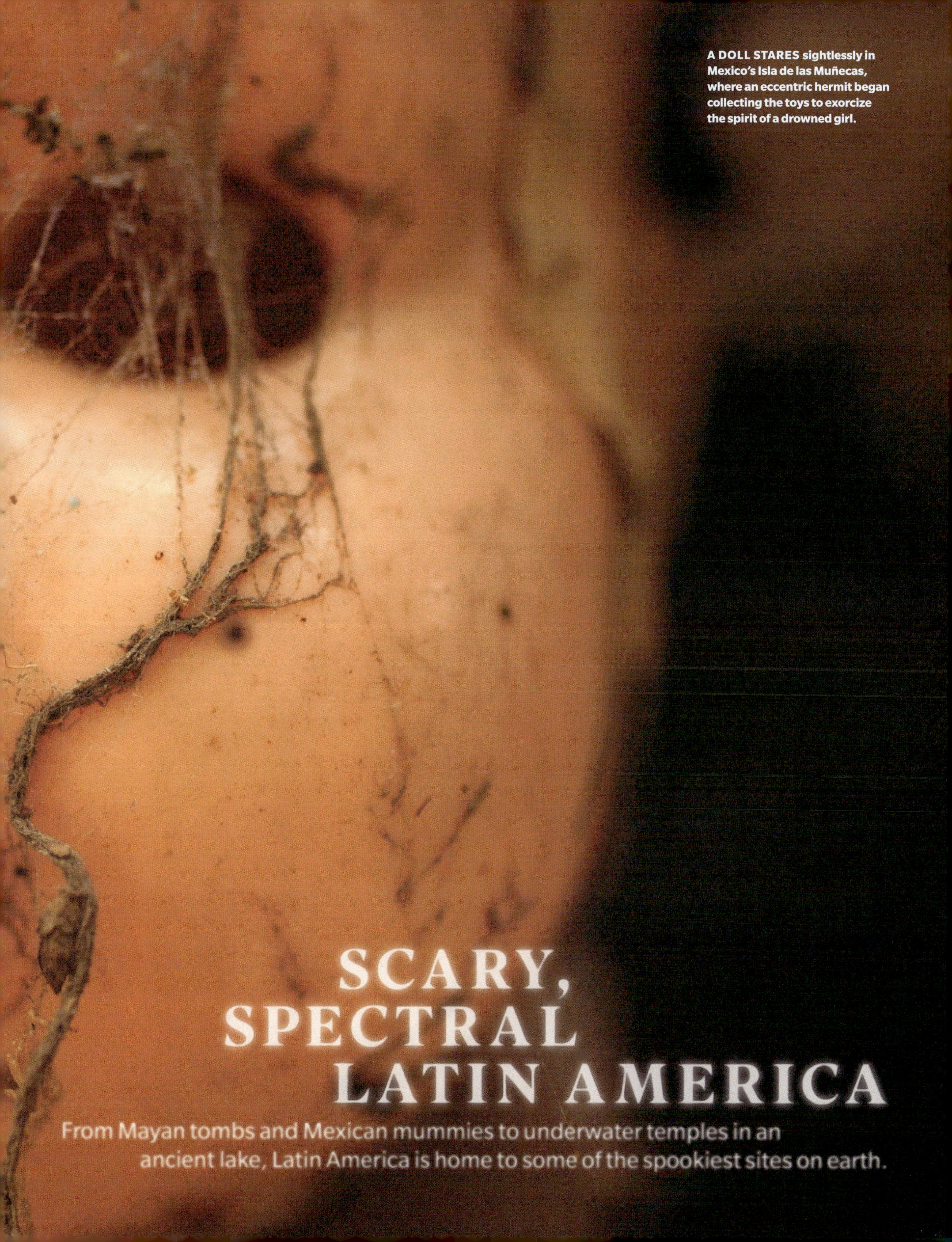

A DOLL STARES sightlessly in Mexico's Isla de las Muñecas, where an eccentric hermit began collecting the toys to exorcize the spirit of a drowned girl.

SCARY, SPECTRAL LATIN AMERICA

From Mayan tombs and Mexican mummies to underwater temples in an ancient lake, Latin America is home to some of the spookiest sites on earth.

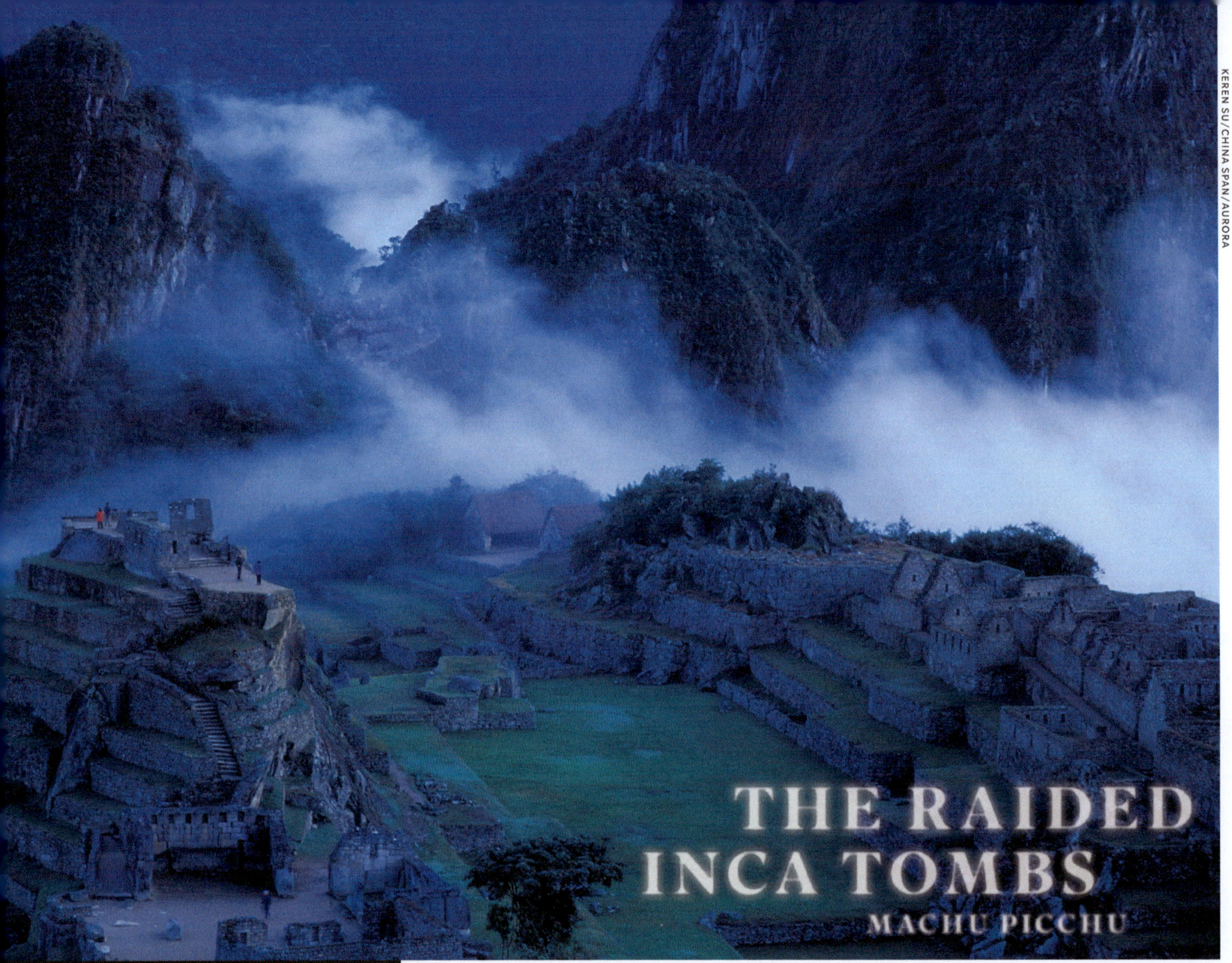

KEREN SU/CHINA SPAN/AURORA

THE RAIDED INCA TOMBS

MACHU PICCHU

ACCORDING TO THE MAN who discovered Machu Picchu, Hiram Bingham, the locals believed "a certain amount of bad luck might happen to their crops should they desecrate the bones of the ancient people buried in the vicinity." That's why the farmers asked for pieces of the bodies' muscles: They wanted to eat them, believing this would ward off a curse. "As Bingham was about to discover for himself," wrote Christopher Heaney in *The Cradle of Gold*, "if there was a curse to Machu Picchu, then this was it: if something can be possessed, then it can be fought over."

"GRAVE ROBBING is at best an unholy venture," wrote osteologist and Yale University professor George Eaton, who was, after all, in a position to know. A year after his colleague Hiram Bingham became the first Westerner to uncover Peru's "lost" city of Machu Picchu, Eaton helped a second Yale expedition unearth 52 ancient Inca graves in 1912.

That August, Eaton and two local Quechuan guides opened their 26th grave, finding a female skeleton with the knees pressed to the chest. Eaton thought it was the body of a priestess, and his unnerved local helpers must have agreed: Soon afterward, one of them did not show up for work, citing pain in his testicles. Then the second man disappeared.

"The fact that the people of Machu Picchu were helping dig up their dead ancestors led them to believe they were cursed," Mark Adams, author of *Turn Right at Machu Picchu*, told LIFE. "At the very least it meant that whatever spiritual significance the remains might have had was gone."

Inexplicably abandoned by the Inca four centuries ago, Machu Picchu is the most famous architectural ruin in the West. It's also one of the most mysterious, a fact that has fueled more than a few theories—from the scholarly to the superstitious. Was it a defensive stronghold or a royal retreat? Was it built by space aliens? Is it the gathering place for the ghosts of Inca priests? But the so-called curse may have been lifted: In 2012, Yale University returned the artifacts that were stolen from Peru nearly one hundred years before. ■

THE SPIRIT STATUES

EASTER ISLAND

ABOUT 2,300 MILES off the coast of Chile, Easter Island (otherwise known as Rapa Nui) is an isolated patch of deforested volcanic land that is one of the world's most remote inhabited islands. Called Te Pito O Te Henu (the Navel of the World) by its Polynesian settlers, it is best known as the site of hundreds of *moai*, the iconic stone heads.

Sculpted from volcanic rock between the 10th and 16th centuries, the moai probably honor the islanders' ancestors (no two heads are the same). Many were somehow moved from the island's quarry to its perimeter—even though they weigh up to 80 tons. (They even have underground bodies!)

No one knows for sure how this feat of prehistoric engineering was accomplished. But some of the island's 5,000 inhabitants insist the statues walked or even flew into place, animated by *mana*, a kind of spiritual force. Some claim they've seen apparitions or heard ancient voices near the moai. Others suggest the heads were moved by extraterrestrials, but we'll leave that to UFO theorist Erich von Dänekin.

The island's history is creepy enough without the paranormal overlay. The original population may have grown too quickly, leading to the dwindling of natural resources (sound familiar?). There is even evidence of cannibalism. But recent theories suggest that an infestation of Polynesian rats may have brought the people to their collective knees. All of this is, of course, enough to give even Stephen King nightmares—with or without the moving statues. ▪

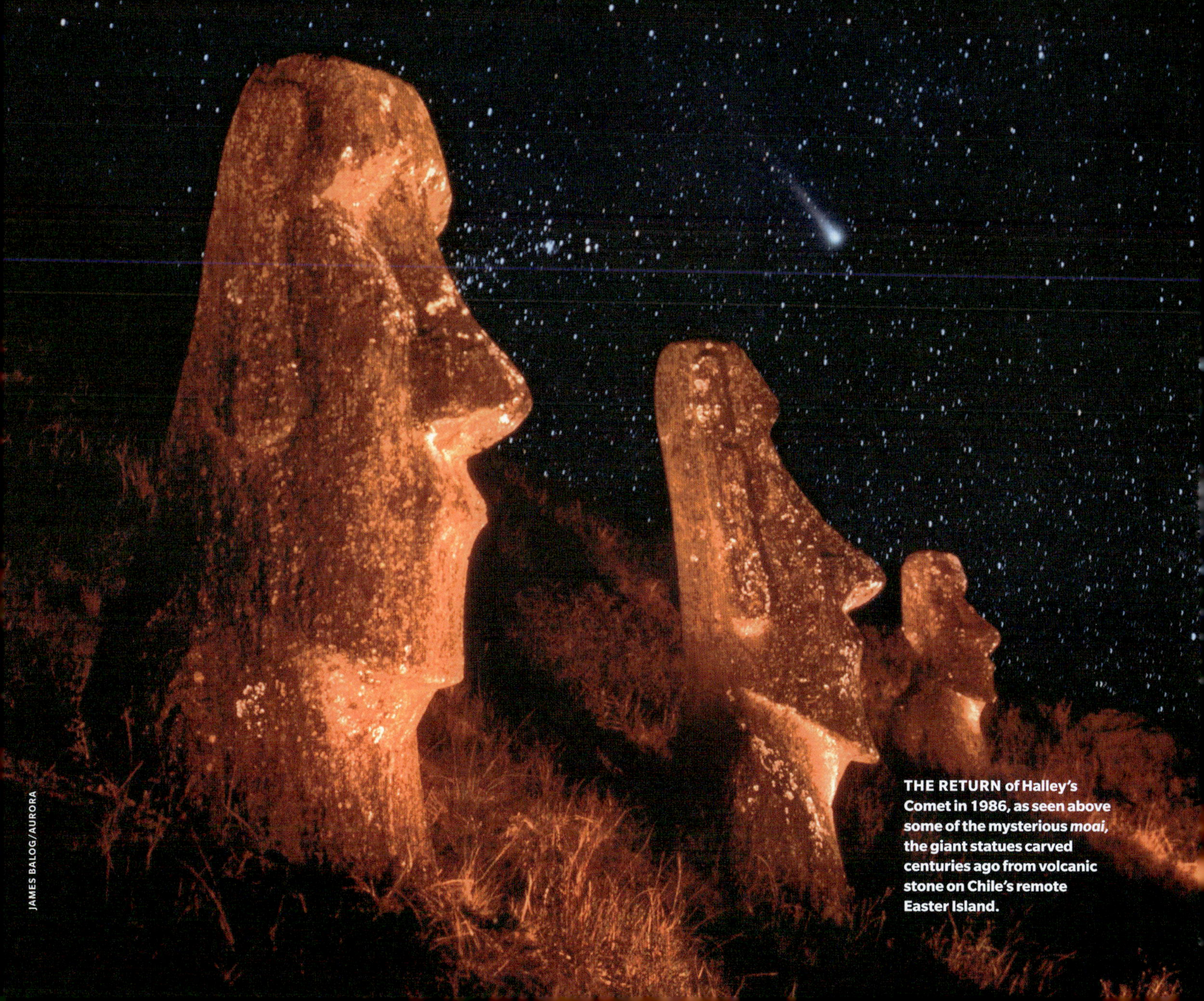

JAMES BALOG/AURORA

THE RETURN of Halley's Comet in 1986, as seen above some of the mysterious *moai*, the giant statues carved centuries ago from volcanic stone on Chile's remote Easter Island.

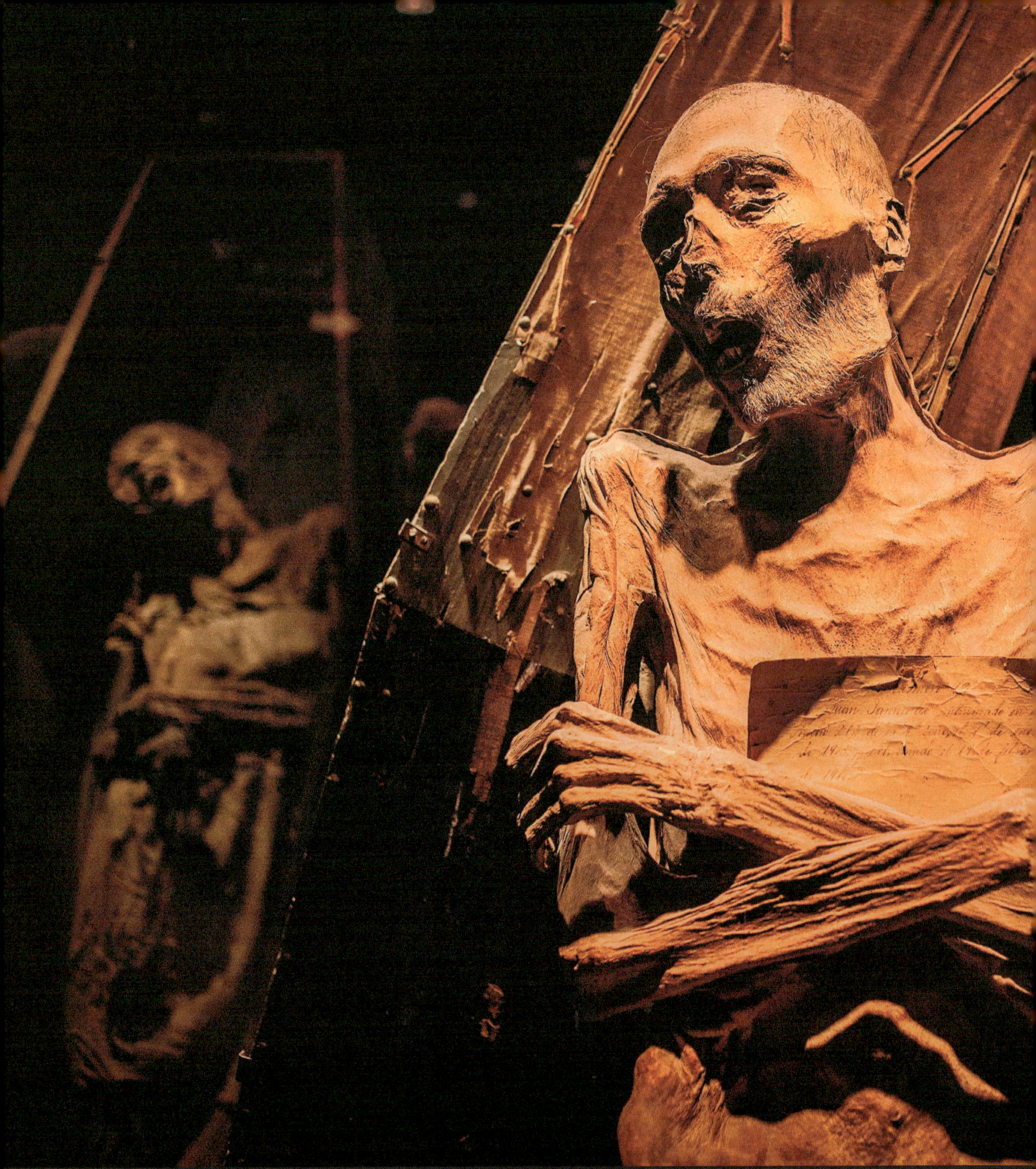

CITY OF THE PLUNDERED DEAD

THE MUMMY MUSEUM

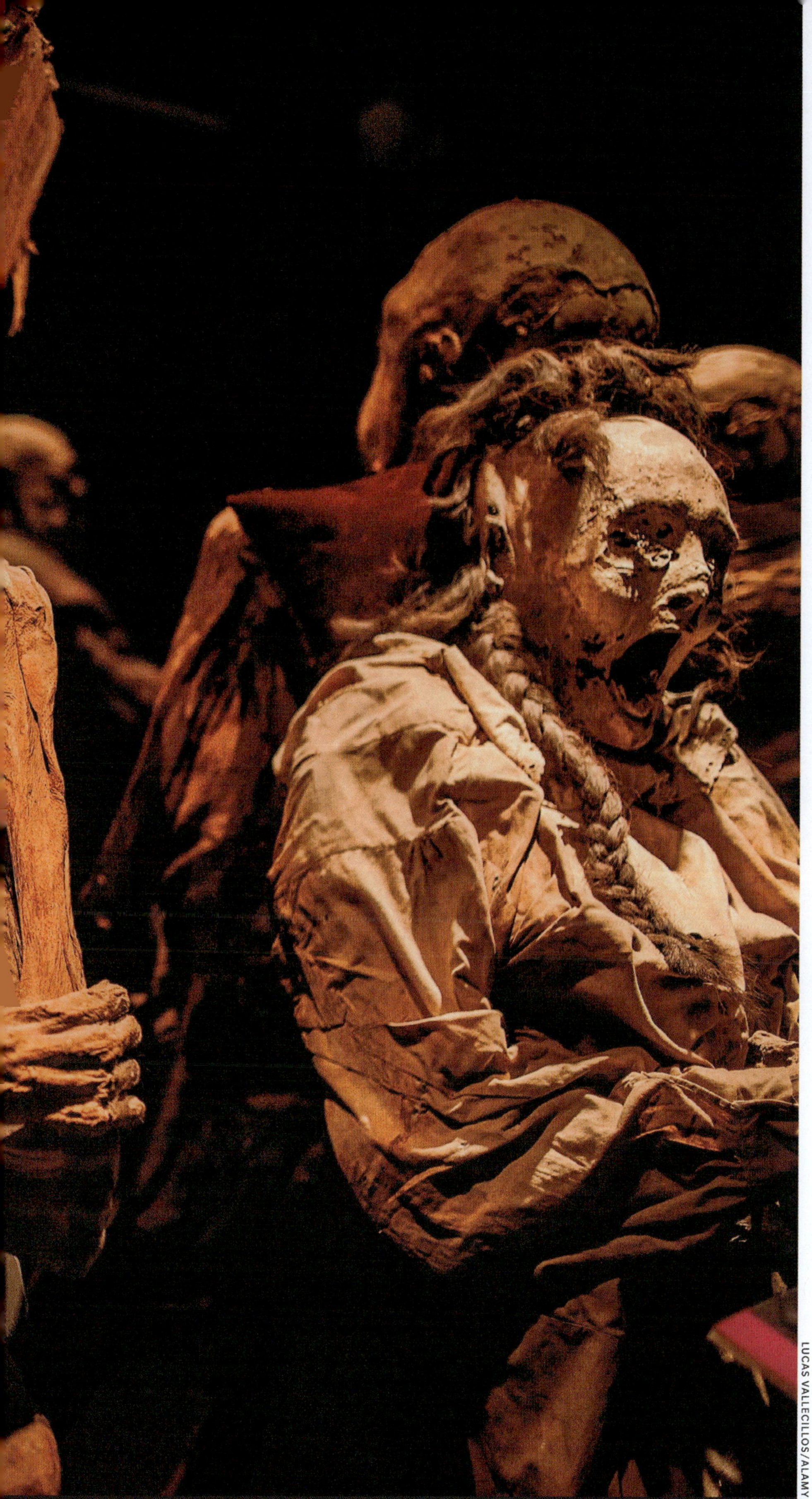

LUCAS VALLECILLOS/ALAMY

SOME OF THE MUMMIES on display at the Mummy Museum in Guanajuato, Mexico. "The experience so wounded and terrified me, I could hardly wait to flee Mexico," author Ray Bradbury wrote after touring the grisly site.

"IN THIS WORLD nothing can be said to be certain, except death and taxes," Benjamin Franklin once wrote. And the two were once gruesomely combined in the silver-mining town of Guanajuato, Mexico. Between the 1860s and 1958, relatives were forced to pay a tax to keep their dead loved ones buried in Santa Paula Pantheon cemetery. If they couldn't afford the fee, the bodies were removed from the tombs and stored in the ossuary.

Because of the dry, hot climate—and the fact that the corpses had been kept in airtight crypts—some of the unearthed souls had become well-preserved mummies. When curious locals began asking to see the bodies, workers started charging for the questionable privilege. And that was the beginning of the Museo de las Momias de Guanajuato, which opened its doors in 1969.

The museum showcases more than 100 mummies in climate-controlled glass cases, their gruesome grimaces the result of hardening tongues and slackening jaws. (No, they were not buried alive, as some have suggested.) There is even a row of babies called *angelitos* and *santitos,* dressed as angels and saints, respectively. The museum also contains what is believed to be the smallest mummy in the world, the remains of a 24-week-old fetus.

Wherever dead bodies have been disturbed, you can be pretty sure there will be ghost stories—and this place is no exception. People have reported seeing the apparition of a tall lady and hearing strange whispering sounds and the cries of babies in the building.

Perhaps trying to justify the display, the museum is careful to say that death is more widely accepted—even celebrated—in Mexico than in many other places. Fair enough, but it's a bit disconcerting to buy sugar skulls and souvenir effigies of mummies in a place where, not so long ago, impoverished people couldn't even pay to keep their loved ones buried. ■

THE HEAVENS . . . AND HELL

CHICHÉN ITZÁ

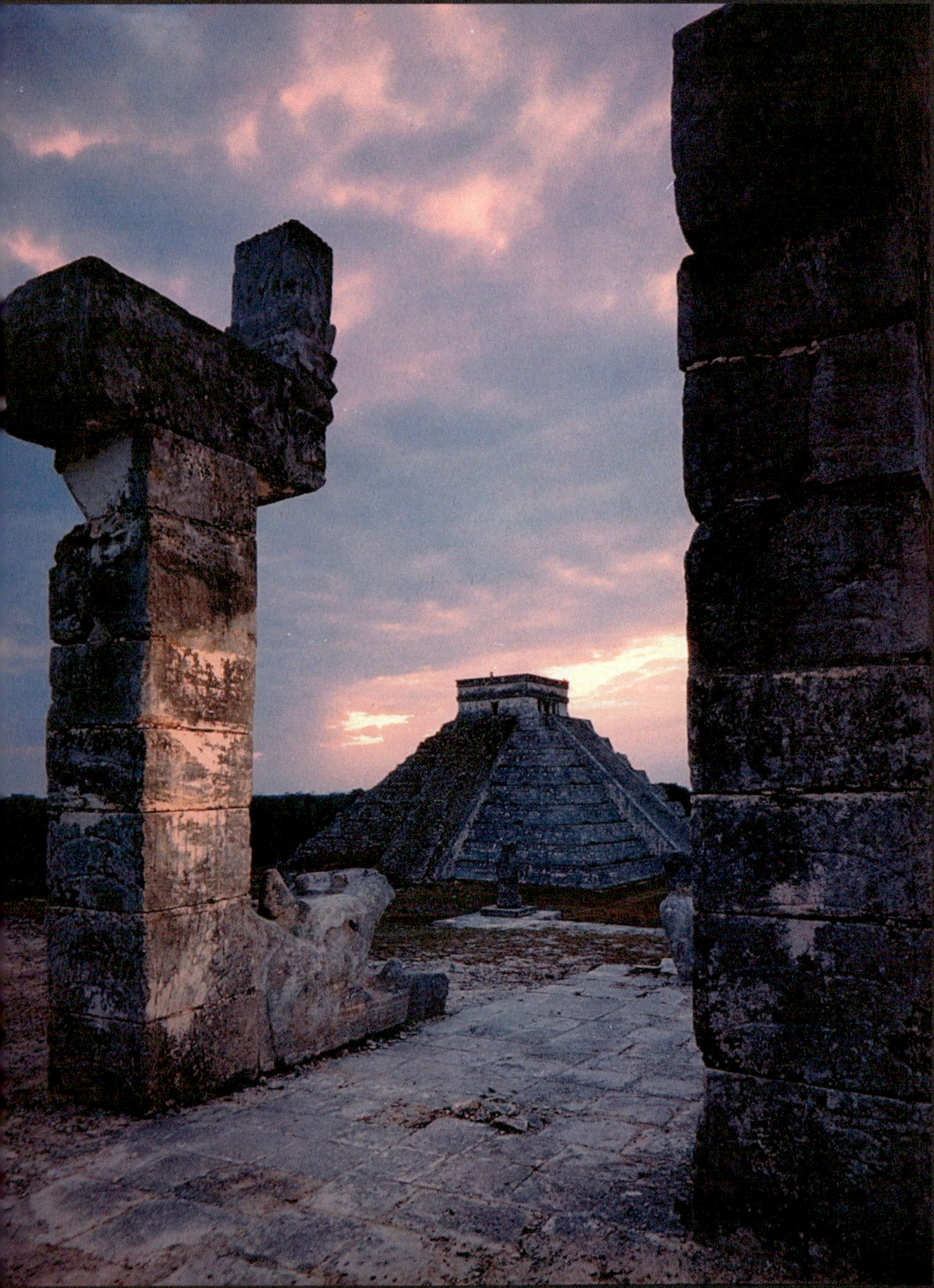

DMITRI KESSEL/LIFE/THE PICTURE COLLECTION

THE ANCIENT Mayan city of Chichén Itzá with El Kukulkan Pyramid—named one of the new seven wonders of the world in 2007—in the background.

IN THE SO-CALLED Dresden Codex, one of four existing pre-Columbian Mayan manuscripts, you will find hieroglyphic divination calendars, descriptions of new-year ceremonies, and instructions on how to find the local rain god, Chaak. The codex was created sometime between A.D. 1200 and 1250 by the astronomer priests who spent dark hours observing the heavens from the observatory in Chichén Itzá, in Mexico's Yucatán Peninsula.

Dubbed El Caracol (The Snail), the observatory is where most hauntings in modern Chichén Itzá are said to occur. "As I strolled down the corridor, I saw a man eyeing me," one tourist is quoted in *The International Directory of Haunted Places.* "He was angry about my being there . . . I sensed that he was not a priest or astronomer but rather some kind of assistant."

Odd, because the observatory was probably not a place of bloodshed—unlike the Great Ball Court, where a lethal game was played (the leader of the losing team was sacrificed, his severed skull used to mold the next ball). And recently the skeletons of six sacrificed humans—including two children—were unearthed from Chichén Itzá's Cenote Sagrado. A volcanic hole leading to an underground water source, the cenote may have been considered a portal to Xibalba, the Mayan underworld, where Chaak lived.

A major urban center since A.D. 750 or so, Chichén Itzá probably began to decline in 1000. Arriving in the 1500s, the Spanish conquistadors destroyed most of the codices, damning them as "devil's books." But thanks to the Dresden Codex, directions to Chaak's domain survive—along with, perhaps, the spirits of ancient astronomers.

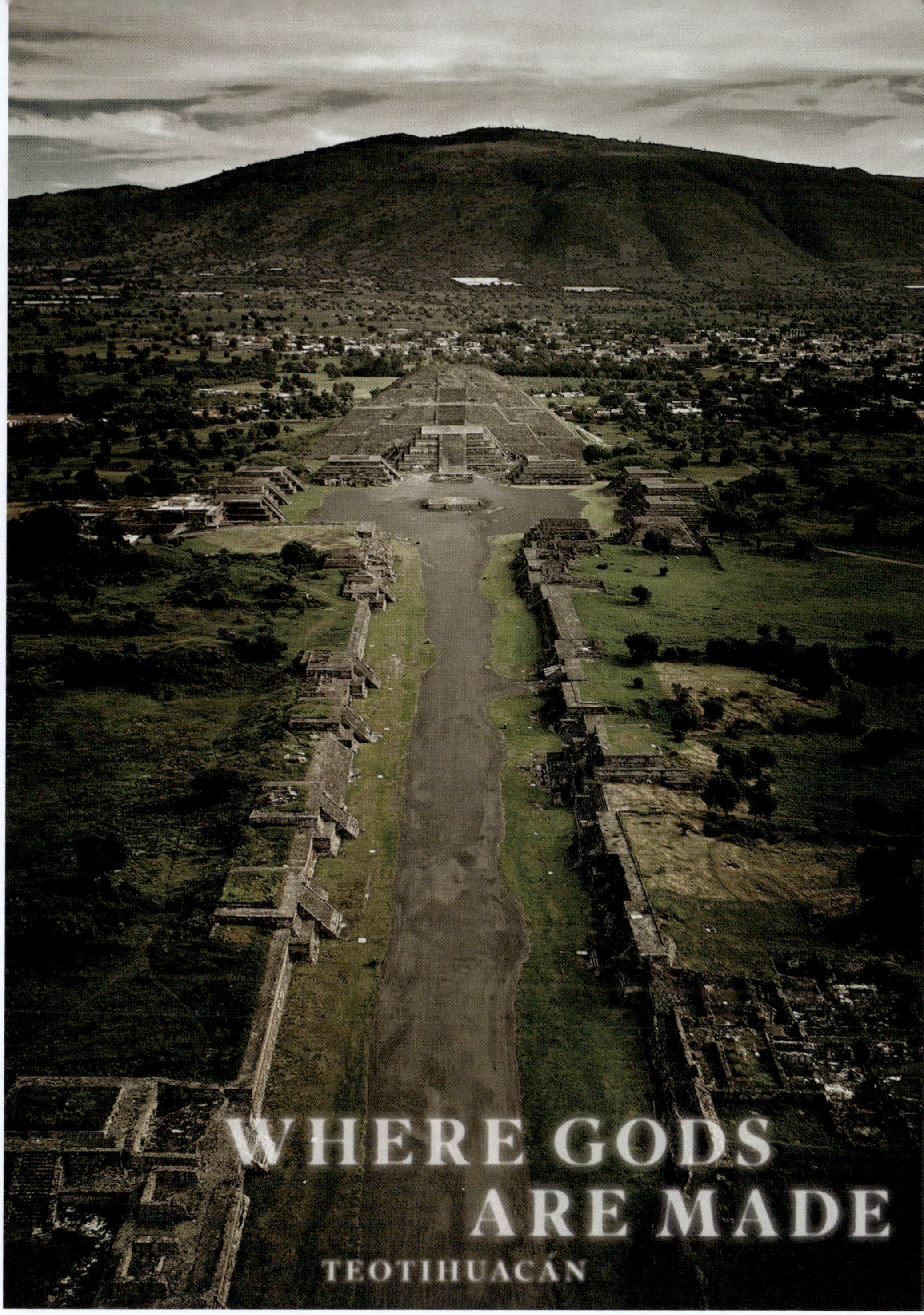

MARCOS FERRO/AURORA

LOOKING DOWN on the Street of the Dead at the Teotihuacán archaeological site, with the Pyramid of the Moon in the distance. The street was named because the structures that flank it were initially (and wrongly) thought to be tombs. The area is where the main excavations have taken place.

WHERE GODS ARE MADE

TEOTIHUACÁN

ABOUT 30 MILES outside Mexico City lie the ruins of pre-Columbian Teotihuacán, once one of the largest and most influential cities in the world. Built between the first and seventh centuries—no one is sure by whom or why—the civilization mostly disappeared after 750, possibly after an all-consuming fire.

When the Aztecs rediscovered the abandoned spot in the early 14th century, they were stunned by its grandeur, calling it "the place where gods are made," or "the City of Gods." But it was also a city of death, filled with evidence of human and animal sacrifice, clearly marking it as a spot of both brutal and sacred significance.

Some of its mysteries are not exactly supernatural: Gold-colored spheres were discovered in a hidden tunnel beneath the Temple of the Feathered Serpent in 2013, and liquid mercury that may indicate the presence of a tomb was found in 2015.

But a few visitors claim to have seen ghosts. Others have spotted the perhaps inevitable, if undocumented, UFOs over the pyramids (check out the videos on YouTube). Purplish, smoky streaks have appeared in photos (ditto). Go ahead: Blame Instagram filters or balloons, but since this place remains a mystery, why should its photographs be any different? ■

THE DROWNED GIRL'S EXORCISM

ISLAND OF THE DOLLS

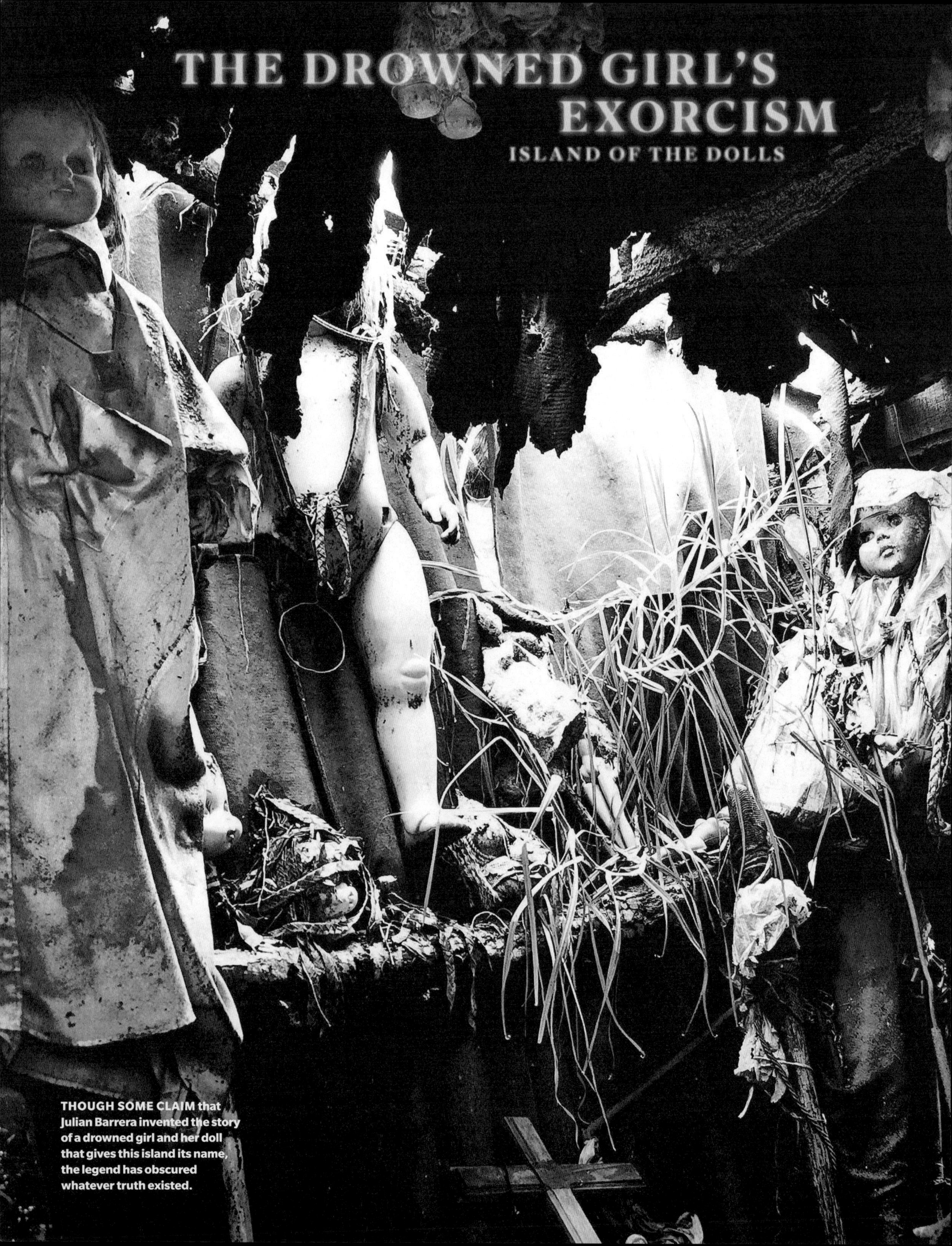

THOUGH SOME CLAIM that Julian Barrera invented the story of a drowned girl and her doll that gives this island its name, the legend has obscured whatever truth existed.

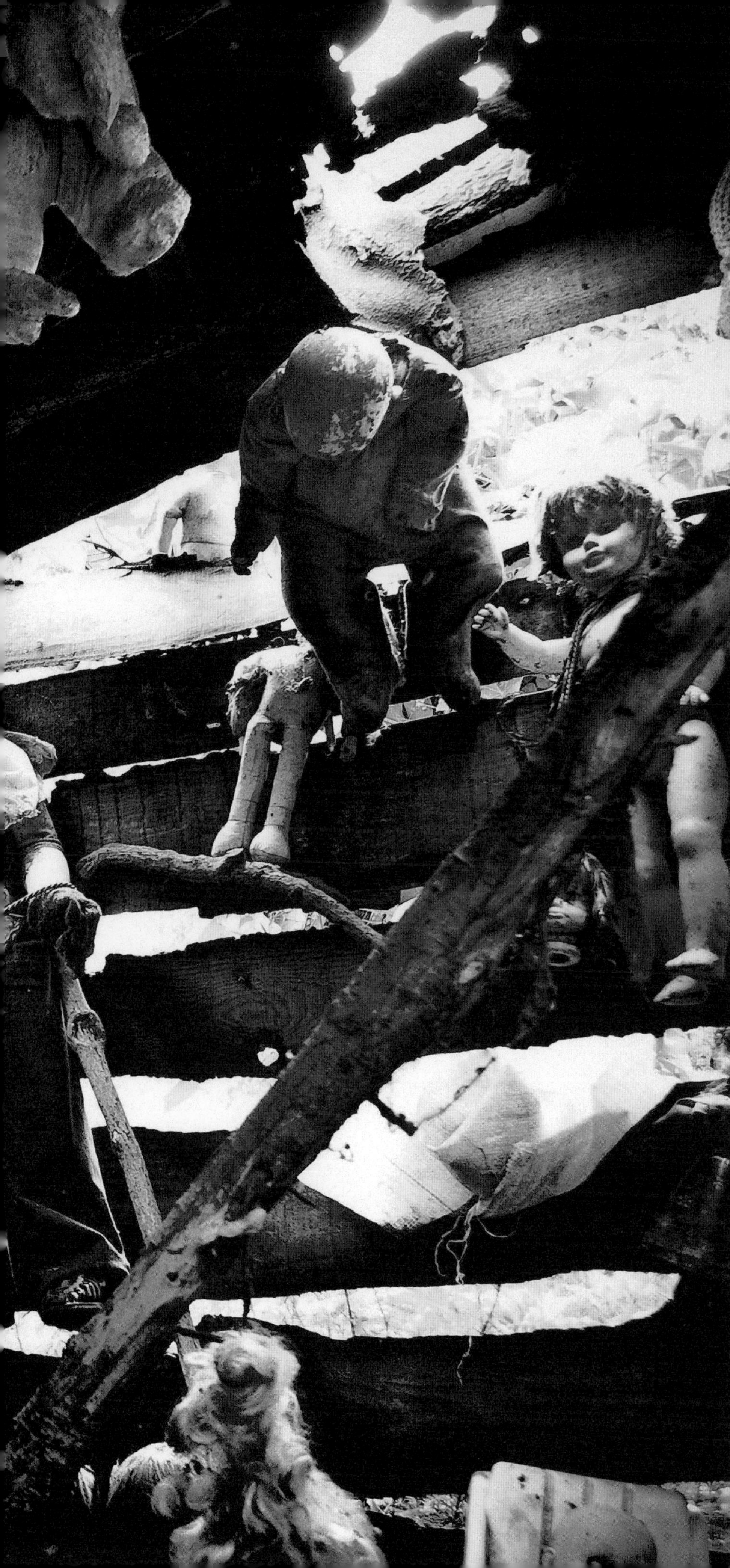

DAVID MAURICE SMITH/OCULI/REDUX

DRIFTING IN A BOAT through a tangle of narrow canals in Xochimilco, a district of Mexico City, you will find yourself heading toward an isolated island. Though it may seem like any other island at first, as you move closer you'll start to see the dolls. Yes, *dolls.* But this is hardly the Island of Misfit Toys—more like Chucky's dream vacation. It is called Isla de las Muñecas (Island of the Dolls), home to thousands of mutilated toys hanging from the trees and lying on the forest floor, eyeless skulls infested by insects.

More than 50 years ago, Julian Santana Barrera, the island's hermit caretaker, allegedly found a drowned girl in a nearby canal, her doll floating alongside her. Later, when he heard crying and footsteps around his shack at night, he became convinced that he was being haunted by the girl's restless spirit. Attempting to appease the ghost, he hung her doll in a tree. When the haunting did not stop, Barrera began hanging more dolls, creating an eerie amalgam of ritual offering and primitive art installation. In time, Barrera came to believe that all the dolls were possessed and that the island was not only haunted but cursed.

Some locals agree. Don't expect your boatman to join you on the island, for instance: Some won't even look at it as they approach. Others say they've seen the dolls moving or opening their eyes. Still others claim the toys whisper and gesture to passersby, as if saying "Join us."

In 2001, Barrera reportedly drowned in the same spot as the girl. Locals believe he, too, now haunts the island, which has become a bona fide tourist attraction. Some visitors bring dolls to add to the growing collection—including a wild-haired Barbie, clearly having left her Dreamhouse far behind. ■

FATAL SHORES

LAKE TITICACA

CARLOS SANCHEZ PEREYRA/DESIGN PICS/GETTY

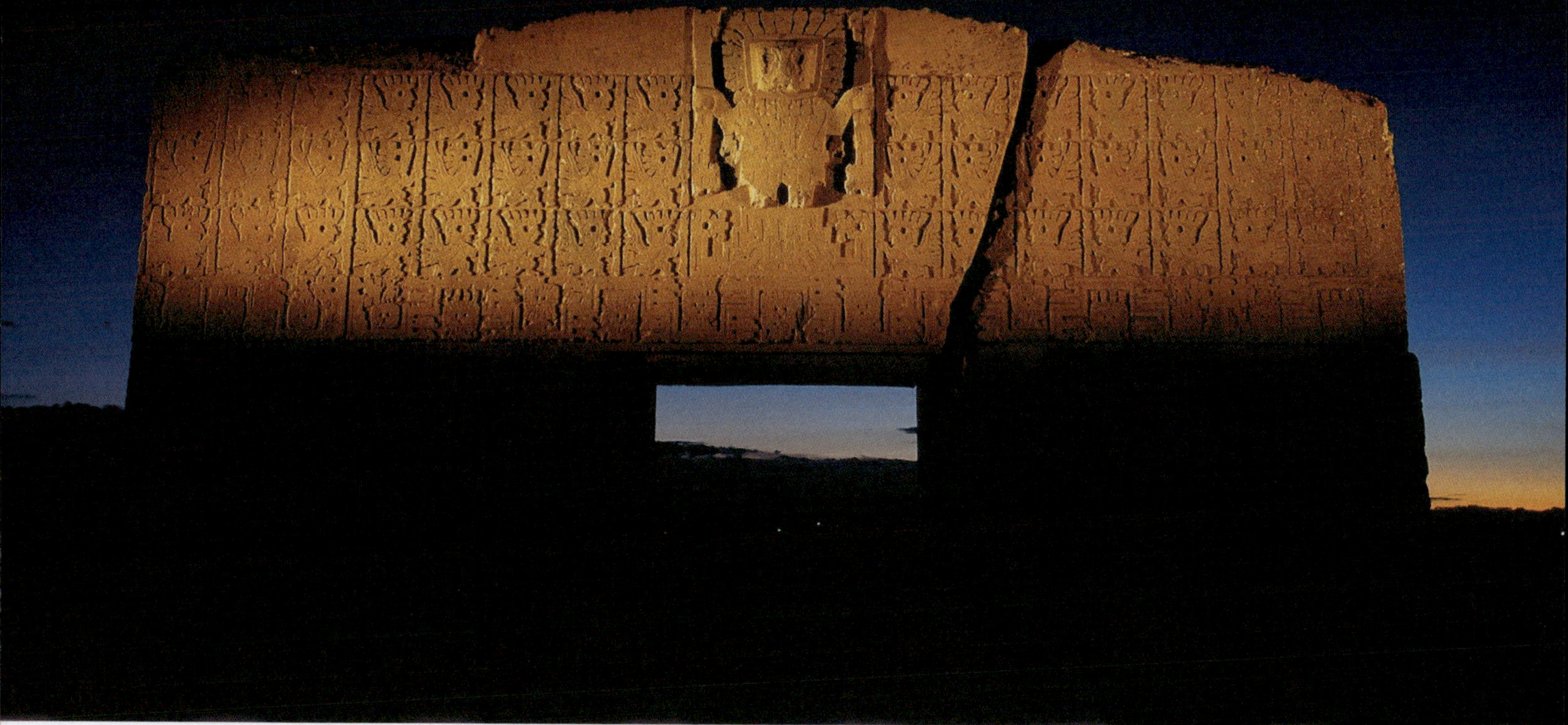

KENNETH GARRETT/NATIONAL GEOGRAPHIC CREATIVE

YOU'RE FLOATING 100 feet below the surface of an ancient lake when, through the watery gloom, you see shapes of things that don't seem to belong here. A terrace, a wall, algae-covered staircases lost in the depths, and a road leading nowhere . . .

Sound like a dream? Or a scene from the latest Indiana Jones film? Maybe, but this actually happened in 2000, when scientists discovered the long-rumored pre-Inca ruins of a 660-foot-long, 160-foot-wide temple under Lake Titicaca, an ancient body of water high in the Andes Mountains on the border of Bolivia and Peru.

The flooded temple is just one of many mysteries surrounding this lake—not least of which is the remains of Tiahuanaco, a sacred ceremonial center near Titicaca's southern shores. Tiahuanaco reached its peak between A.D. 400 and 900 before collapsing in the first half of the 12th century. (Like the submerged temple, some of Tiahuanaco's ruins are underground—in March 2015, a buried pyramid was found.)

Though some have said the Inca built the city, Tiahuanaco probably predates them by at least 1,000 years. (The Inca believed Lake Titicaca was the birthplace of the sun and that they were its children.) Some have suggested the Egyptians were somehow involved in its construction. And the ghosts of the ancient race have reportedly been seen in the environs—particularly inside the Kalasasaya, one of the ruins' main buildings.

In Tiahuanaco lie the ruins of Pumapunku, thought—by some—to have been built by (wait for it) extraterrestrials. Yes, we've heard this before: Ancient megaliths seem to automatically signify the presence of otherworldly astronauts. But UFOs have been spotted all over the lake area, where (so the legend goes) the sun sent the founders of the Inca civilization. ■

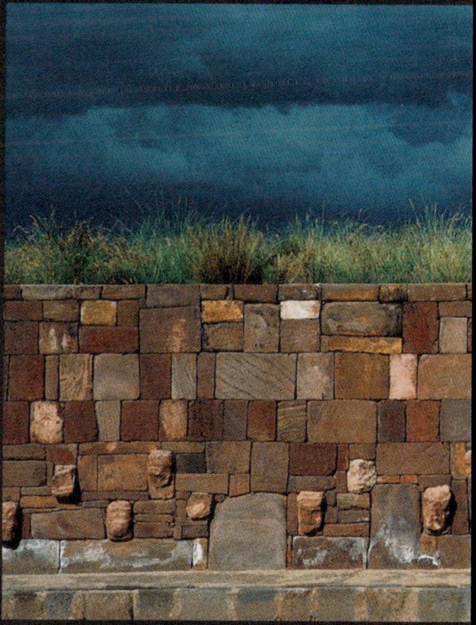

© WOLFGANG KAEHLER

OPPOSITE PAGE: The shores of mysterious Lake Titicaca. Top: The Gate of the Sun at Kalasasaya Temple in Tiahuanaco, a pre-Columbian city near Lake Titicaca, was carved from a single block of stone. The temple was part of an astronomical observatory. Above: The sculptured heads set in the walls probably reflect the civilization's practice of displaying the trophy heads of slaughtered enemies.

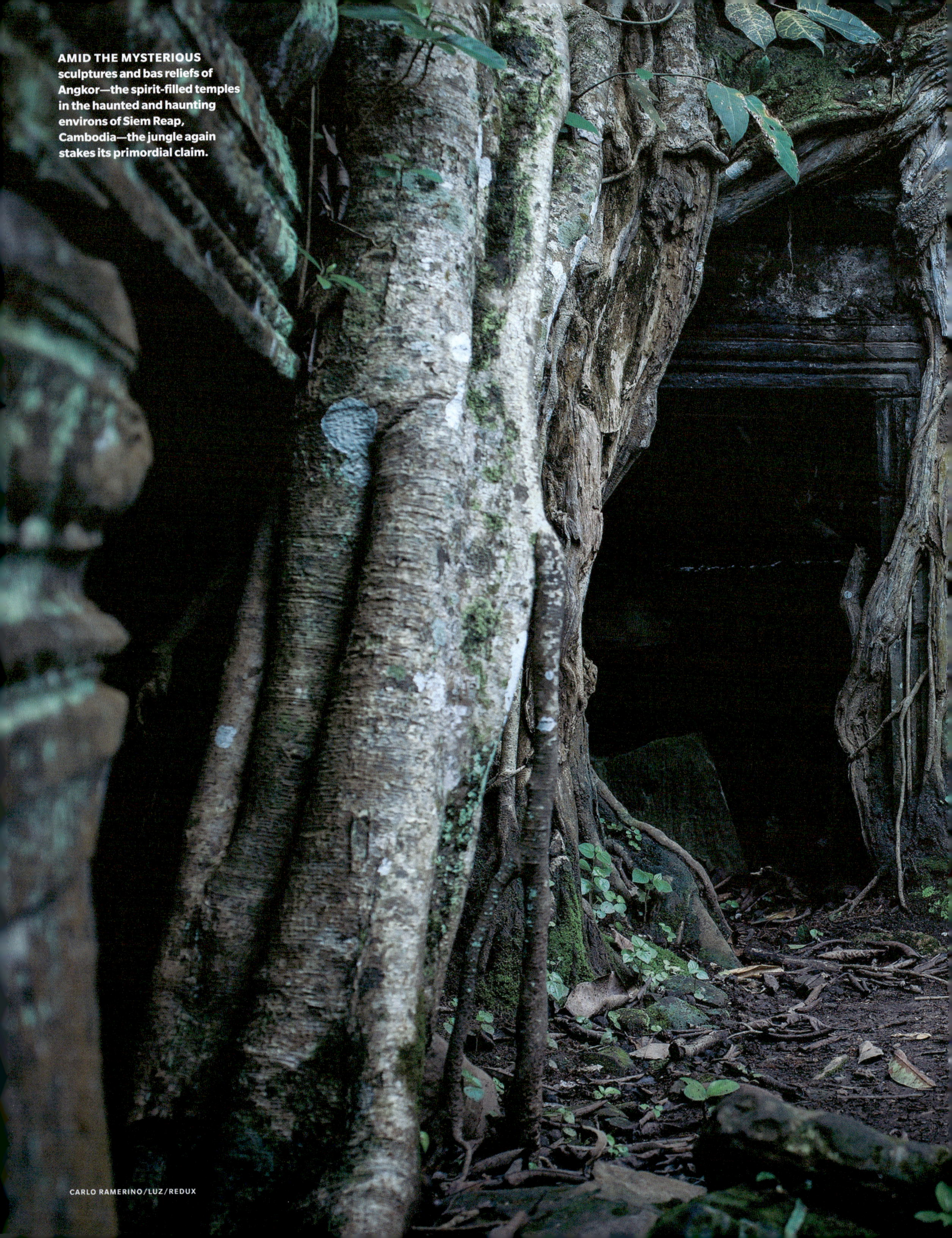

AMID THE MYSTERIOUS sculptures and bas reliefs of Angkor—the spirit-filled temples in the haunted and haunting environs of Siem Reap, Cambodia—the jungle again stakes its primordial claim.

CARLO RAMERINO/LUZ/REDUX

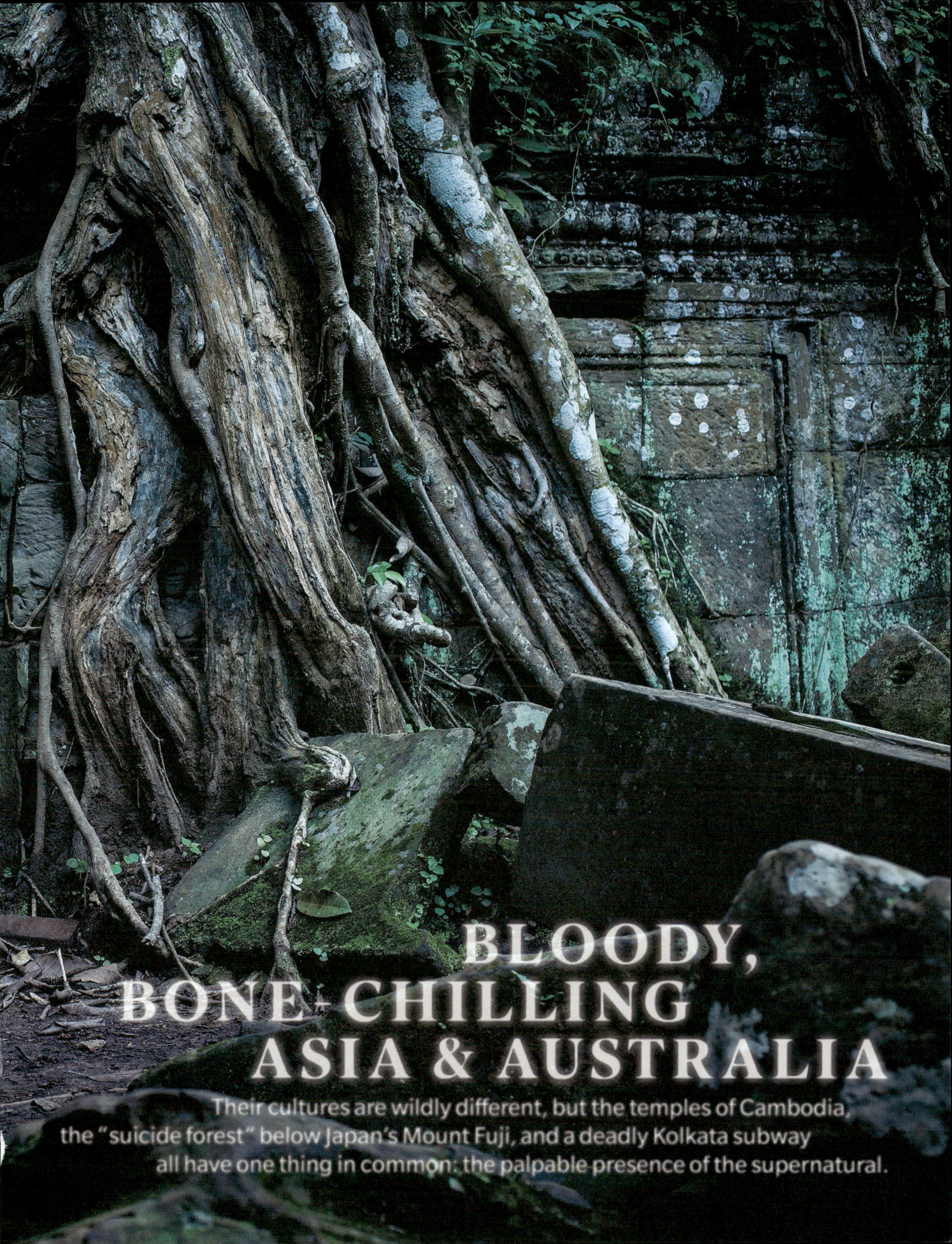

BLOODY, BONE-CHILLING ASIA & AUSTRALIA

Their cultures are wildly different, but the temples of Cambodia, the "suicide forest" below Japan's Mount Fuji, and a deadly Kolkata subway all have one thing in common: the palpable presence of the supernatural.

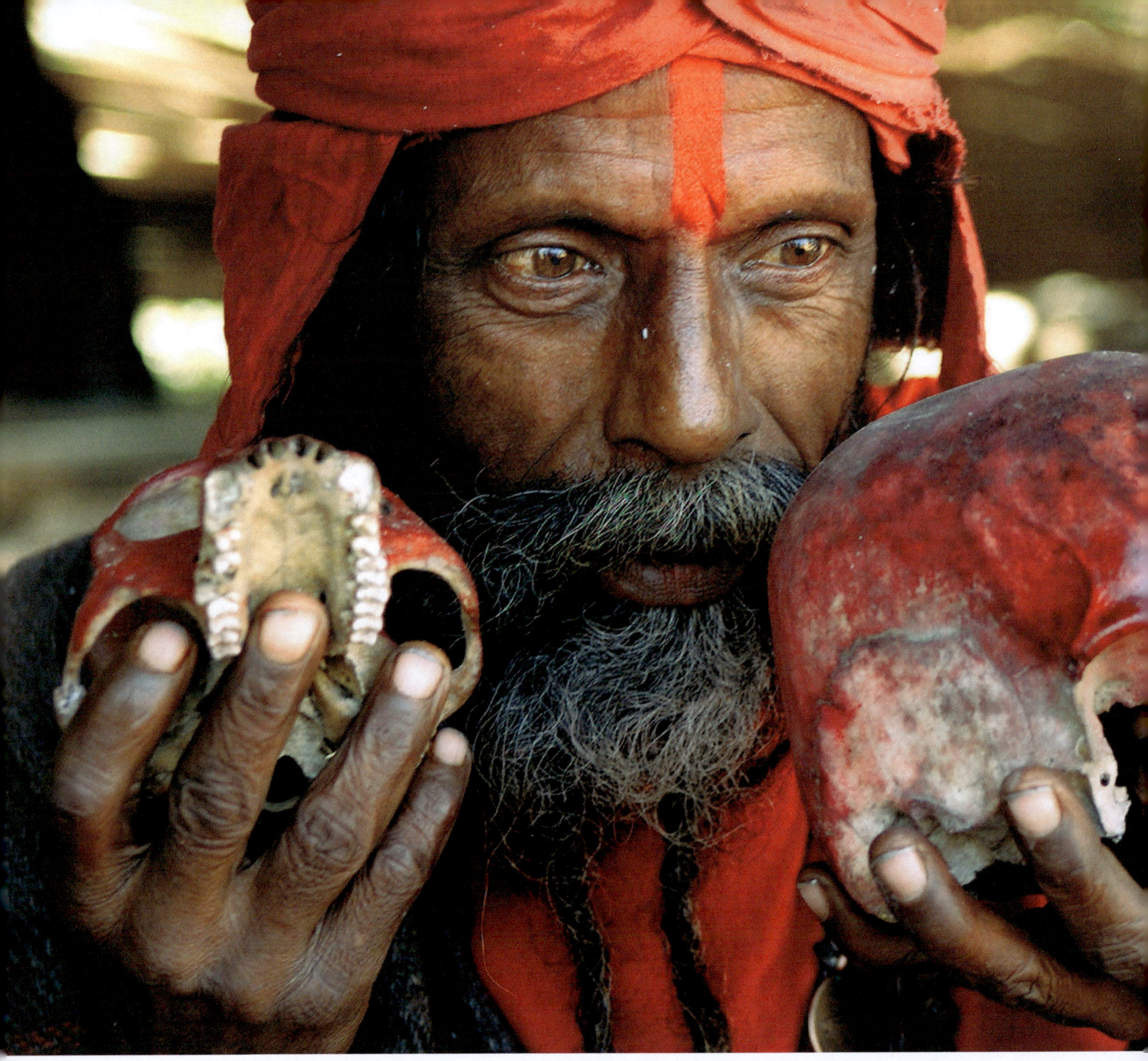

ON MAY 7, 2015, a subway motorman pulled the emergency brake between Kolkata's Netaji Bhavan and Rabindra Sadan stations, bringing his train to a sudden halt. The reason? He'd seen a man walking along the tracks just ahead. But after a search for the figure turned up nothing, the motorman and the local press were moved to label the entity a "ghost."

Commonly called the "Suicide Paradise" because so many people kill themselves there, the Rabindra Sadan subway station is just one of many supposedly haunted spots in India's largest city, the capital of West Bengal. "Haunted houses in India don't have just one ghost," wrote Sandip Roy, a former resident of Kolkata. "It could be a whole family . . . But you have to watch out for the very dangerous *nishi,* who call people by name in the dead of night and lead them away, never to be seen again."

One of the most commonly

AT LEFT: A man performs black magic inside a makeshift tent in Kolkata. Below: The city's Howrah Bridge, under which the hands of suicides are sometimes seen waving in the water at night. "The ghost belief is stronger here than almost anywhere else in India," Soumen Kotal, cofounder of the Paranormal Research Society of India, told the *Los Angeles Times*.

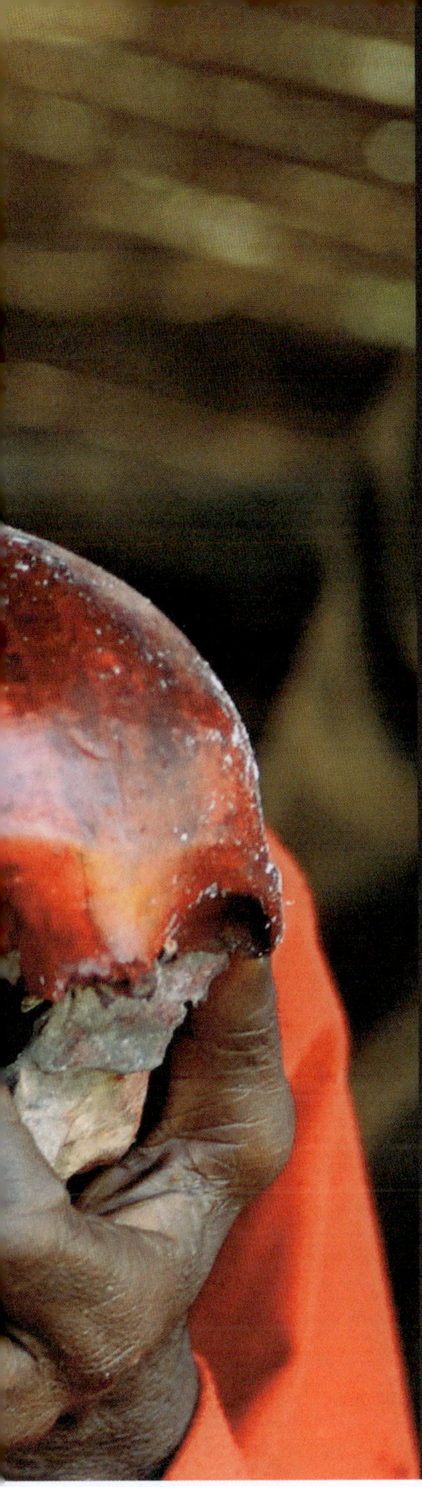

SUCHETA DAS/REUTERS

CREEPY KOLKATA

WEST BENGAL, INDIA

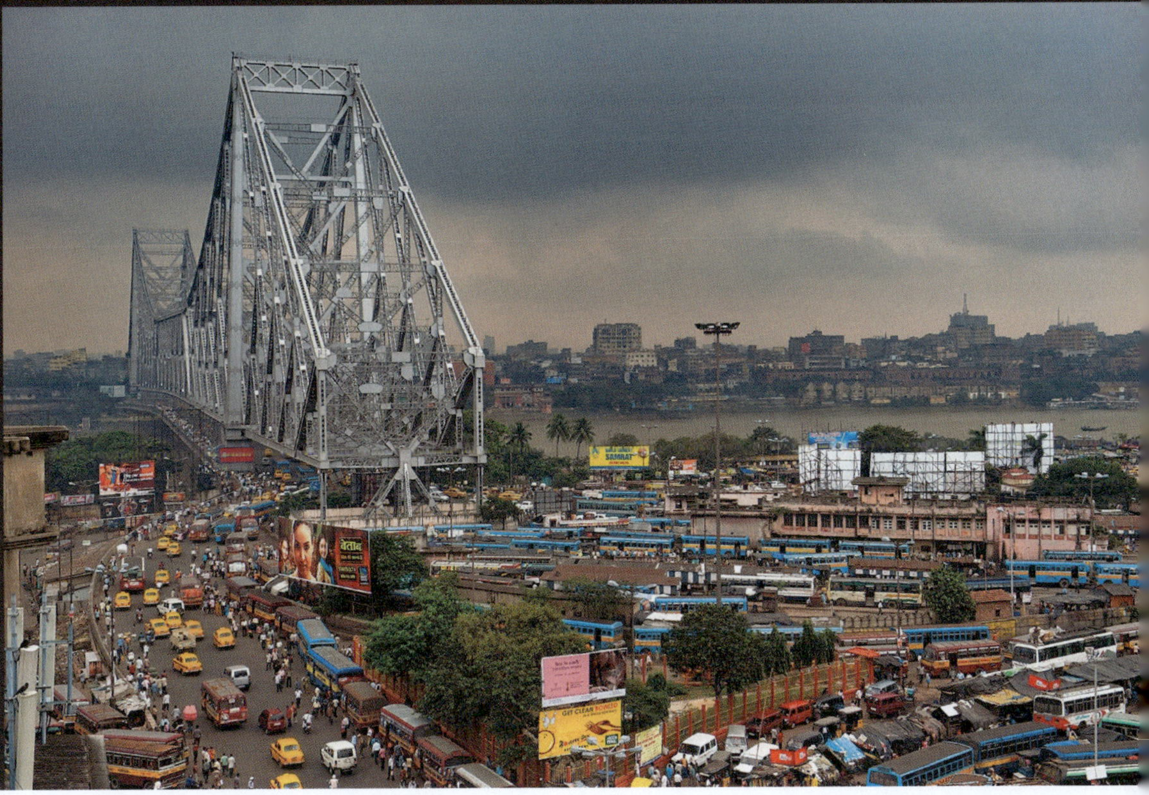

STEVE RAYMER/NATIONAL GEOGRAPHIC CREATIVE

noted spook sites here is the Writer's Building, formerly home of the British East India Company's administrative staff. In December 1930, three Indian freedom fighters shot Lieutenant Colonel N.S. Simpson, the inspector general of prisons known for torturing prisoners. No one claims that Simpson's ghost haunts the old structure, but sounds of crying spirits allegedly disrupt the night.

The obsessively neat wife of British colonial administrator Lord Metcalfe is said to roam the halls of the National Library, sometimes whispering in readers' ears. Other spooky spots include the South Park Street Cemetery, perhaps haunted by the many British soldiers who are buried there, and the Royal Calcutta Turf Club, where a ghostly white mare supposedly gallops around the racecourse at night. Under the Howrah Bridge, a favored spot for suicides, wrestlers who practice on ghats (the stairs descending to the Hugli River) have seen hands flailing in the water at night.

Like many ancient cities, Kolkata is also supposedly home to its share of black magic. The Aghoris, members of a tantric Hindu sect whose holy men eat human flesh at cremation grounds, are said to frequent the crematorium at Nimtala ghat. As the Bengali writer Trailokyanath Mukhopadhyay once wrote, "There is no dearth of darkness in our country." ■

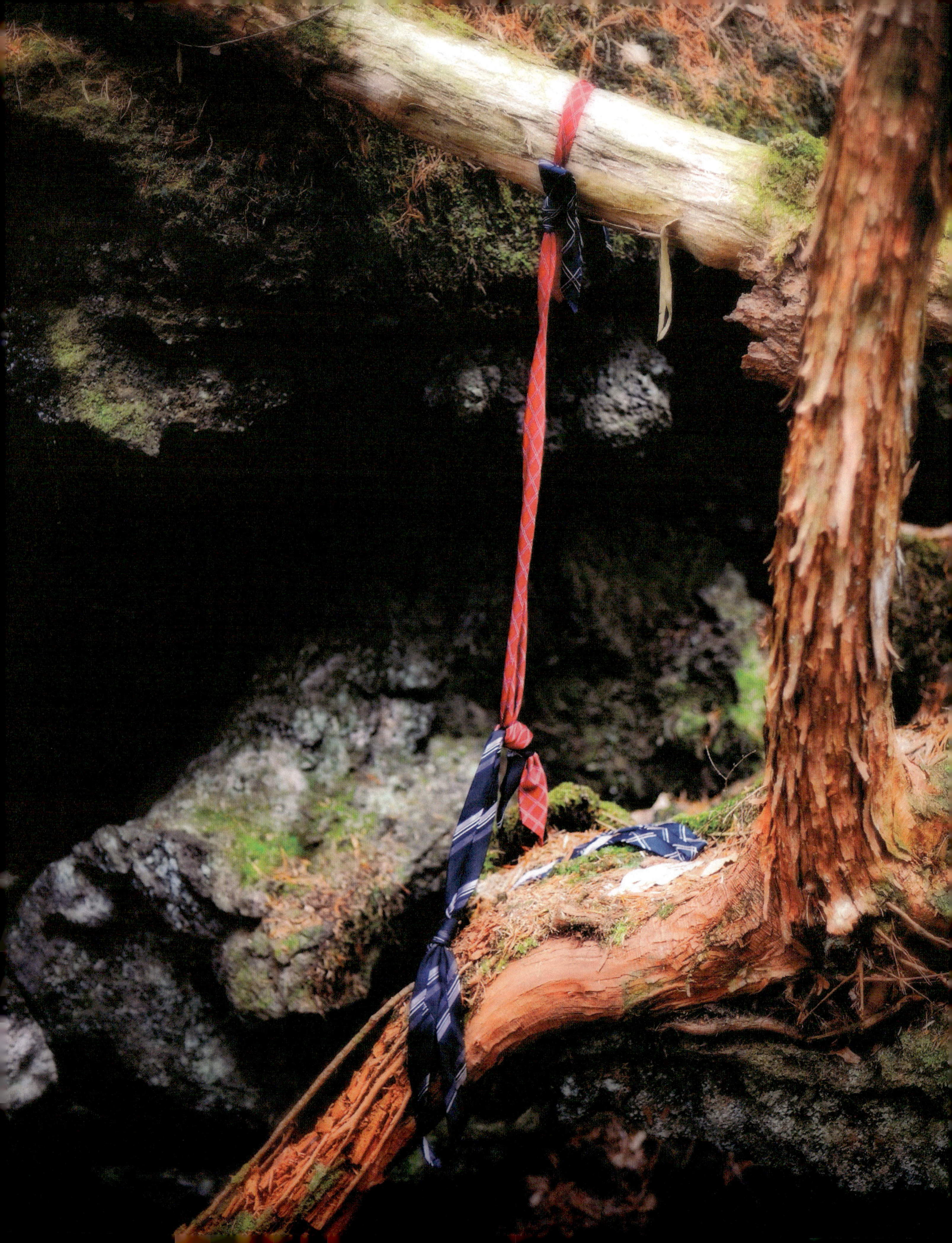

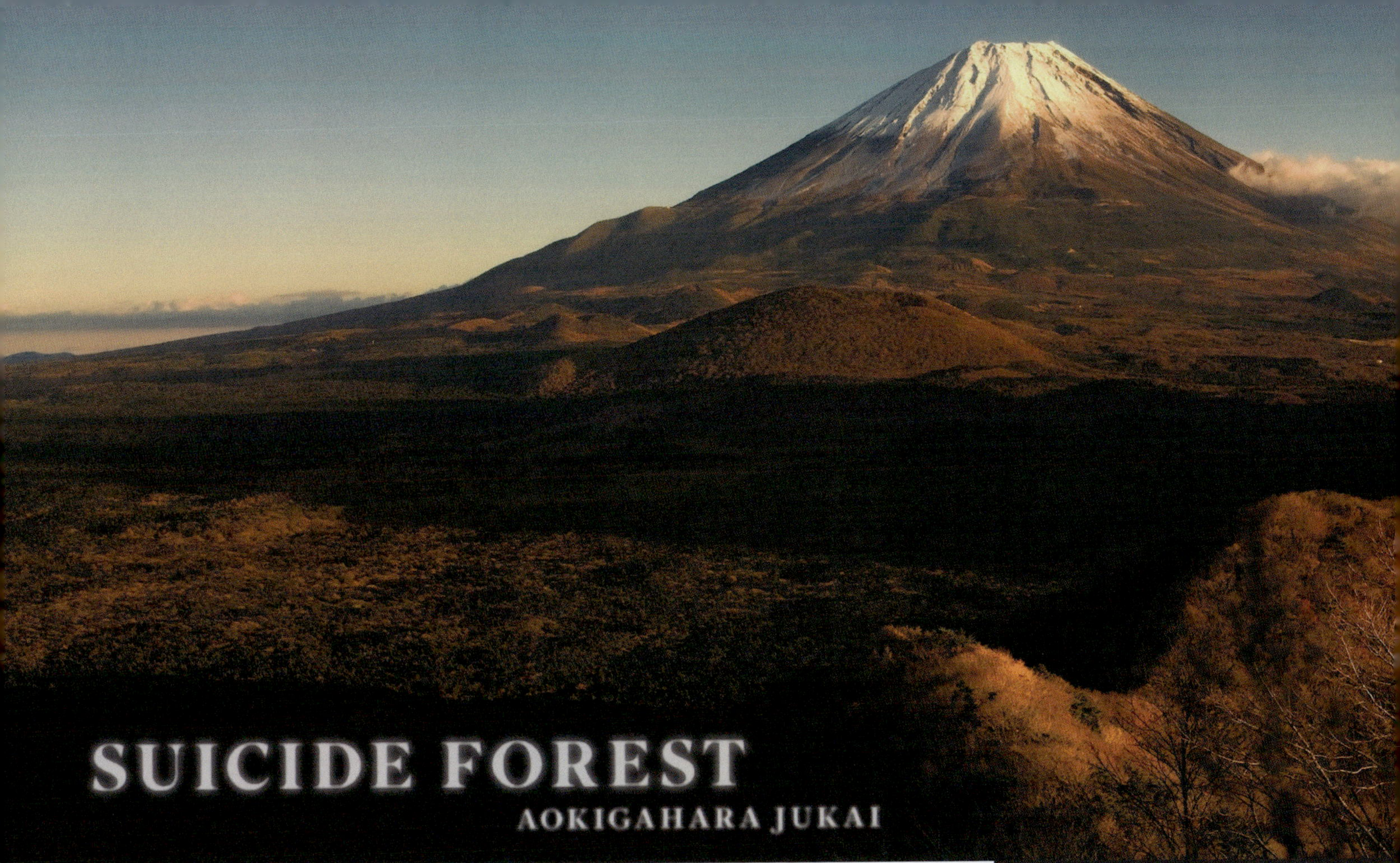

SUICIDE FOREST

AOKIGAHARA JUKAI

ROB GILHOOLY (3)

"YOUR LIFE is a precious gift from your parents. Please think about your parents, siblings, and children. Don't keep it to yourself. Talk about your troubles."

So reads a sign in Aokigahara Jukai, a dense 14-square-mile volcanic forest at the northwest base of Mount Fuji in Japan's Yamanashi Prefecture. Though Jukai means "Sea of Trees," Jukai is known as the Suicide Forest, the most popular suicide destination in Japan. (At least 100 bodies are found every year.)

Deep in these quiet woods, you can find tents, clothes, skeletons, and even copies of Wataru Tsurumi's controversial 1993 bestseller, *The Complete Manual of Suicide,* which recommends Jukai as a good place to go out. (Along with two novels that depict "romantic" suicide pacts in these woods, Tsurumi's book is one reason the forest continues to attract so many lost souls.)

Not long ago, a park geologist found a doll nailed upside-down on a tree—the sign of a curse, he said.

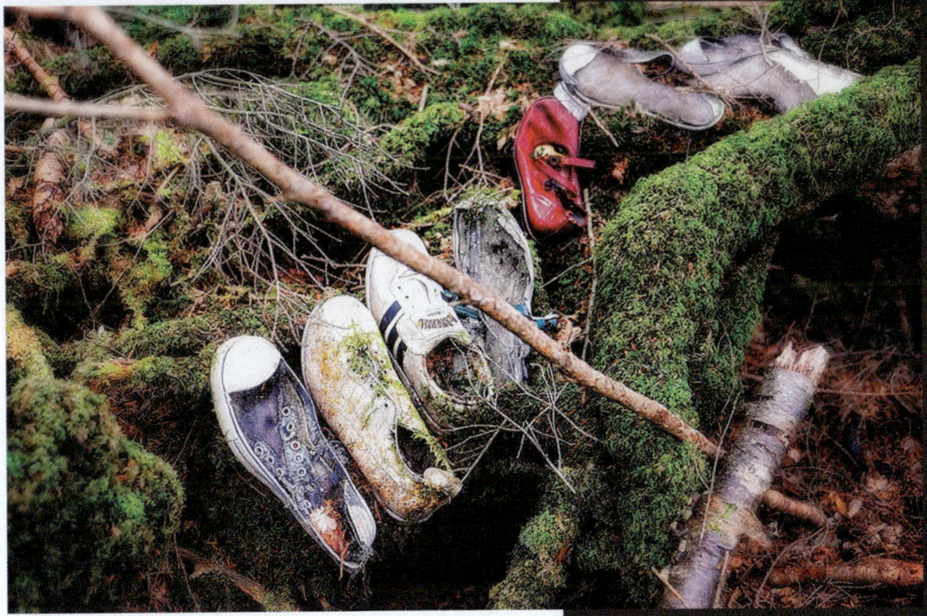

Indeed, the area has a reputation for being haunted by *yurei*—unhappy, angry spirits with white clothes and long black hair. (Think the ghost girl in *The Ring.*) Some say their anguished howls are often heard between two and three a.m.—a time when it's too late, in more ways than one, to "talk about your troubles." ■

OPPOSITE: A necktie noose hangs in Jukai, where signs warn visitors to stay on the marked paths. The suicidal wander off anyway, though some unravel rolls of tape, so they can find their way back—in case they change their minds. Top: Mount Fuji towers above Jukai. Above: Shoes that probably belonged to a woman, man, and two children.

THE LOST TEMPLE

ANGKOR WAT

WERNER BISCHOF/MAGNUM

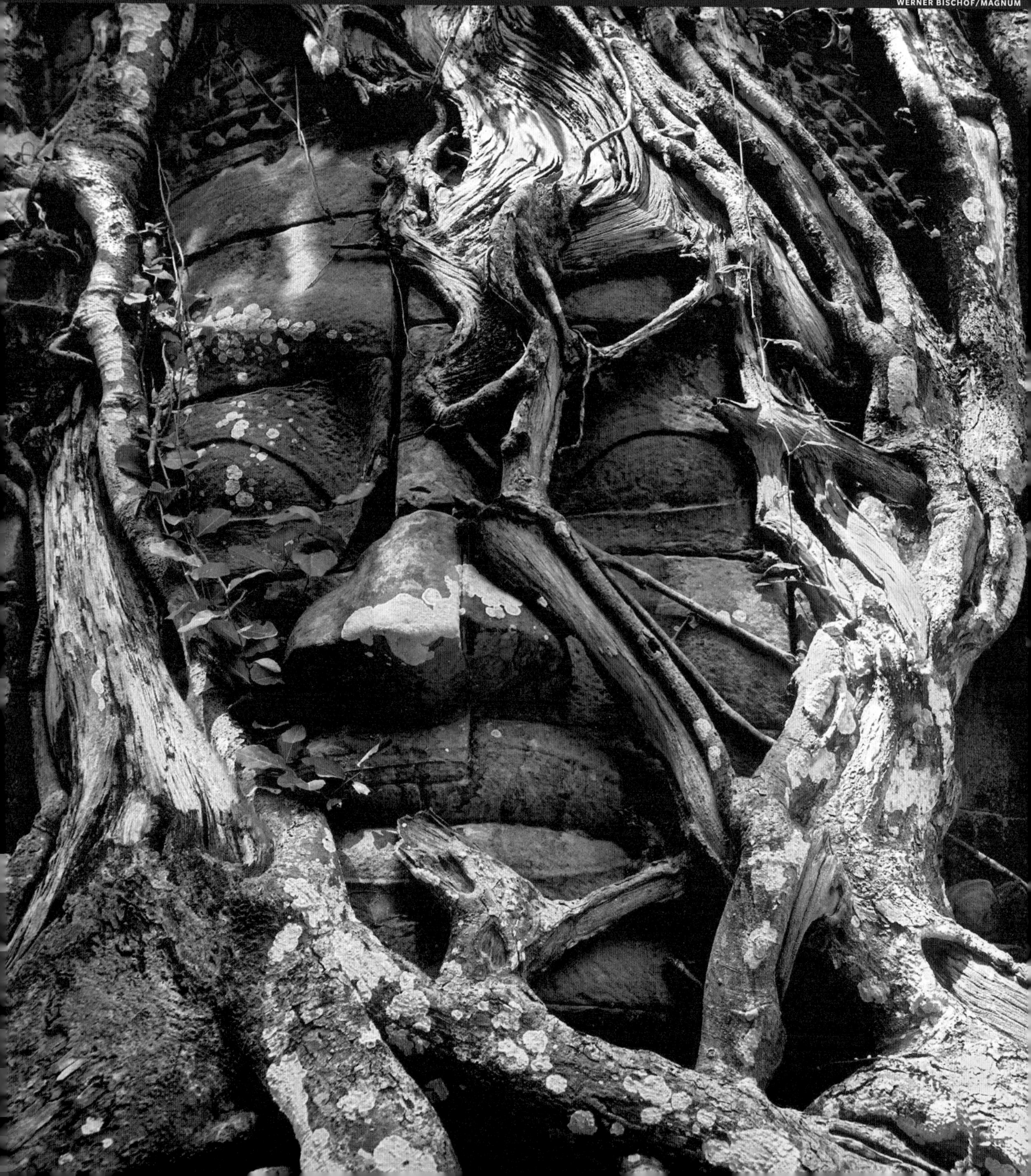

DEDICATED to the Hindu god Vishnu, Angkor Wat was built near Siem Reap, Cambodia, in the 12th century, probably as a funerary temple for King Suryavarman II. Part of Angkor Archaeological Park, a 154-square-mile area containing remains from the Khmer Empire, which lasted from the 9th to the 15th centuries, Angkor Wat fell into neglect and was mostly unknown to the West until the mid-1800s.

An earthly microcosm of the Hindu universe, Angkor Wat is both the world's largest religious monument and an architectural work of art, filled with narrative bas-relief marvels and stunning sculpture, such as the heads that smile so mysteriously they might just make the Mona Lisa look like Kim Kardashian.

The temple creates an overwhelming sense of awe and disorientation among its many visitors—so much so that people have felt themselves walking in the realm of the spirits . . . and even getting lost there. One tourist said that he became separated from a friend during his visit, calling her to no avail—only to discover later that they were both in the same area. Though she did hear someone distantly shouting her name, "why," her friend later asked, "didn't we see each other?"

A belief in ghosts and other supernatural creatures is pervasive in Cambodia, particularly among still largely agrarian areas like Siem Reap. "The people that live in the city don't believe in ghosts, but in the forests near the temples it's common to believe," villager Ngan Thea told *The Phnom Penh Post.* "The forest is a quiet place, so strange things always happen at night."

Locals even create weapon-bearing scarecrows called *ting mong* to scare evil spirits away. "So many ghosts here, you know," one woman said to journalist Andrew Lam after he saw fiery orbs outside his bedroom in a house just outside Siem Reap one night. "Their souls have not gone to heaven. They are still very angry." ■

HUGH SITTON/CORBIS/GETTY

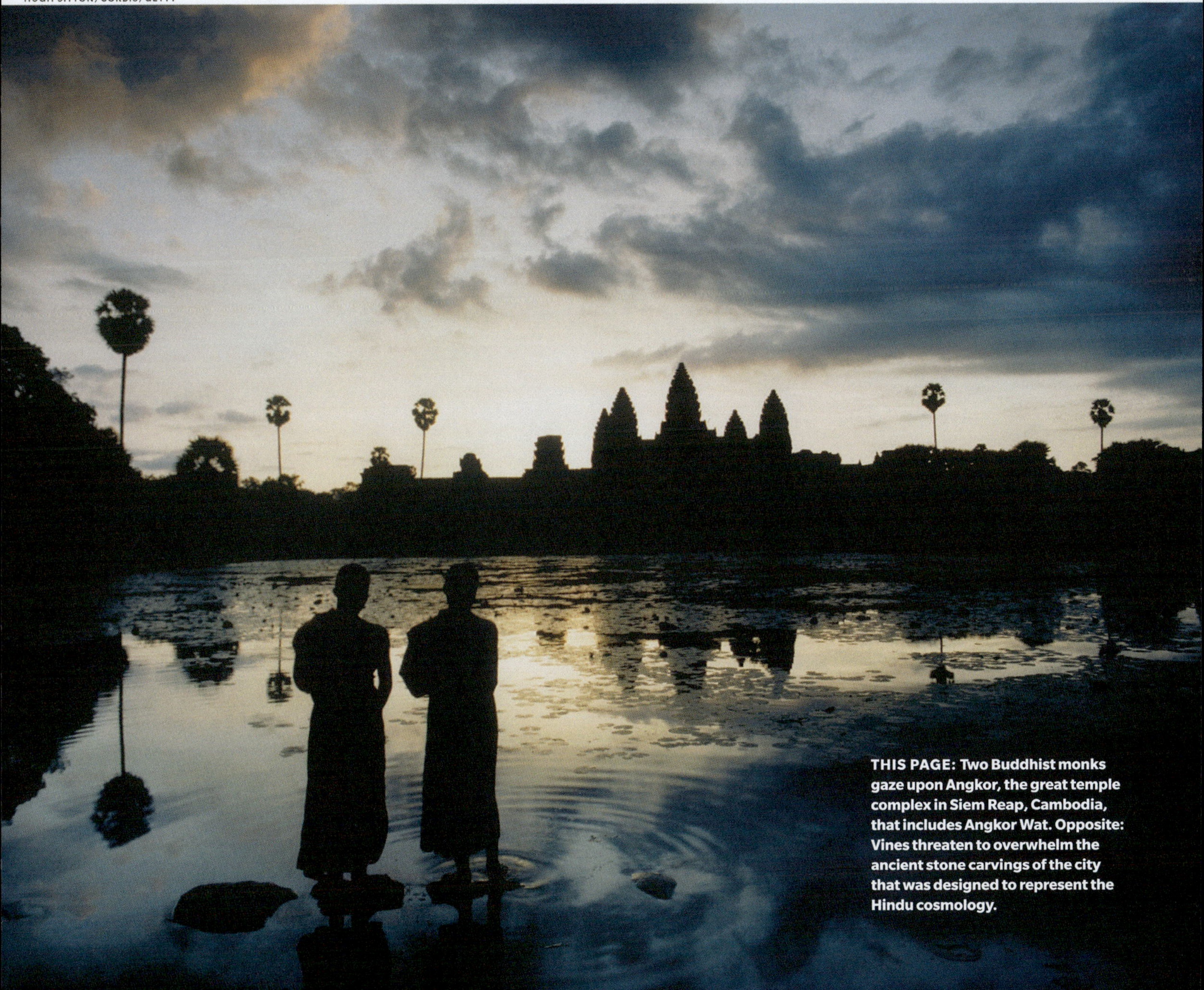

THIS PAGE: Two Buddhist monks gaze upon Angkor, the great temple complex in Siem Reap, Cambodia, that includes Angkor Wat. Opposite: Vines threaten to overwhelm the ancient stone carvings of the city that was designed to represent the Hindu cosmology.

THE GREAT WALL

CHINA

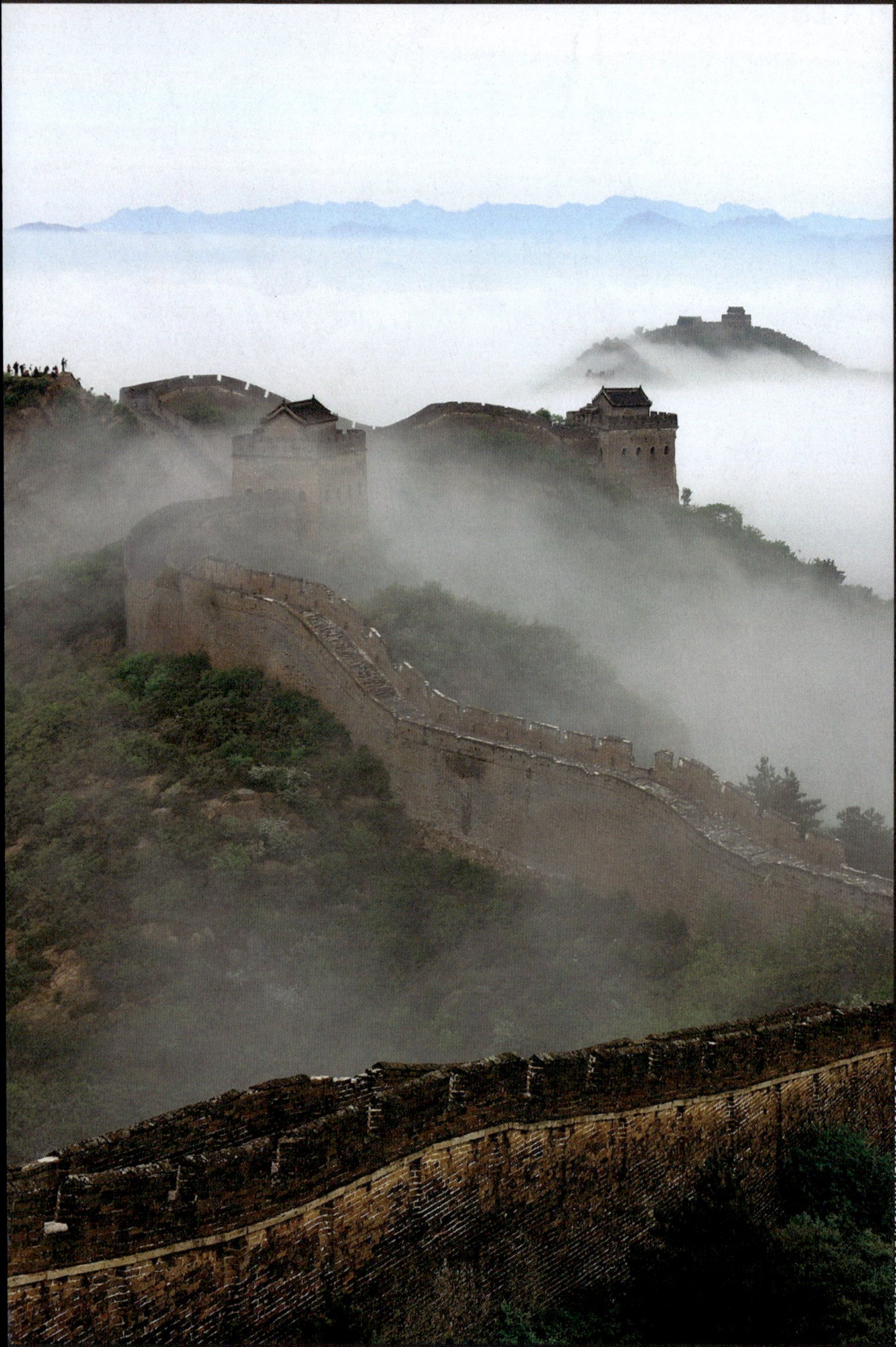

GUO ZHONGXING/XINHUA/EYEVINE/REDUX

CLOUDS HOVER over the Jinshanling Wall after rainfall near Chengde, in north China's Hebei Province. Along with the Gubeikou Wall, Jinshanling is one of the supposedly haunted "Wild Wall" sections of China's Great Wall.

STRETCHING MORE than 5,500 miles from near the North Korean border to the Gobi Desert, the Great Wall of China was constructed over more than 2,200 years to protect the country against invasions from northern nomadic tribes. Not a wall so much as a series of fortifications erratically erected by discrete states, *changcheng* ("long wall") was completed during the Ming Dynasty (1368–1644), when it become the world's largest man-made object.

But as with most epic human achievements, building it took a very human toll. Some 400,000 people, laboring by hand, are said to have died during its construction. At one point, even boys were enlisted, which reportedly made some women fearful of giving birth to sons. (This in a culture that saw girls as disposable, no less.)

With all that suffering and bloodshed, it's no wonder that the fortifications are said to be haunted. Some visitors have claimed they felt uneasy or sick while exploring its paths, though one could presumably chalk that up to the pork dumplings. Others have seen what they said were ghosts of fallen workers, some of whom are known to even punch or kick. (Here's a tip: Fireworks are said to keep them at bay.)

The structure's most haunted areas include Crouching Tiger Mountain and Coiling Dragon Mountain—part of the unrestored and rugged sections collectively know as the "Wild Wall." Dating from two discrete dynasties, they lie in Gubeikou's Yanshan Mountains, about 90 miles from the tourist-packed ramparts of Beijing. In the relative quiet of these remote, rugged remains—mostly free from cell phones and tour groups—the presence of the past is palpable, as are perhaps the ghosts of the men who sacrificed their lives to build these ancient battlements. ■

THE FORBIDDEN CITY

BEIJING

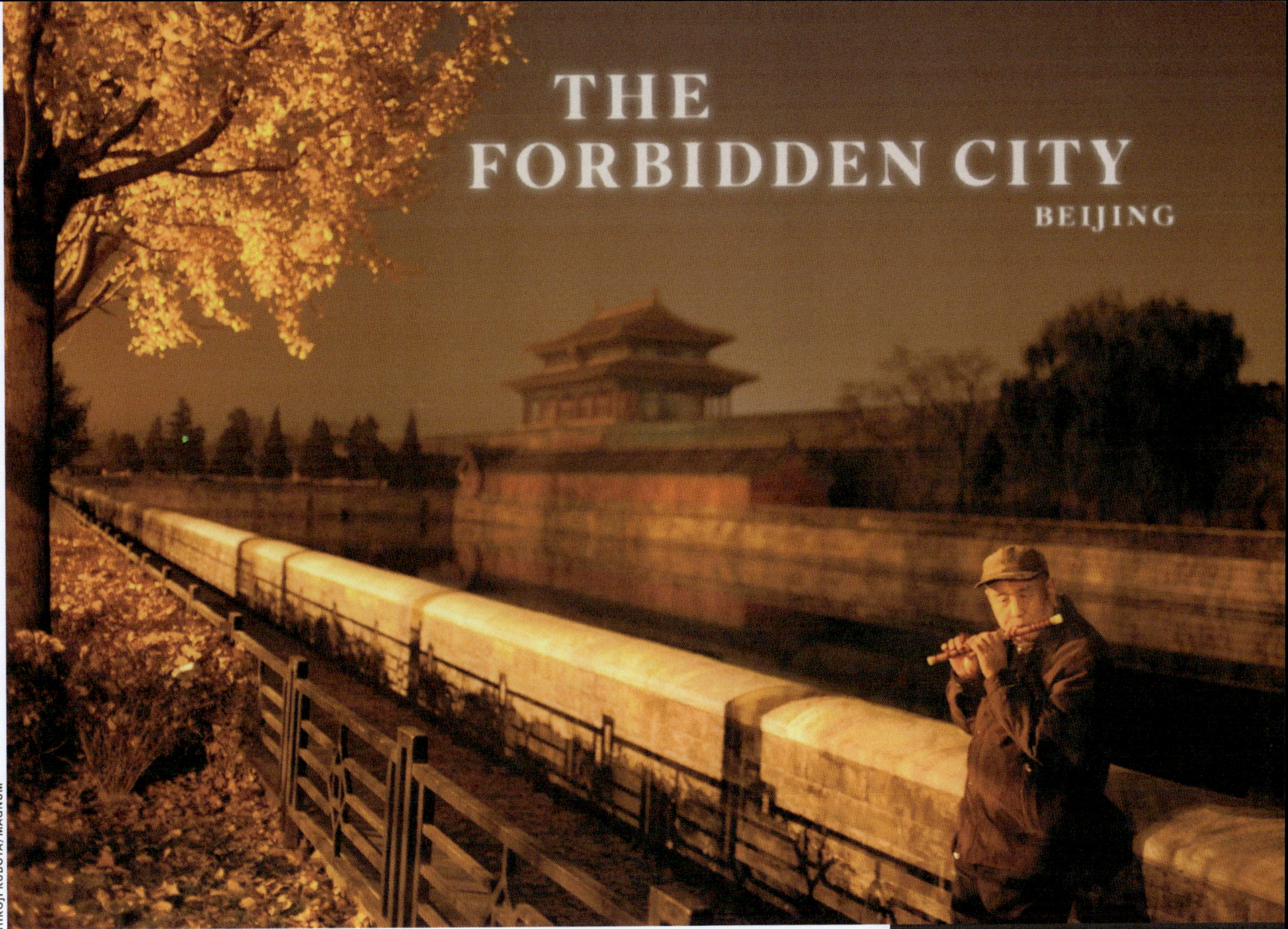

HIROJI KUBOTA/MAGNUM

"IT IS MINE! IT IS MINE!" a disembodied voice was reportedly heard to declare in Beijing's Forbidden City during an exhibition of concubines' jewelry. But greedy ghosts don't need the lure of jade to hunger for what they've lost. After closing, gatekeepers at one of the world's largest palaces supposedly hear music and see ladies-in-waiting wandering the grounds with eunuchs. And when one recent tourist asked a guide why the floors were raised under the doors, he was told, "Because ghosts can't jump." (That same tourist later posted what he claimed to be the photo of a ghost he had captured in one of the rooms.)

If any structure in the world has the right to be haunted, it's the 9,000-room imperial palace that served 25 Chinese emperors from the Ming Dynasty to the end of the Qing Dynasty (about 1421 to 1911). It has, needless to say, seen more than its share of intrigue and violence—not to mention everyday heartache and greed. (Which spectral concubine wanted her jewelry back?)

Indeed, the palace was created in a cauldron of grief and bloodshed. After his nephew became emperor in the late 14th century, Prince Zhu Di rebelled, assisted by eunuchs, killing his relatives' loyalists and establishing a new stronghold as the Yongle Emperor in Beijing, where he embarked on the creation of the fabled city.

As to Beijing itself? There are plenty of supposedly haunted spots—Gongwangfu Mansion and Liuyin Street among them. But we so often associate hauntings with decaying old buildings, and Beijing—like the rest of China—is determined to raze reminders of its past in the name of "progress."

Case in point: In 2001, the Forbidden City became home to a Starbucks. ▪

A MAN PLAYS flute before sunrise in Beijing's legendary Forbidden City, where guards claim to have seen odd animals at night—and where ghostly women cry in the concubine quarters.

BELOW: THE LAST PHOTO ever taken of British mountaineers George Mallory (left) and Andrew Irvine as they prepare to attack Everest in June 1924. Bottom: The purported hand and scalp of a yeti lie in Nepal's Pangboche Monastery. Opposite: The road to Everest.

THE DEATH ZONE

MOUNT EVEREST

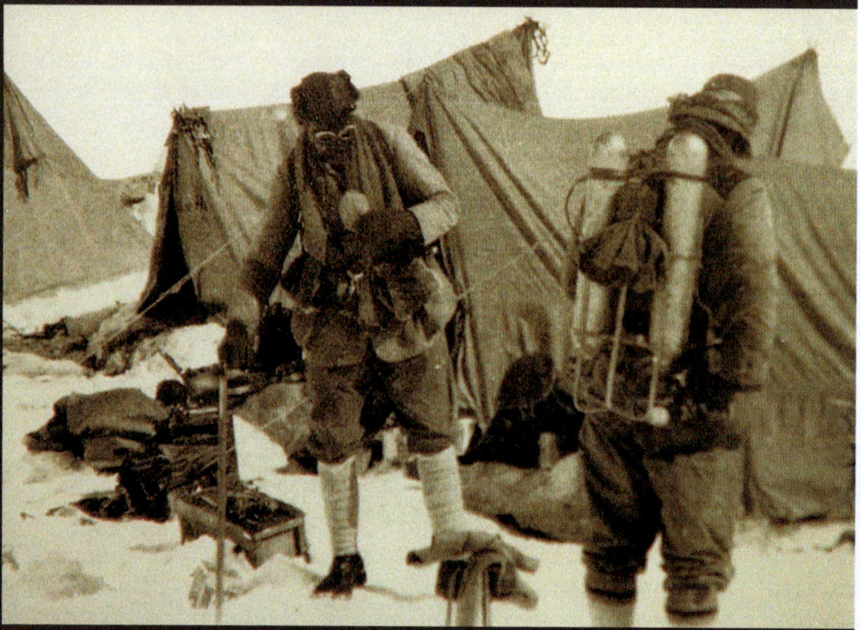

STR/AP

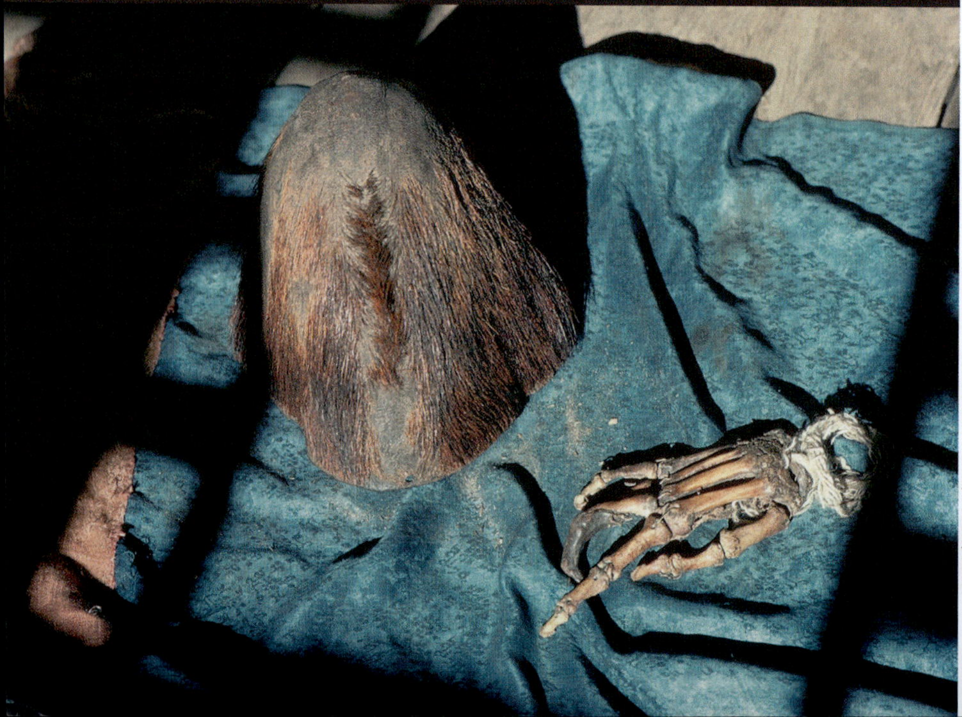

EARL & NAZIMA KOWALL/CORBIS/GETTY

ON JUNE 8, 1924, climbers Andrew "Sandy" Irvine and George Mallory left their camp not far from the summit of Mount Everest in a final attempt to reach the top. They never returned. Though Mallory's well-preserved body was discovered in 1999, Irvine's corpse has never been found. But some say his restless ghost continues to haunt the world's highest mountain.

In June 1933, British climber Frank Smythe climbed as high on Everest as anyone had before, but after two exhausting nights in the so-called Death Zone—"not for flesh and blood," he later said—he became convinced that a pulsating spirit hovered alongside him.

In 1975, Dougal Haston and Doug Scott, the first Britons to reach the top of Everest (unless, of course, Mallory and Irvine achieved it), claimed they felt a presence in their snow hole the night before they summited. Scott said the presence, which he also felt on the way down, was "helpful," giving him "confidence and advice." Another expedition member said that he'd been "followed by the appearance of a man . . . definitely a human figure with arms and legs."

If Irvine's ghost does indeed haunt Everest, he may well have company. The mountain is filled with the restless spirits of people who have died while climbing it, according to Pemba Dorji, who broke the record for fastest summiting (eight hours, 10 minutes) in 2004. "I saw some spirits in the form of black shadows coming toward me, stretching their hands and begging for something to eat," said Dorji.

All of these visions can, of course, be easily explained as hallucinations induced by hypoxia, thin air, exhaustion, and the limits of human endurance. But the Everest area has long been considered a holy and haunted place in Nepal and Tibet.

The Himalayas are also said to be home to the legendary Abominable Snowman, also known as the yeti. Supposed yeti remains—including a "sacred" finger and the so-called

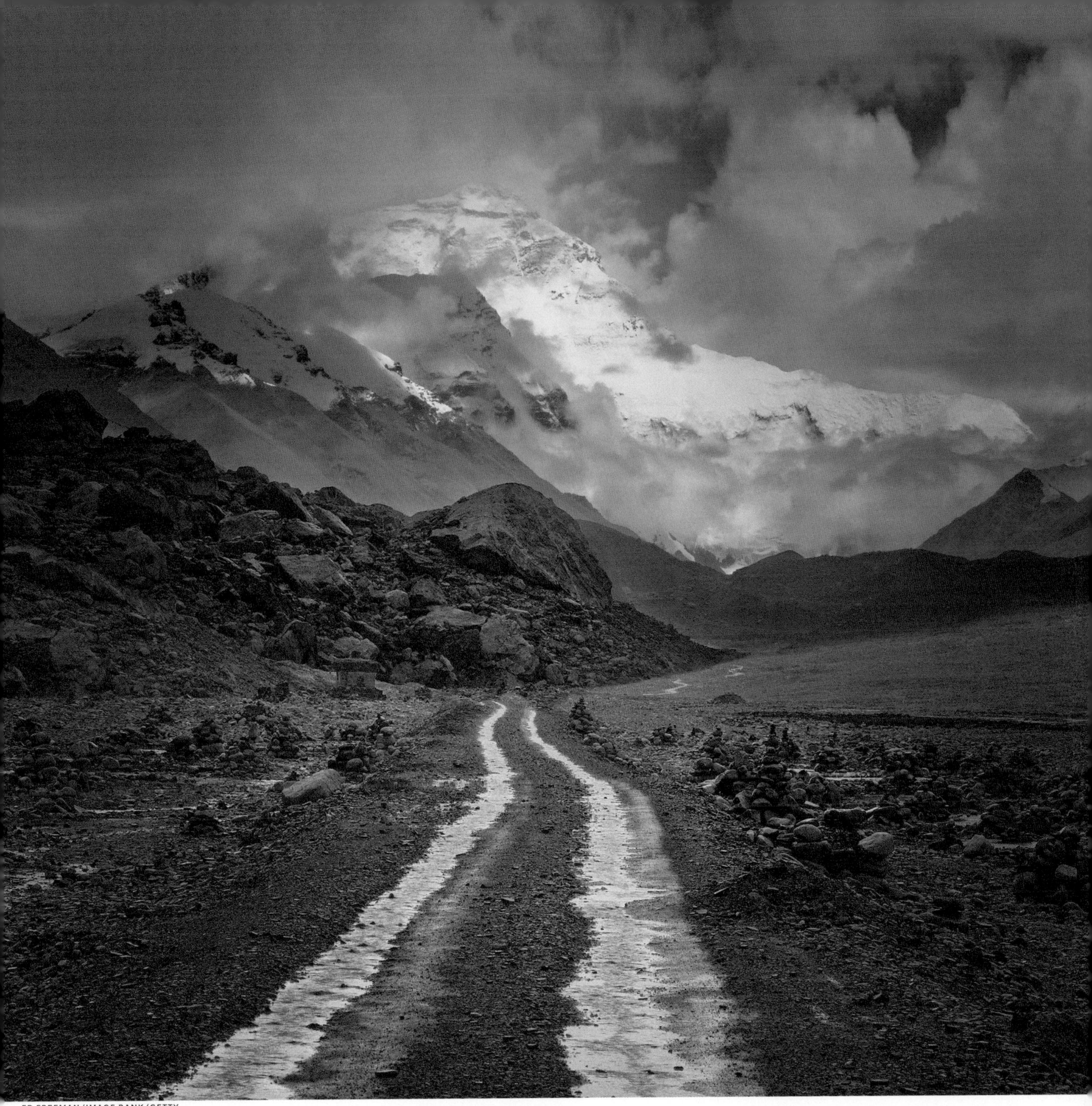

ED FREEMAN/IMAGE BANK/GETTY

Pangboche hand—are kept in a number of Tibetan Buddhist monasteries. In the wake of the 1922 British Everest expedition, 20 local boys said they encountered seven yetis at the base of the mountain's North Col while searching for supplies the climbers had left behind. And explorer Eric Shipton took pictures of what some believed to be yeti footprints in the Everest environs in 1951.

In 1986 in Tibet, Reinhold Messner, the first to climb Everest without bottled oxygen and the first to summit the world's 14 highest peaks, saw a strange creature: It "towered menacingly," he later wrote, "its face a gray shadow, its body a black outline. Covered with hair, it stood upright on two short legs and had powerful arms." Sadly for aficionados of the outré, Messner later identified the creature as a rare Tibetan bear.

But the unforgiving mountain hardly needs ghosts and monsters in order to strike fear in the hearts of climbers. The actuality, as one writer said, is that "the scariest stories on Everest are true." ■

UNEARTHLY INN

HOTEL TAKARA

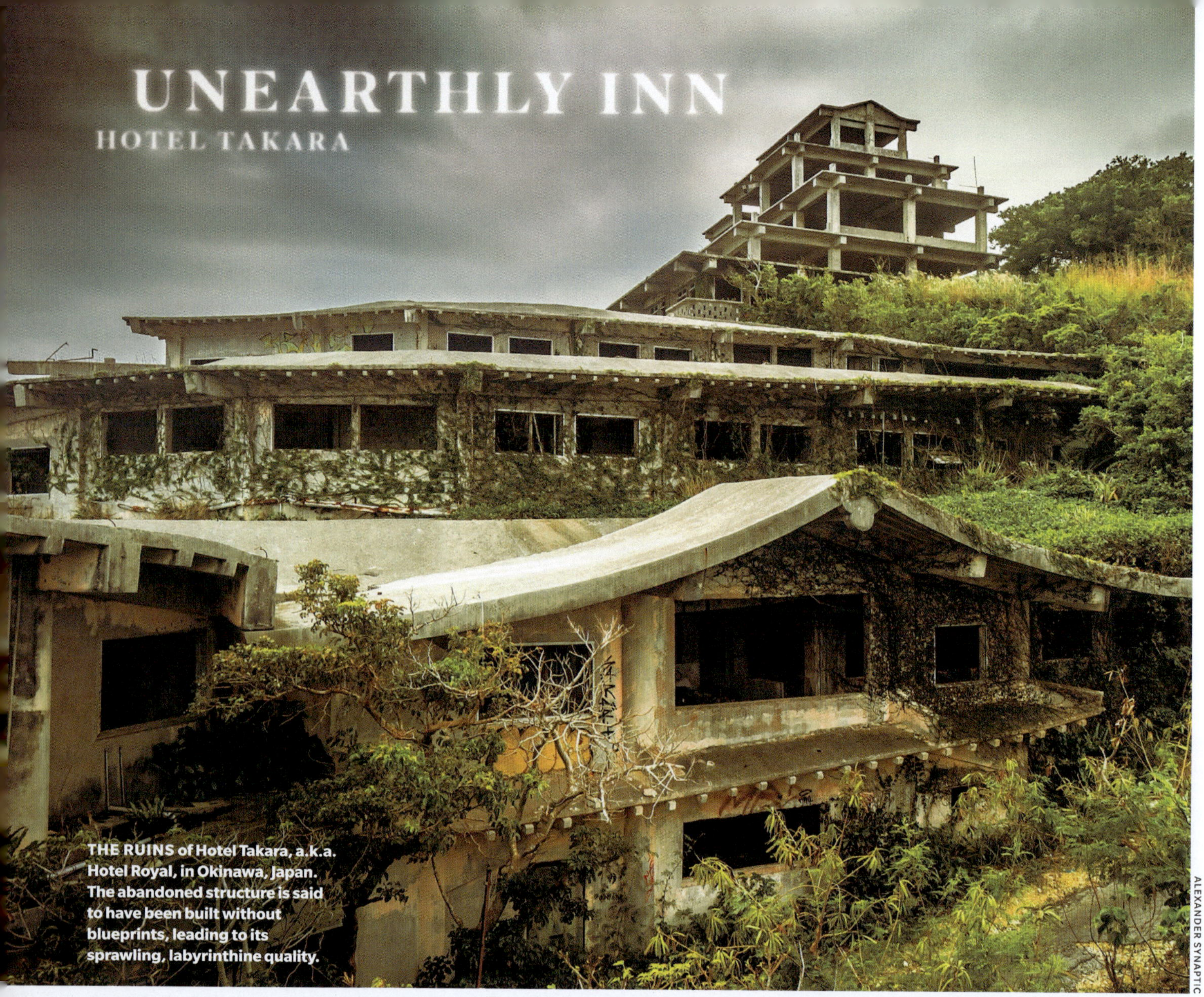

THE RUINS of Hotel Takara, a.k.a. Hotel Royal, in Okinawa, Japan. The abandoned structure is said to have been built without blueprints, leading to its sprawling, labyrinthine quality.

ALEXANDER SYNAPTIC

"KEEP OUT!" "Do not enter!" and "Denger!" [*sic*] read signs posted outside the abandoned Hotel Takara near the restored ruins of the 14th-century Nakagusuku Castle in Okinawa, Japan. Physical danger aside, the hotel—also known as the Royal—has become the kind of haunt that local teenagers use to dare and scare themselves. In the process they've created a campfire story that has been enshrined as fact, thanks in part to repeated iterations on our modern collective campfire known as the Internet.

Here's how the legend goes: In the mid-1970s an unnamed businessman from Naha financed the construction of the hotel on the hill with prime views of Okinawa. Hoping to cash in on the crowds coming to the 1975 Okinawa International Ocean Exposition, he hatched plans for a complex that included a water park, a petting zoo, and a nightclub. But local Buddhist monks warned him that the site was sacred. It was also, they said, too close to a number of old tombs and a cave inhabited by restless spirits.

But the businessman paid no attention—until a series of freak accidents claimed the lives of some workmen. After his remaining employees resigned, too terrified to face the spirits, the owner moved into his uncompleted project—and slowly went insane, ending his days as a gibbering hermit in the empty rooms.

Certainly accidents on the site have continued through the years. When a serviceman stationed in Okinawa was injured in the unfinished hotel in 2009, for instance, it was put off-limits to Marines, though not because of any curse: The dilapidated condition of the structure alone is enough to explain most mishaps.

Whether or not the Hotel Takara is haunted—or just a real estate gambit gone bust—the spot is undeniably creepy, even in the daylight. Its rubbish-filled abandoned halls are festooned with graffiti and spider webs, and it isn't hard to mistake a tattered curtain for a ghost. Or maybe it's that businessman from Naha. ■

THE DEMONIC DOMAIN

RUINS OF BABYLON

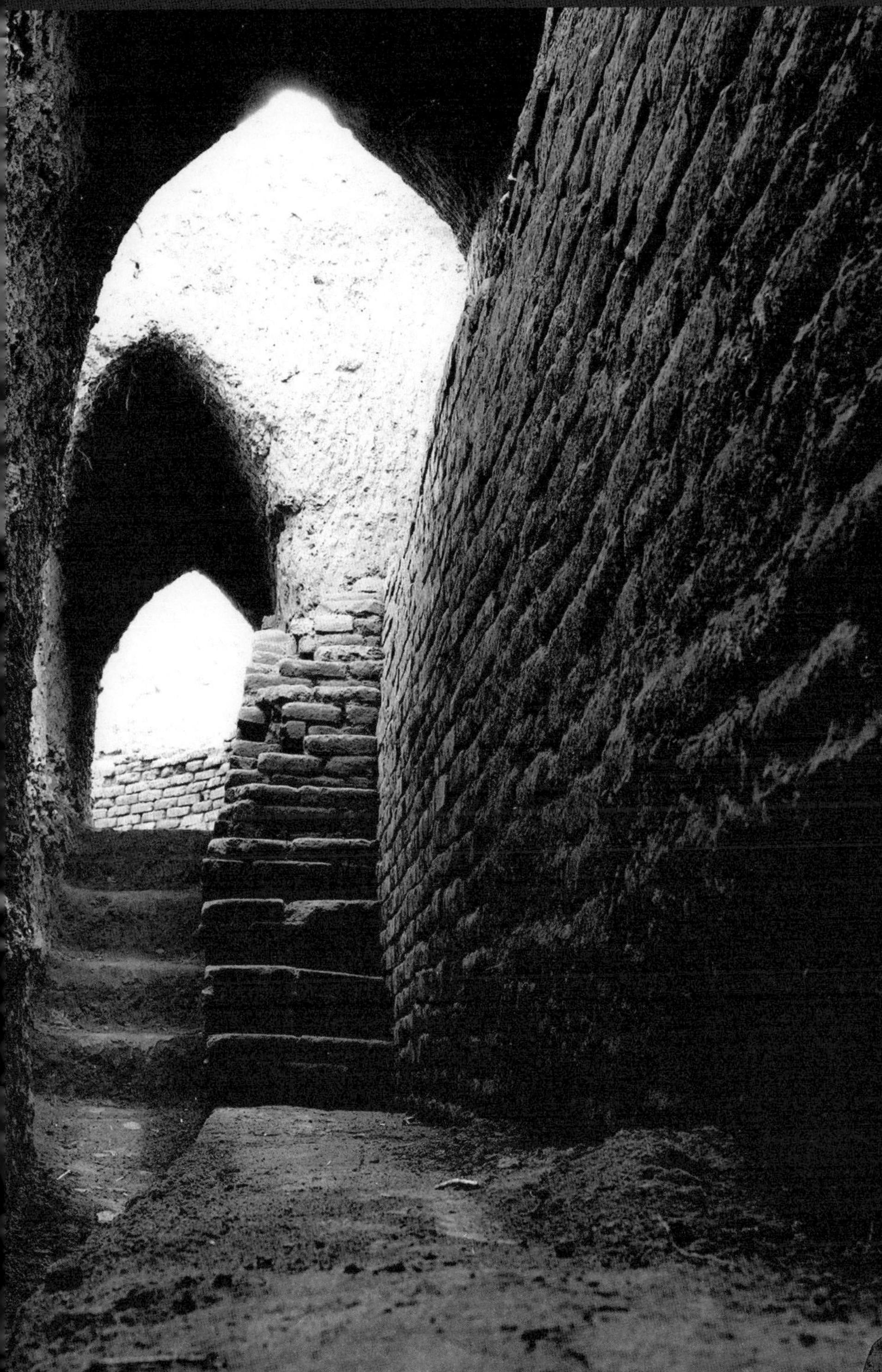

DEAGOSTINI/GETTY

"BABYLON the great is fallen, is fallen, and is become the habitation of devils, and the hold of every foul spirit," reads Revelation 18:2, a prophecy eerily

ABOUT 60 MILES from Baghdad lies what's left of Babylon, the city where Hammurabi and Nebuchadnezzar once ruled, now a patch of barren land and plundered treasure. The legendary Hanging Gardens of Babylon (one of the seven wonders of the ancient world) are lost to history, of course, but the famed Ishtar Gate was taken by the Germans in the early 20th century, and Turks used bricks still marked with Nebuchadnezzar's name to build dams on the Euphrates.

In 1985, Saddam Hussein began remaking the site in his own megalomaniacal image. The American invasion put an end to this in 2003, but the troops brought their own depredations, building a helicopter landing pad over ruins and crushing ancient pavement with heavy vehicles. It wasn't long before graffiti marked the site ("Hi Vanessa. I love you. From Saddam's palace") and priceless cuneiform tablets started showing up on eBay.

Ancient Babylonians believed the destruction of sacred idols meant their divinities had abandoned them to evil forces, and it's not hard to imagine that this ravaged wasteland is haunted by the likes of their *ekimmu,* the restless spirits of souls who were not properly buried; *utukku,* demons who haunt abandoned places; and *alu,* faceless creatures who crush sleeping humans. (Let's not forget that Pazuzu, the possessing spirit in *The Exorcist,* was a Babylonian demonic god.)

Jinn, supernatural creatures of Arabic mythology, may also linger here, since they're known to haunt ruins—and, no, this isn't just an ancient superstition. In November 2014, the residents of Kut, a city about 90 miles from the Babylonian ruins, became convinced that jinn were burning their houses (you can find a

THE "CURSE" OF THE ROCK

ULURU

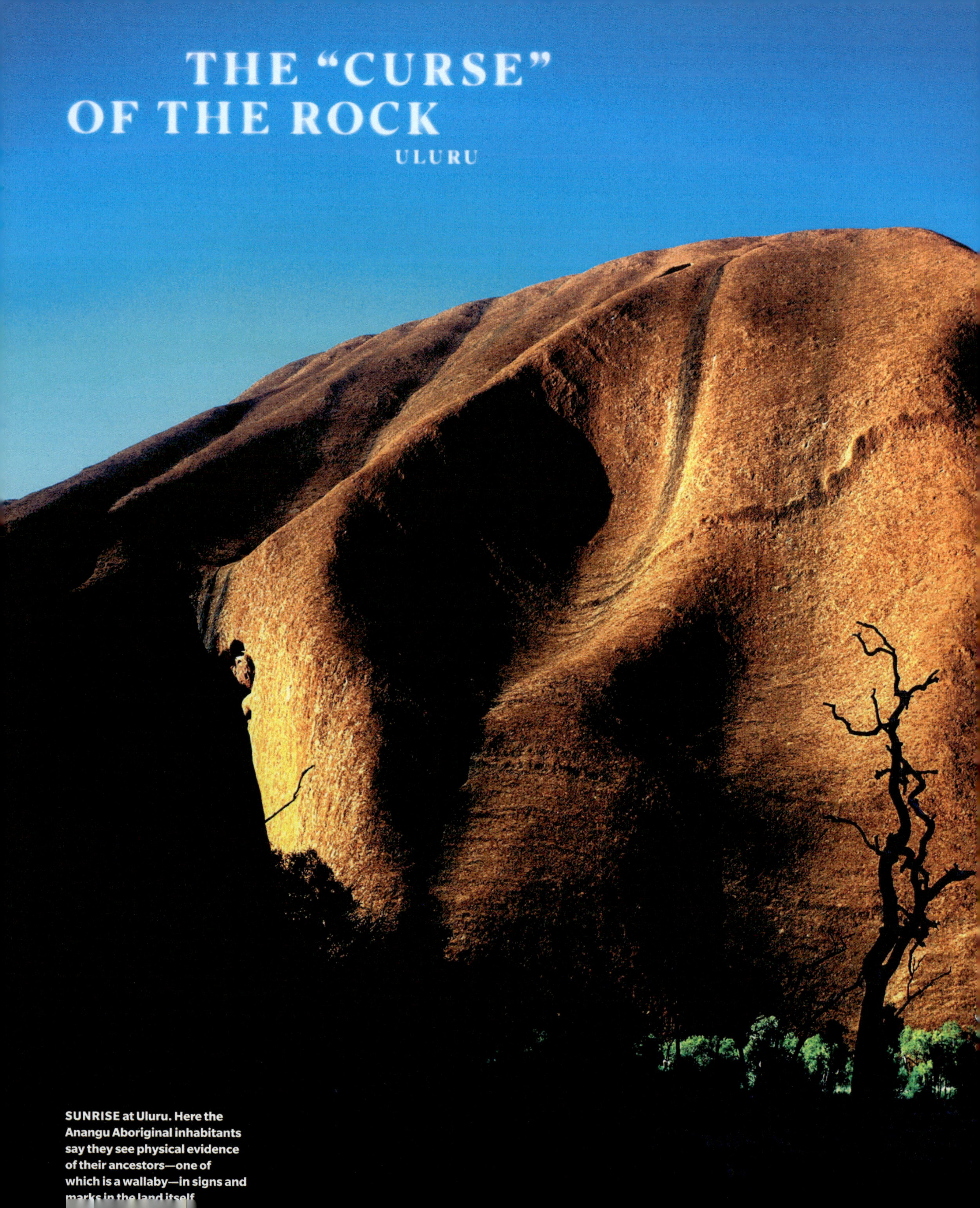

SUNRISE at Uluru. Here the Anangu Aboriginal inhabitants say they see physical evidence of their ancestors—one of which is a wallaby—in signs and marks in the land itself.

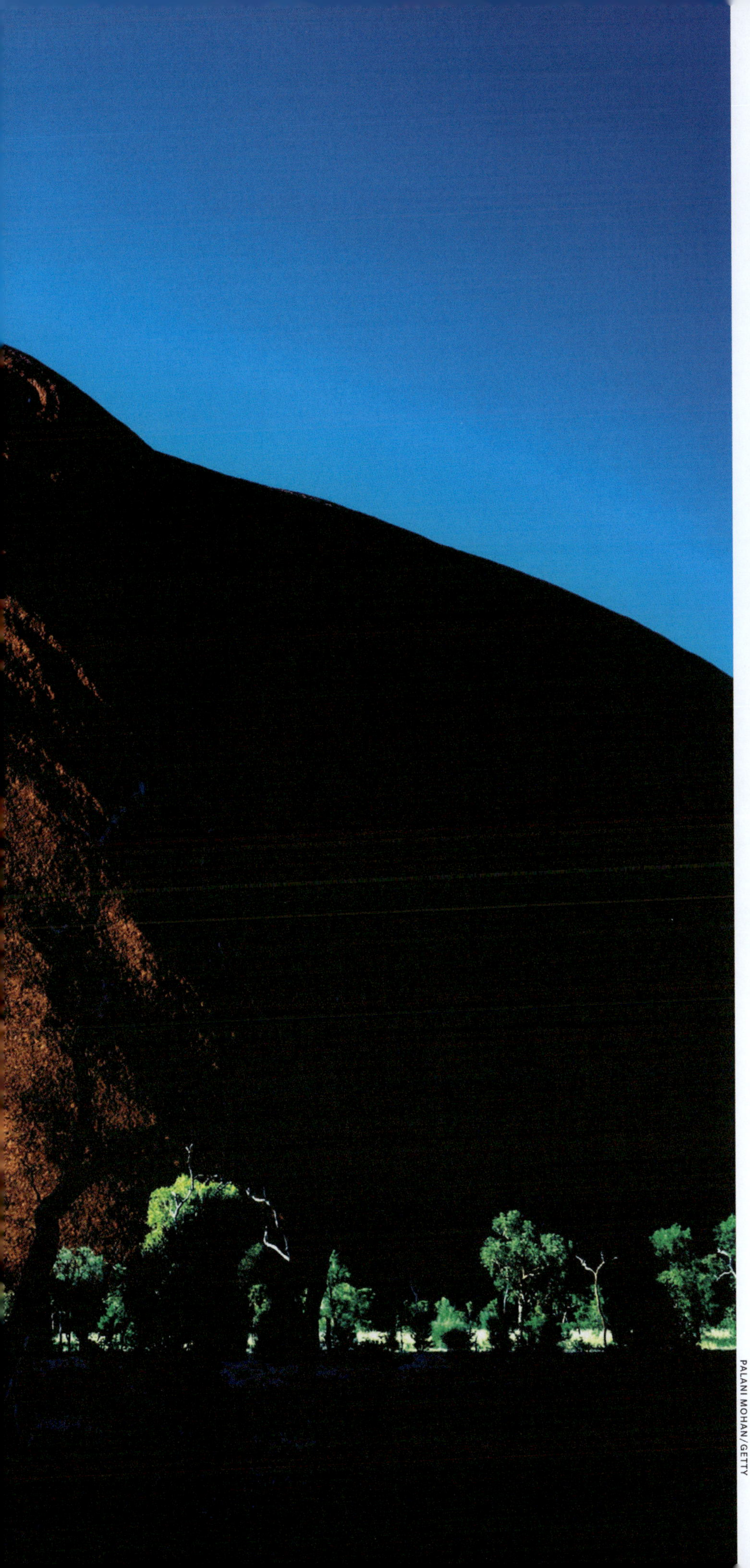

PALANI MOHAN/GETTY

EVERY DAY, RANGERS in Uluru-Kata Tjuta National Park in Australia's Northern Territory receive rocks in the mail. Yes, *rocks.* Ranging from small chips to 70-pound boulders, the stones are sent from all over the world by tourists who have stolen them from Uluru, also known as Ayers Rock, the park's sublime centerpiece, and returned them because they were "cursed."

Many of these packages contain apologies, but about a quarter list the tragedies the writers say followed the thefts. "Things were good in my life before I took some of Ayers Rock home with me," one British tourist wrote, "but since then my wife has had a stroke and things have worked out terribly for my children—we have had nothing but bad luck."

Others describe breakups, illnesses, and even deaths. "It's just a weird phenomenon," one park manager said of the rocks. "We stack them up in boxes and every now and then we try and return them [to the mountain] . . . so that people's bad luck is dissolved."

Formed hundreds of millions of years ago, Uluru and its environs have been home to the Aboriginal Anangu people for 10,000 years. The 1,150-foot sandstone monolith is a literally haunted place for the Anangu, animistically inhabited by hundreds of ancestral beings (plants, people, and animals). It is also, they say, honeycombed with hidden sacred "songlines," paths that reflect the creation of the world and that are literally reflected in songs. The Anangu call their sacred sites "my grandmother" or "my grandfather," so climbing Uluru is—for them—a sacrilegious act of desecration, if not the prelude to a curse. "You shouldn't climb," one Aborigine said. "It's not the real thing about this place. The real thing is listening to everything."

But the tourists keep climbing—and pocketing rocks, returning them to rangers when and if the "curse" follows them home. There's no evidence the atonement works, however. "I haven't had anyone write and say, 'Since I returned the rock we won the lotto,' or anything," one park manager said. ■

HAIR-RAISING, HAUNTED EUROPE

The continent where history and legend often intersect is home to some of the world's greatest ghost stories, along with goblins, vampires, and more than a few doorways to the underworld.

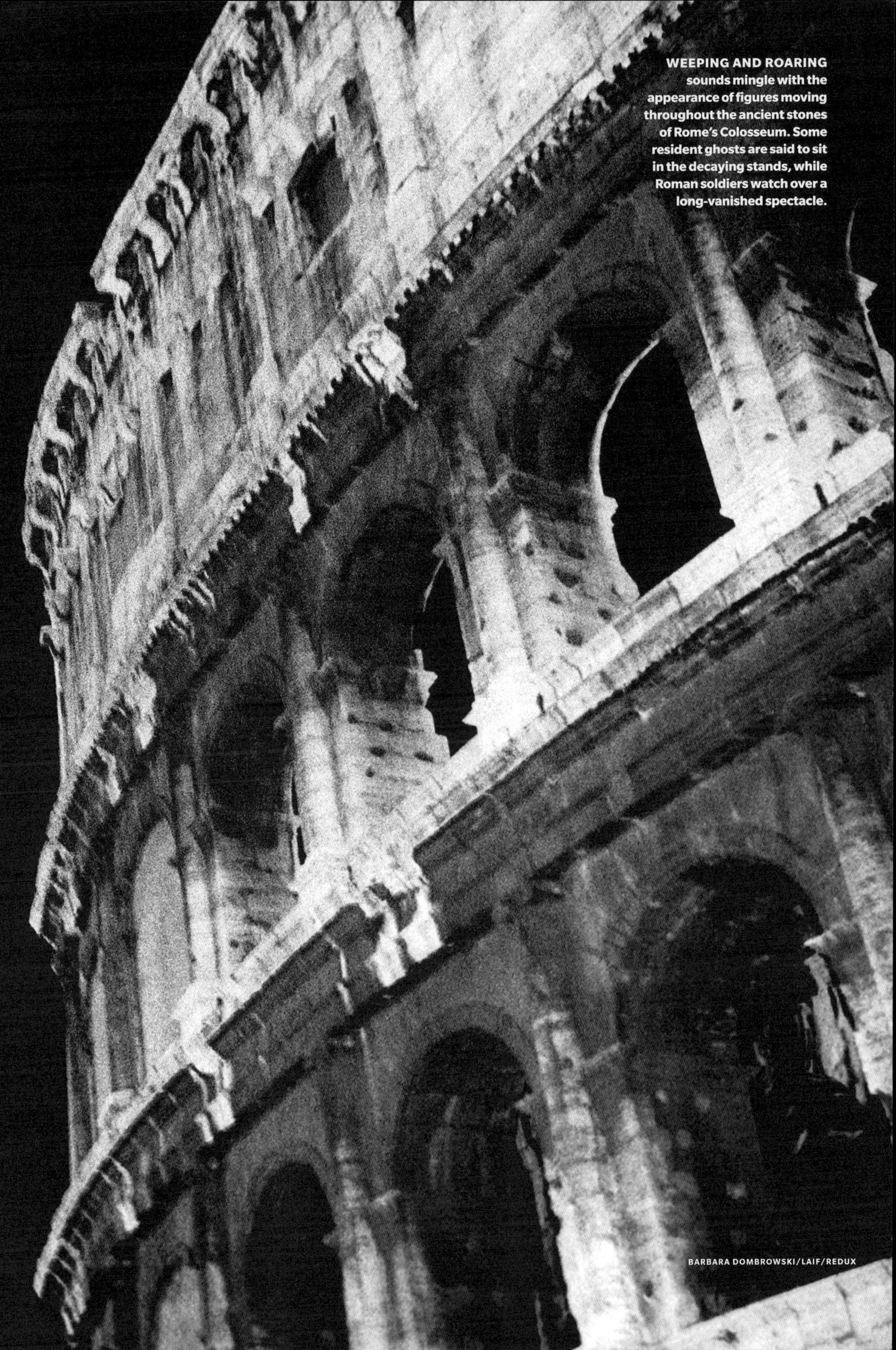

WEEPING AND ROARING sounds mingle with the appearance of figures moving throughout the ancient stones of Rome's Colosseum. Some resident ghosts are said to sit in the decaying stands, while Roman soldiers watch over a long-vanished spectacle.

BARBARA DOMBROWSKI/LAIF/REDUX

RIGHT: THE NOTORIOUSLY haunted catacombs of Paris. Below: A statue in the gardens and park of the château of Versailles, supposedly haunted by the ghost of Marie Antoinette. Bottom: Graves in Père-Lachaise cemetery.

PARANORMAL PARIS

FRANCE

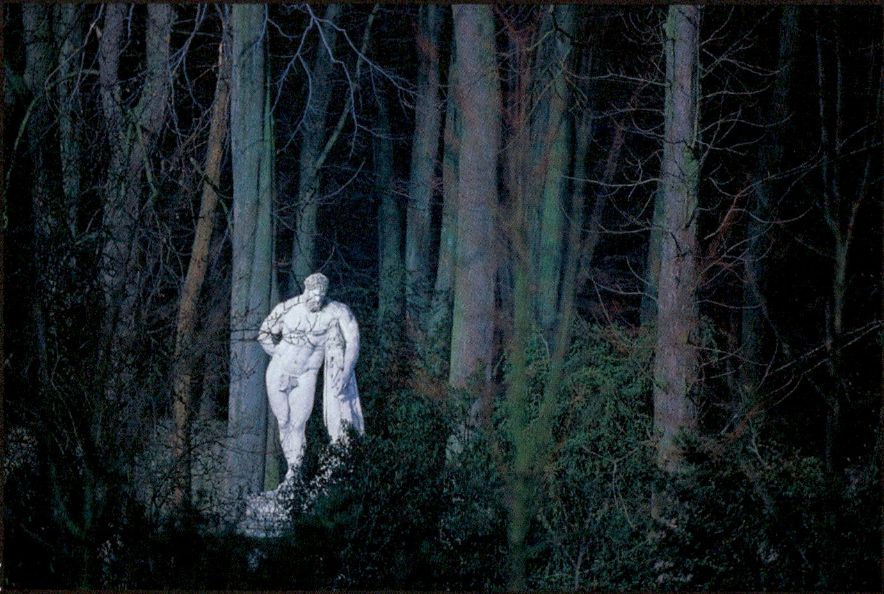

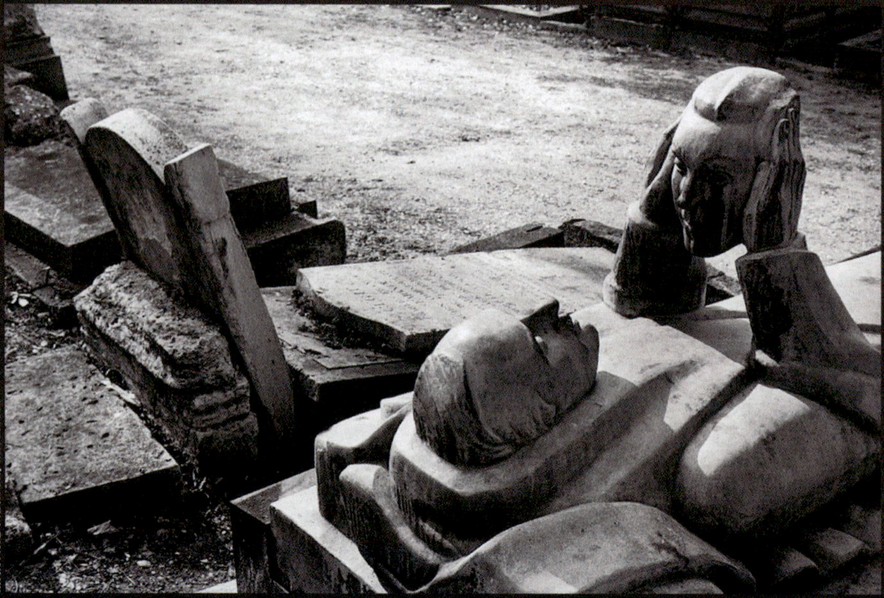

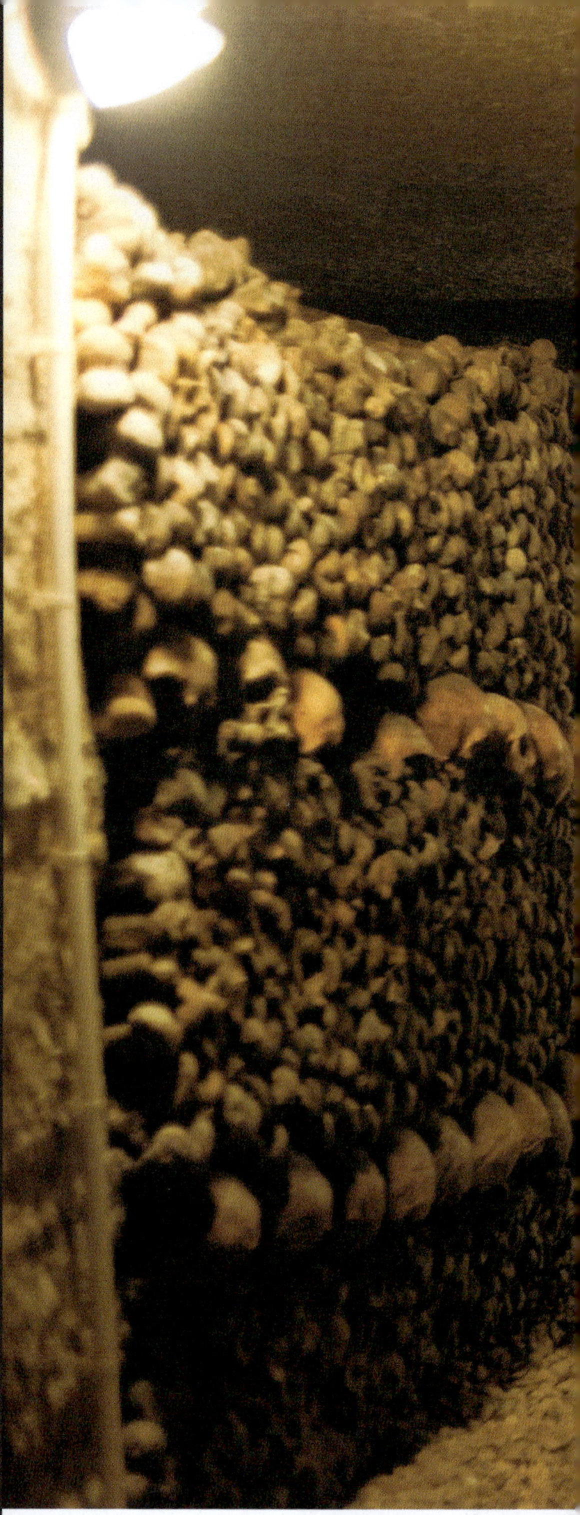

XAVIER POPY/REA/REDUX

ON JULY 14, 1931, as Paris celebrated Bastille Day, Princess Anna Obolensky Troubetzkoy fell almost 1,000 feet from the third platform of the Eiffel Tower. She had recently gotten married and seemed in good spirits–surely it was an accident. But letters later found in her purse proved that she'd killed herself. One of hundreds of people who have jumped from the Iron Lady since it was built in 1889,

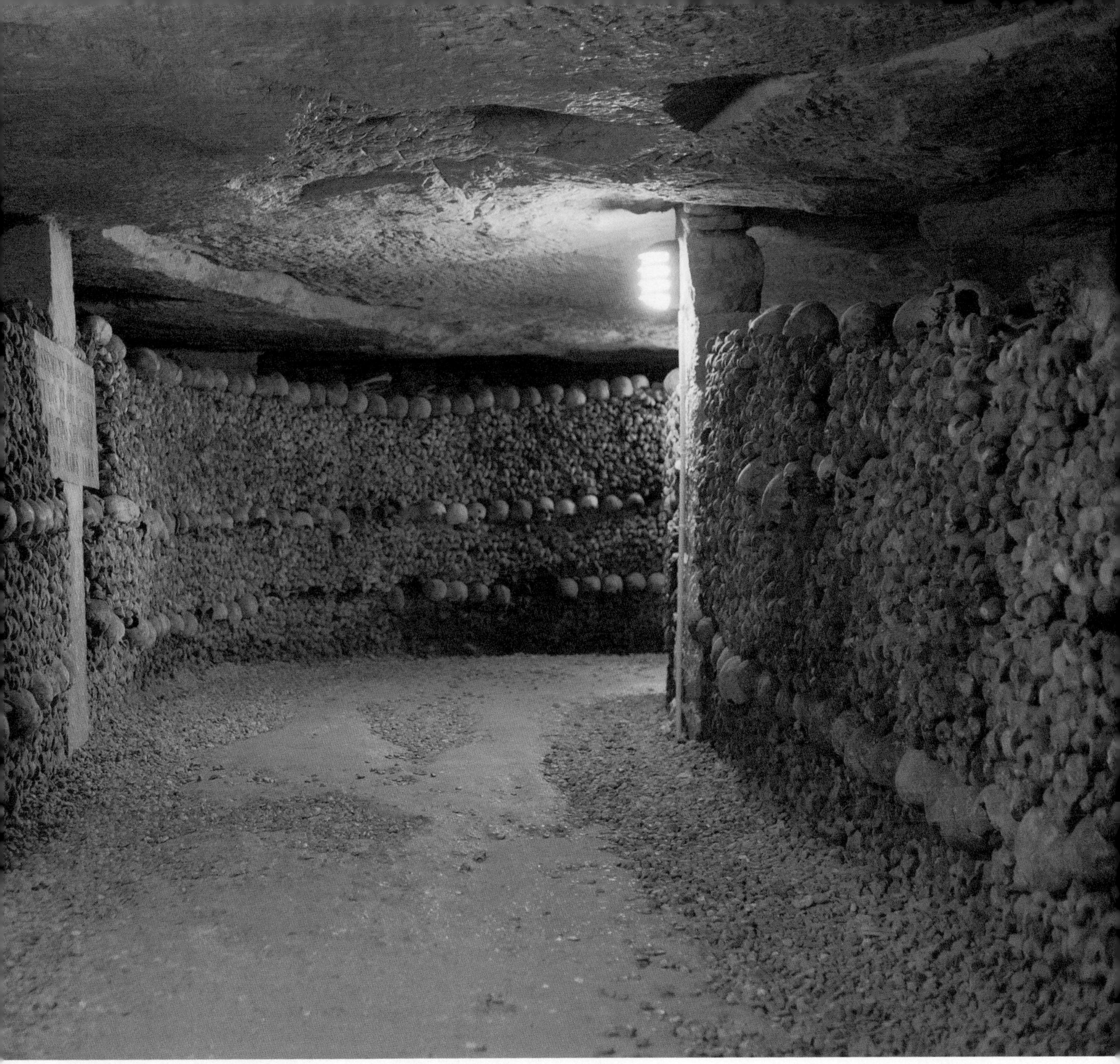

the princess is now said to be among the many souls who haunt France's national symbol.

No matter where you look, the City of Lights has a dark side—from spirits in the Louvre, which some have called the city's most haunted building, to the eerie catacombs, and even nearby Versailles. No, the orbs and ectoplasmic shades sometimes seen in the museum's medieval section are not, in fact, art installations but perhaps the spirits of people who were once imprisoned there. One particularly well-known entity is the "Little Red Ghost," reportedly seen by the likes of Catherine de Medici and Napoleon.

Plenty of spooky places figure in great works of French literature. Notre Dame Cathedral is known for its Hunchback, and the Opera has its Phantom. But in "real life" those structures are reportedly haunted by, respectively, robed figures with tall pointed hats and the ghost of a suicidal woman who roams the streets outside, searching for the man who jilted her.

Though the famously practical Parisians see Père-Lachaise—in all its Gothic splendor—as nothing more or less than a cemetery, it is said to be haunted by Oscar Wilde, Marcel Proust, Jim Morrison, and a number of, shall we say, lesser mortals. ■

SINCE THE MIDDLE AGES, Catholic pilgrims have traveled to Station Island in the middle of Lough Derg, in County Donegal, Ireland. There, they spend three days fasting and praying at the site where, according to legend, Christ showed Saint Patrick a cave leading straight to purgatory. The opening is supposedly now covered by a monastery, so if the dead ever decide to walk the earth they probably won't start here.

But the island is only one of many places where a gateway to the underworld supposedly exists. In 2013, archaeologists unearthed "Pluto's Gate," which the people of the Phrygian city of Hieropolis (in present-day southwest Turkey) believed to be an entrance to the netherworld. "This space is full of a vapor so misty and dense that one can scarcely see the ground," wrote one Greek geographer. "Any animal that passes inside meets instant death."

And in the early 1970s, the Derweze Crater, a fiery desert sinkhole, opened in Turkmenistan. Though it's known locally as the "Door to Hell," its hellish aspect has more to do with natural gas deposits than demons: It was created when the ground gave way under a Soviet drilling rig.

Other supposedly infernal entrances include Iceland's Mount Hekla volcano; Houska Castle north of Prague; the Bloody Hell Pond in Beppu City, Japan; and Lake Avernus near Naples, Italy, which the Romans considered the entrance to Hades. (It is referred to as such in Virgil's *Aeneid*.)

Some otherworldly openings are a lot closer to home. There are supposedly seven gates to hell in the woods of York County, Pennsylvania, for instance, and anyone who passes through all of them goes straight to ... well, you know. (Locals insist no one who made it past five gates has ever returned.) In the dilapidated cemetery of tiny Stull, Kansas, lore has it that hidden steps descend to the Gates of Hell. And voodoo tradition holds that seven portals to hell exist throughout New Orleans.

Then there are the hells that exist in name only—Hell, California; Hell, Michigan; Hell, Grand Cayman, Cayman Islands. But if you find yourself in Hell, Norway, relax: There, the word simply means "luck." ■

PILGRIMS PRAY AT DAWN and fast for three days at the holy site of St. Patrick's Purgatory on Station Island in Lough Derg, County Donegal, Ireland. Note that no one is wearing shoes, which are not allowed on the island.

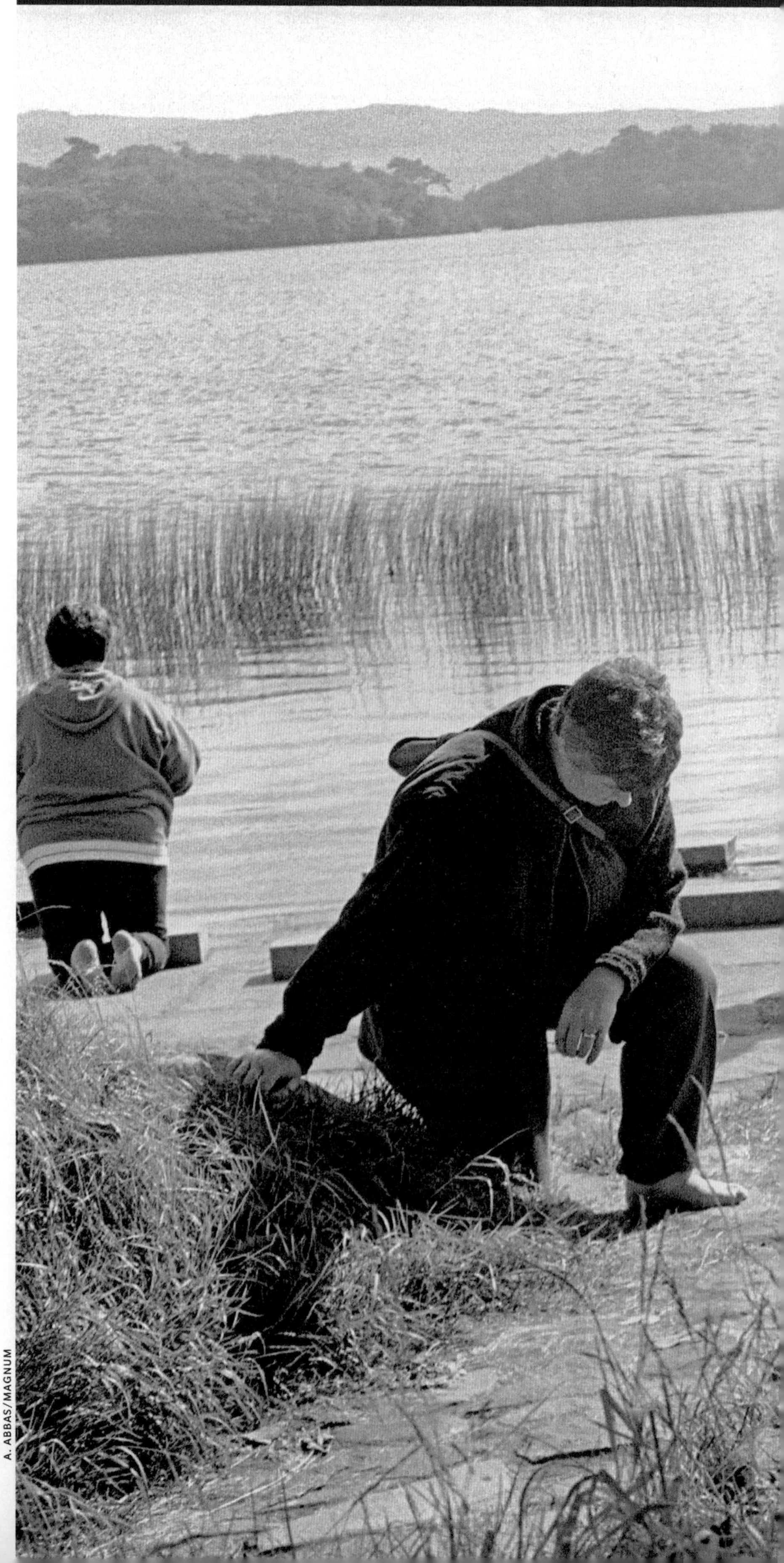

A. ABBAS/MAGNUM

THE DOORWAY TO HELL

ST. PATRICK'S PURGATORY

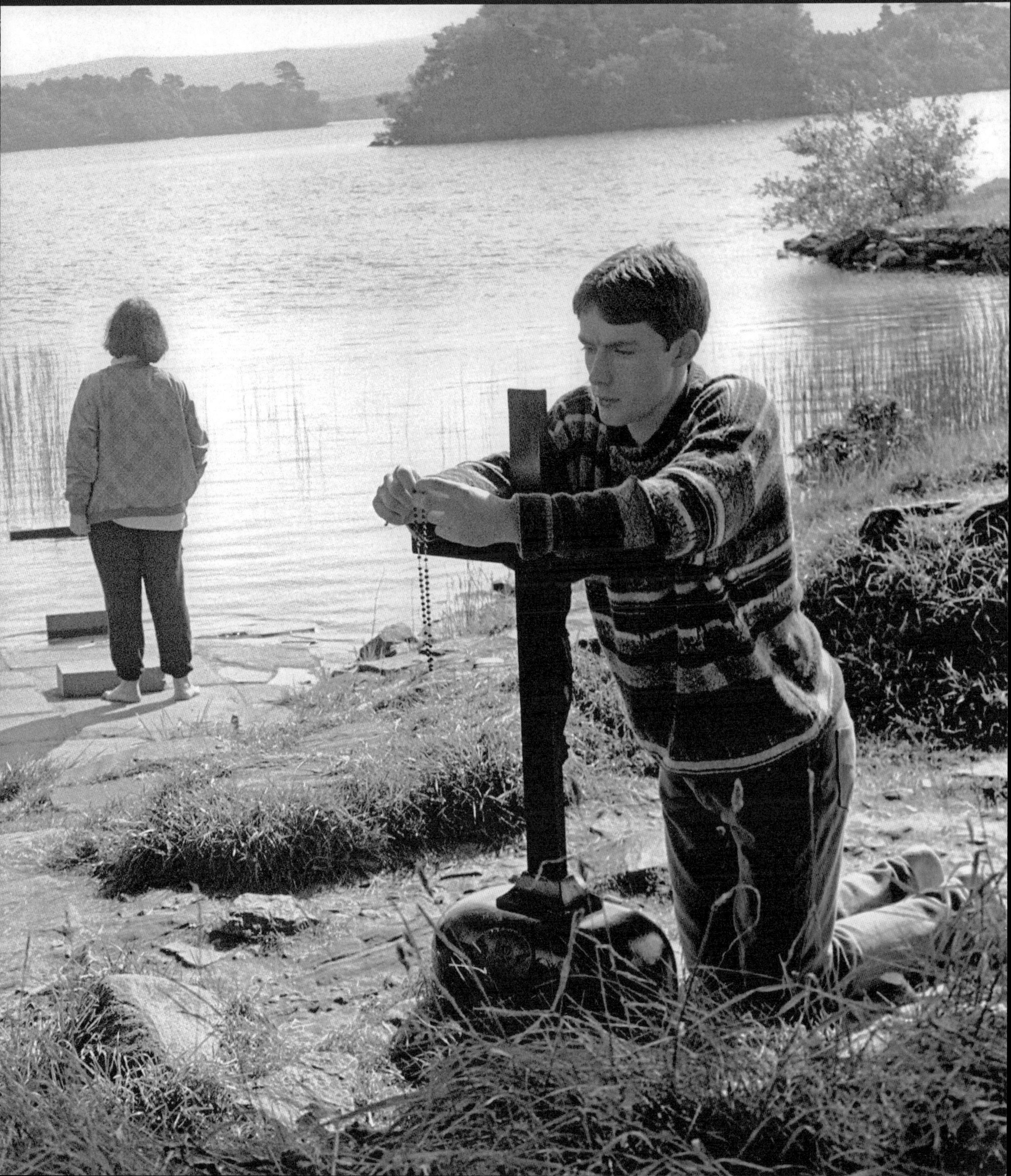

DRACULA'S LAIR

BRAN CASTLE

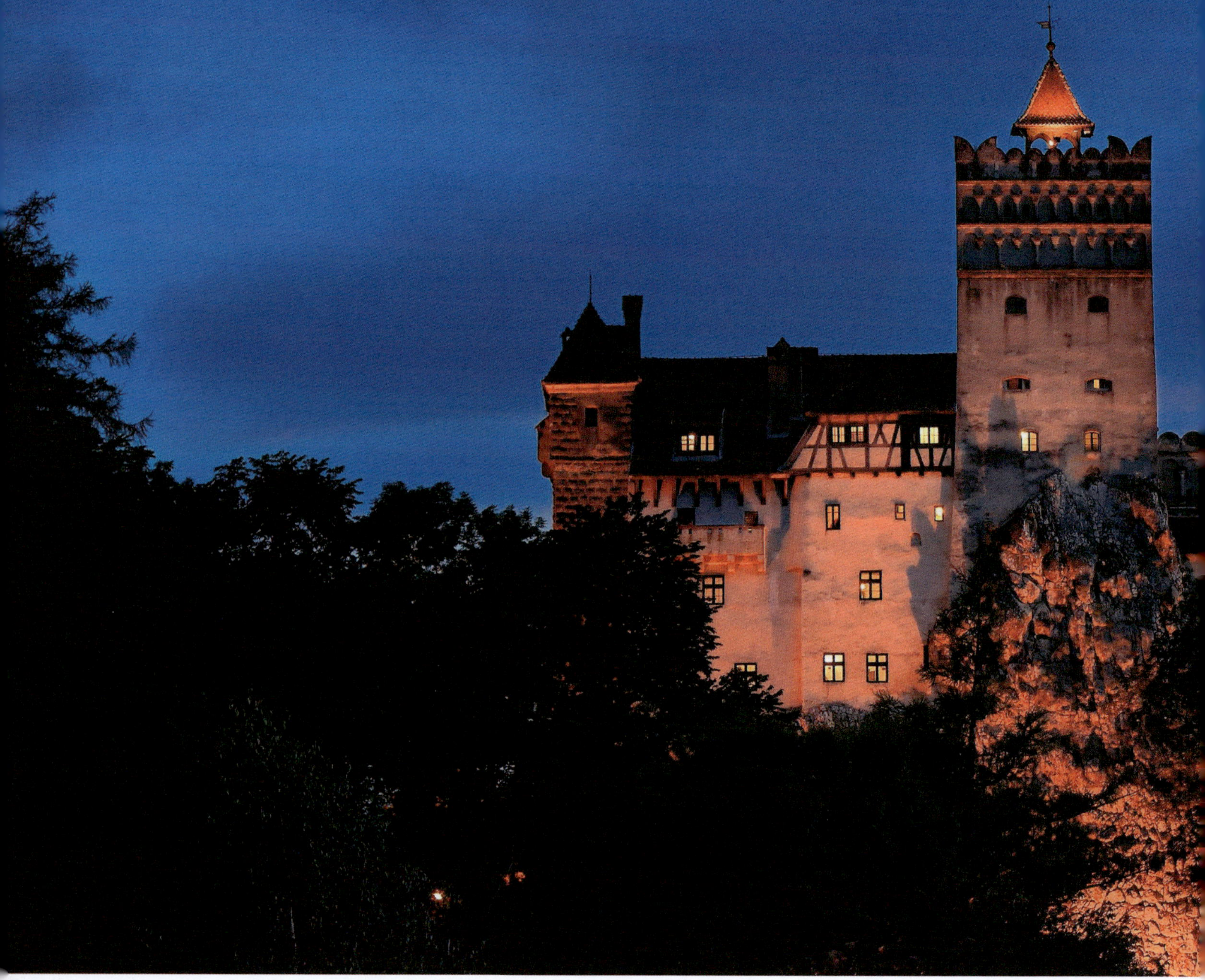

THOUGH TRANSYLVANIA'S Bran Castle has long been known as Dracula's Castle, the "real" home of the man who inspired the bloodthirsty count is actually in Wallachia, Romania. Now a ruin, it once belonged to 15th-century prince Vlad Tepes (a.k.a. Vlad the Impaler, a.k.a. Vlad III Dracula), who was known for such atrocities as impaling his enemies on spears. (Hence his nickname.)

Completed in 1388 on a cliff between Magura and Dealul Cetatii, Bran Castle is the only structure in Transylvania that matches the description of Dracula's domain in Bram Stoker's classic 1897 novel. But Stoker never visited Romania, and his book was based on 19th-century tomes that depicted the country as a backwater filled with superstitious peasants. In his novel, he called Transylvania "this cursed land, where the devil and his

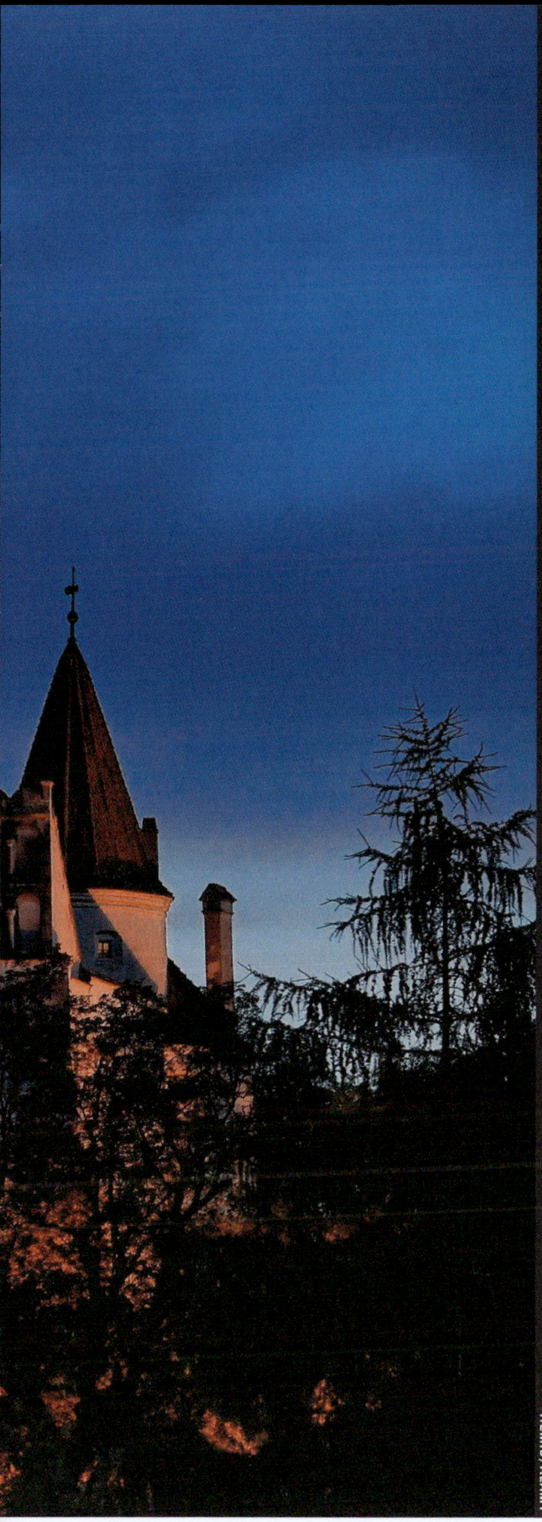

HEMIS/ALAMY

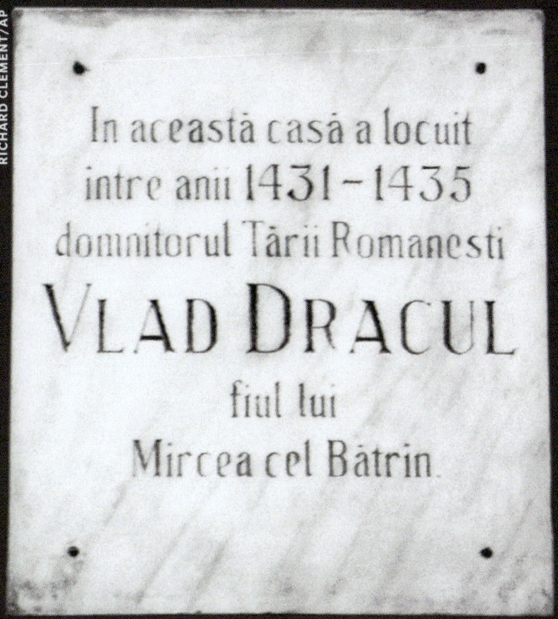

RICHARD CLEMENT/AP

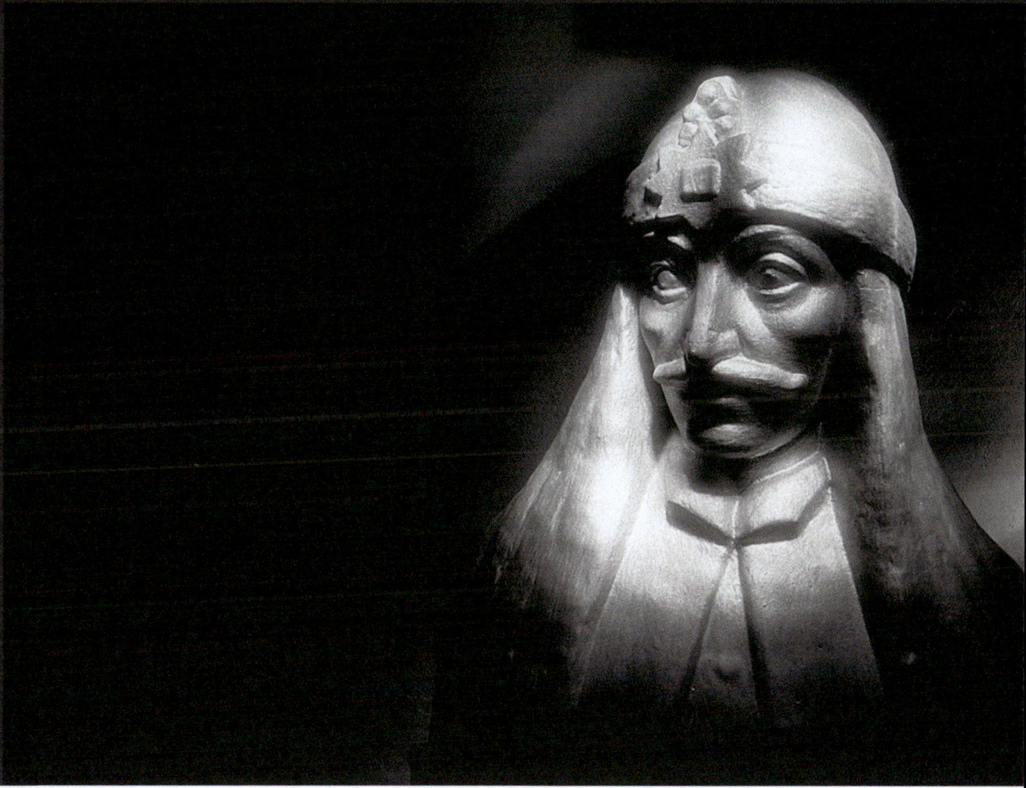

BERTHOLD STEINHILBER/LAIF/REDUX

NEAR LEFT: A PLAQUE for Vlad III Dracula, the bloodthirsty Transylvanian prince who may have inspired Bram Stoker's famous character, marks the house, in Sighisoara, Romania, where he first lived as a child. Below: A statue of Vlad in the house. Far left: Bran Castle. Stoker never visited Romania but may have been inspired by seeing an illustration of the castle in a book.

children still walk with earthly feet!"

That skewed impression continues, more or less, to this day. "The mist-covered mountains are real," a 1994 LIFE article read, "the crumbling castles are real, the howling wolves, swooping bats, peasants making the sign of the cross, all real."

Maybe. But many Romanians resent the characterization of their country as a doom-haunted land of mystery and superstition. "I hardly heard anything about vampires, werewolves or any of that," said Trent Leinenbach, a Brigham Young University student who spent time researching folktales in Romania. "[Romanians are] aware that it's something they are known for . . . but they don't seem to be extremely interested in that side of the folklore."

Still, many older Transylvanians continue to believe in the existence of ghosts, vampires, werewolves, witches, and forest spirits (such as the *strigoi,* humans whose souls leave their bodies at night to wreak havoc among the living). These legends are rapidly dying out, though. Which is partly why Britain's Prince Charles (a descendant, believe it or not, of Vlad the Impaler!) has established a foundation to preserve Romanian heritage. "I do have a bit of a stake in the country," he said. "Transylvania is in my blood." ■

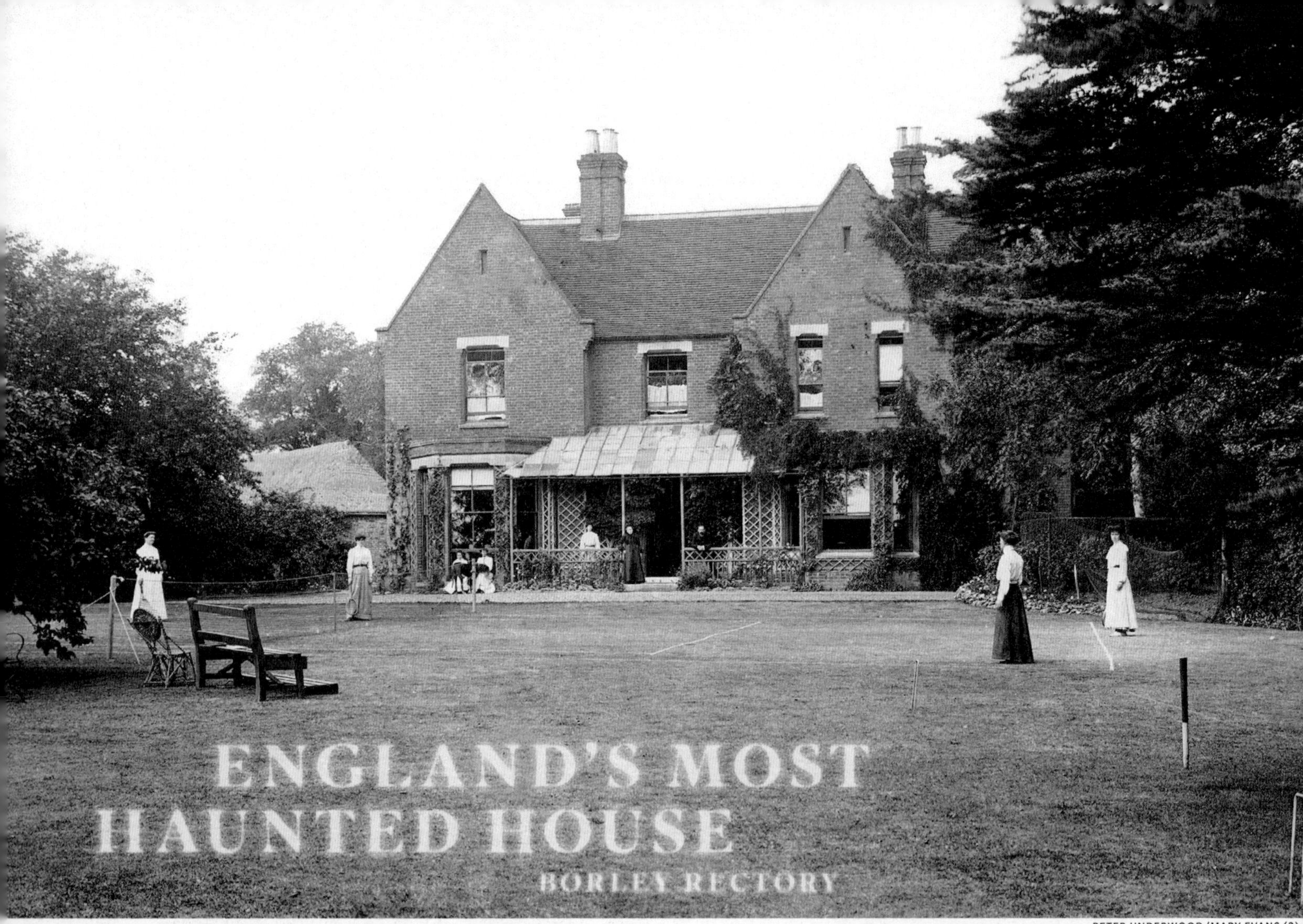

ENGLAND'S MOST HAUNTED HOUSE

BORLEY RECTORY

PETER UNDERWOOD/MARY EVANS (2)

IN 1863, BORLEY RECTORY was built in Essex, England—allegedly over the remains of a Benedictine monastery. According to local legend, that was where a monk and a nun were murdered after falling in love and trying to elope. (Their coachman didn't fare much better.)

The house's first residents and locals claimed to see the nun's ghost walking on a path that became known as—what else?—the Nun's Walk. Among other phenomena, a ghostly figure was always seen looking though a window. (Sensibly, they barred it shut.) But none of this became widely known until the late 1920s, when the new rector, the Reverend Guy Eric Smith, began to witness the spectral events and became distressed.

So he reached out to controversial psychic researcher Henry Price. But when Price arrived to investigate, all hell broke lose—literally—leading him to call Borley "the most haunted house in England." Keys flew from locks. And pebbles and coins rained from nowhere. Soon after, the Smiths fled the house when publicity made Borley arguably the first mass media–covered haunting, the precursor to the likes of *The Amityville Horror.*

In 1930, a new rector moved in but left in 1935 after the supposed spirits became particularly attached to his wife, Marianne, writing messages on the walls: "Marianne, please help get" and "pleas for help and prayers." After Price took up residence in 1937, intending to conduct further experiments, a message in a séance predicted that the rectory would be destroyed in a fire.

Nearly one year later a fire gutted Borley Rectory.

In 1944, the building's remains were demolished. A LIFE photographer visited and shot the site, and one of his images captured what appeared to be a brick levitating in a doorway—Borley's "last phenomenon," Price called it. Except, of course, that it wasn't: The haunting continued in nearby Borley Church.

Over the years, many people came forward either denying the events or alleging fraud. But at least one observer, occult expert Ellic Howe, was convinced that the haunting was legitimate. "Suppose for a moment that Price was quite aware that he was setting the stage for a colossal hoax," Howe wrote. "If he had that sort of thing in mind he never gave the game away—or at least not to me. His acting must have been consummate. But I don't think he was acting."

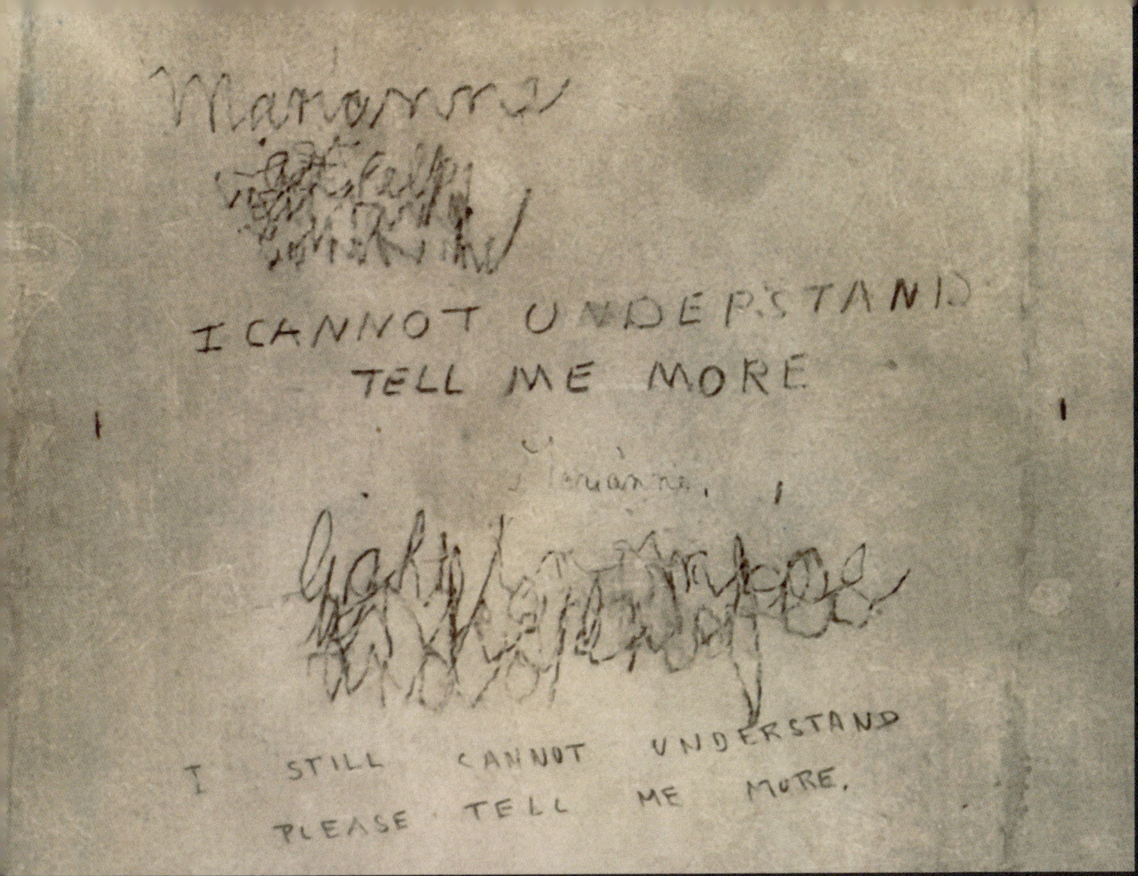

OPPOSITE PAGE: Borley Rectory around 1892, when the original occupant, Henry Bull, was in residence; in the garden, the Bull family plays tennis. Left: The spirits seemed particularly enamored of one rector's wife, Marianne, often addressing her with incomprehensible messages. Below left: Noted psychic researcher Harry Price with his Ghostbusters paraphernalia. Price was almost single-handedly responsible for the rectory's reputation as "the most haunted house in England." Below right: While covering a story on the burned rectory's demolition, LIFE photographer David E. Scherman snapped this shot that showed, he claimed, a brick floating in the black entryway seen in the center of this photo.

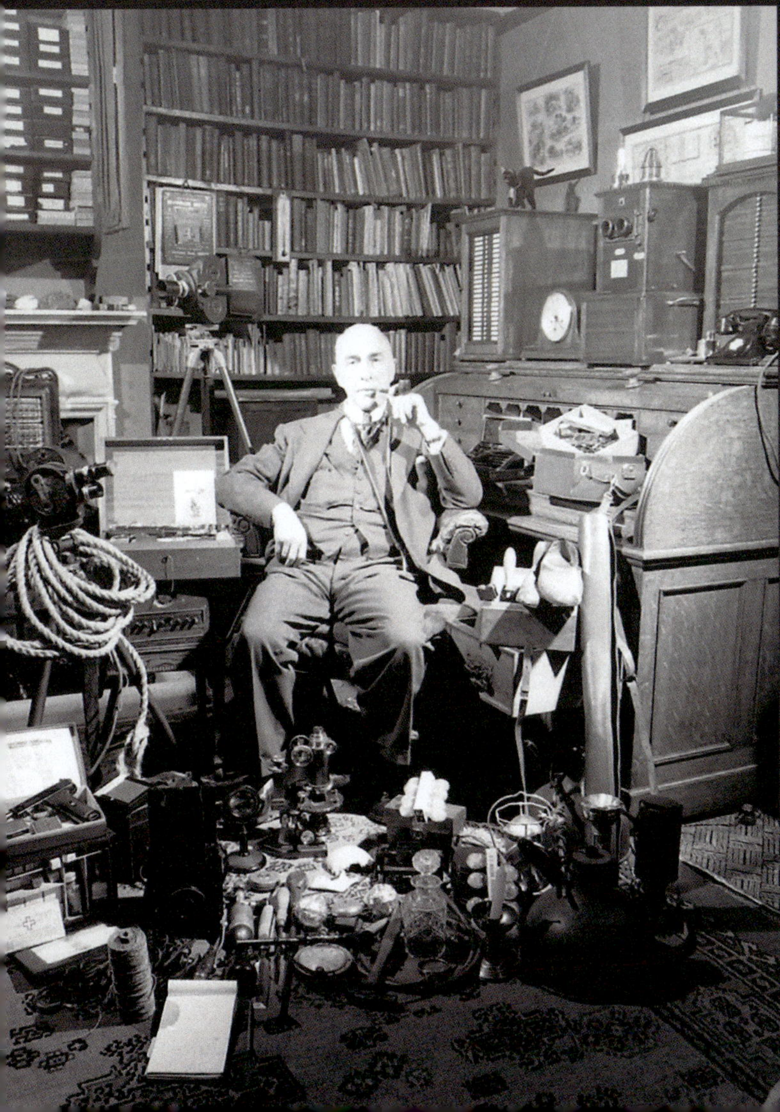

DAVID E. SCHERMAN/LIFE/THE PICTURE COLLECTION (2)

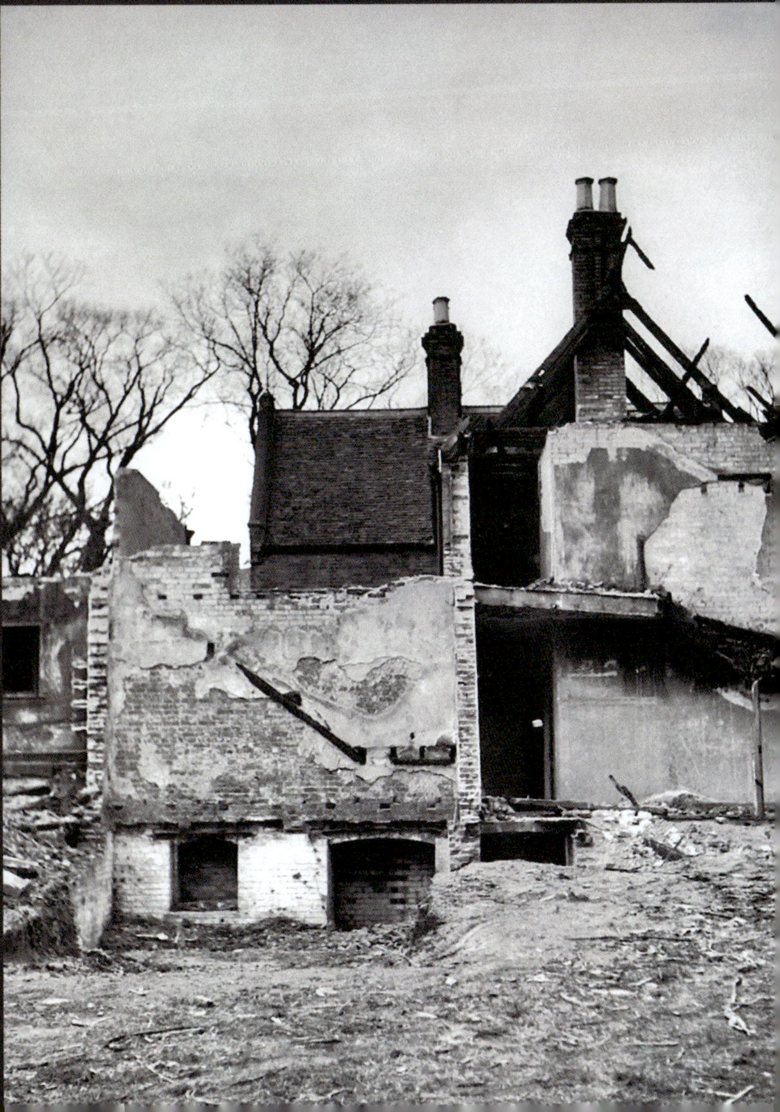

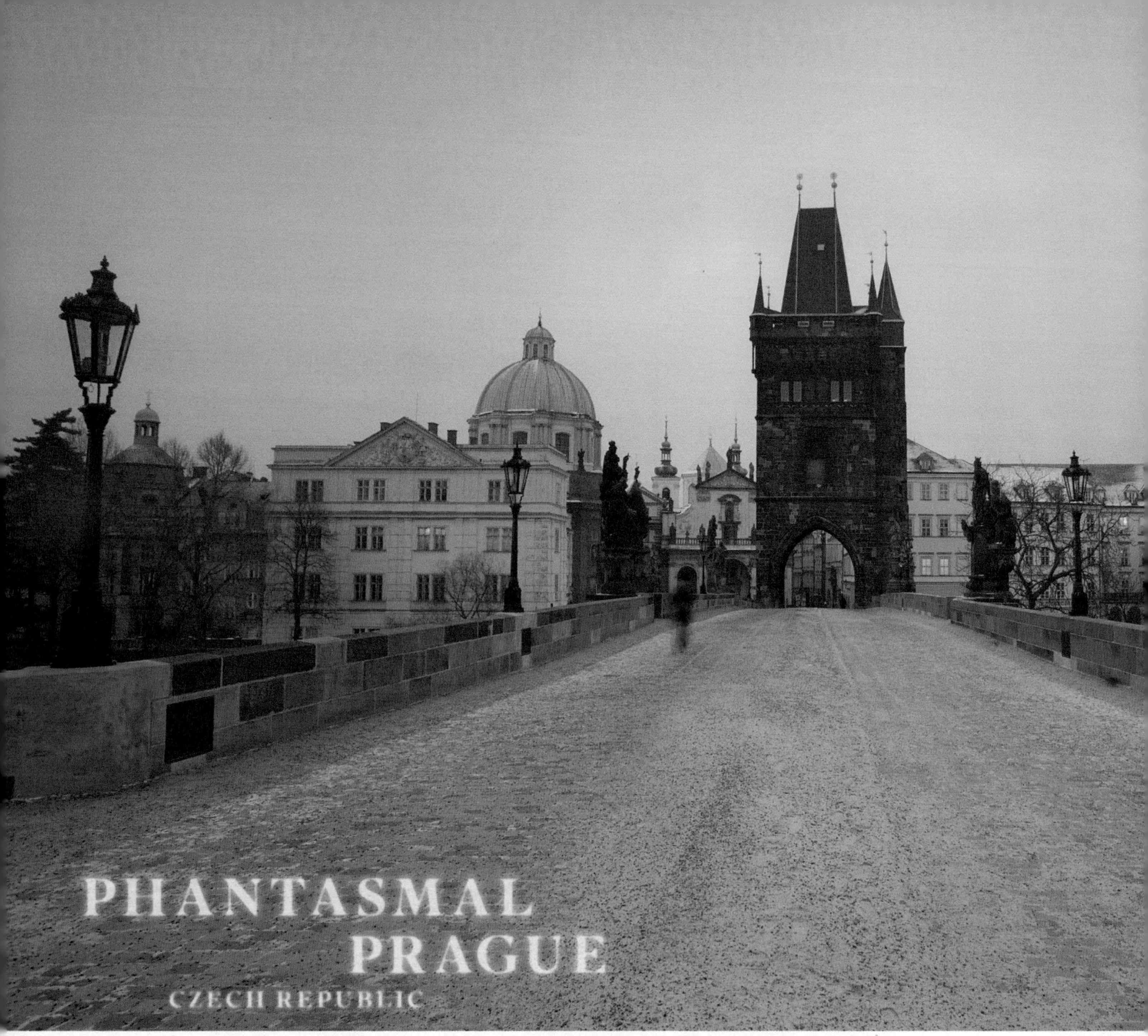

PHANTASMAL PRAGUE

CZECH REPUBLIC

"I FELT AS IF THE HOUSES were staring down at me with malicious expressions full of nameless spite: the doors were black, gaping mouths in which the tongues had rotted away," wrote Gustav Meyrínk of early 20th-century Prague in his classic mystical novel, *The Golem.*

A sort of Biblical Frankenstein, the Golem is a mythical creature referred to in the Bible and the Talmud and supposedly fashioned from clay by wise men. One of its creators was Rabbi Judah Löw ben Bezalel during the reign of Rudolph II in the late 16th century. The rabbi's aim: to protect Prague's Jewish Quarter from pogroms and anti-Semitism. Given the events of subsequent centuries, he wasn't entirely successful.

Maybe that's why the Golem is never seen on the streets of this Bohemian city. However, plenty of other supernatural beings are. If Prague isn't the most haunted metropolis in Europe, it certainly offers one of the widest varieties of otherworldly entities. Here, you will find not just the ghost of the Headless Templar and a benevolent spirit in the Convent of St. Agnes but reignited pagan fires on Petrín Hill, a goblin that lives under the Charles Bridge, and a skeleton that begs drunks for money.

Prague may be one of the few cities with a monument to a ghost: The statue of a man named Jáchym Berka stands on Platnérská Street in the city's Old Town. His story goes like this: Returning from a war,

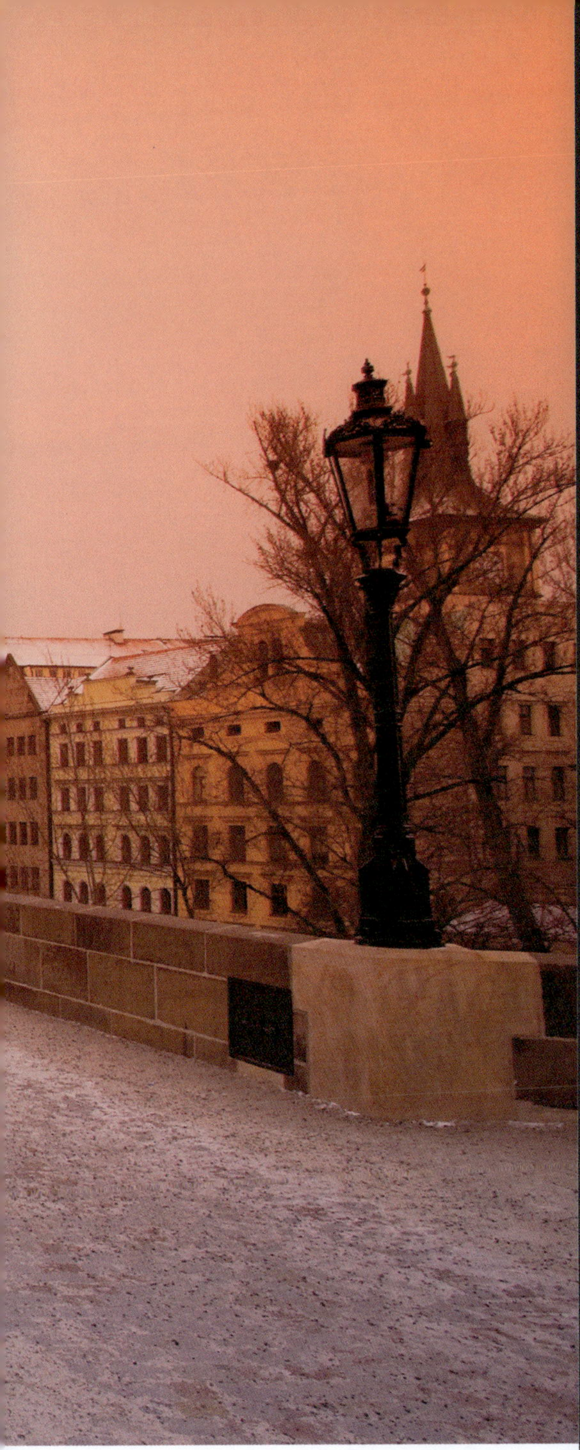

HULTON-DEUTSCH/CORBIS/GETTY

AT LEFT: PRAGUE'S famous Charles Bridge, shown here uncharacteristically empty of tourists—but perhaps not of spirits. Below: Tombstones in the ancient Jewish cemetery, where the rabbi who created the famous Prague golem is buried. Bottom: A reliquary, used as a sort of casket for a body part—in this case, the skull of Saint Ludmila. It can be seen in the Convent of St. Agnes, said to be haunted by a ghost.

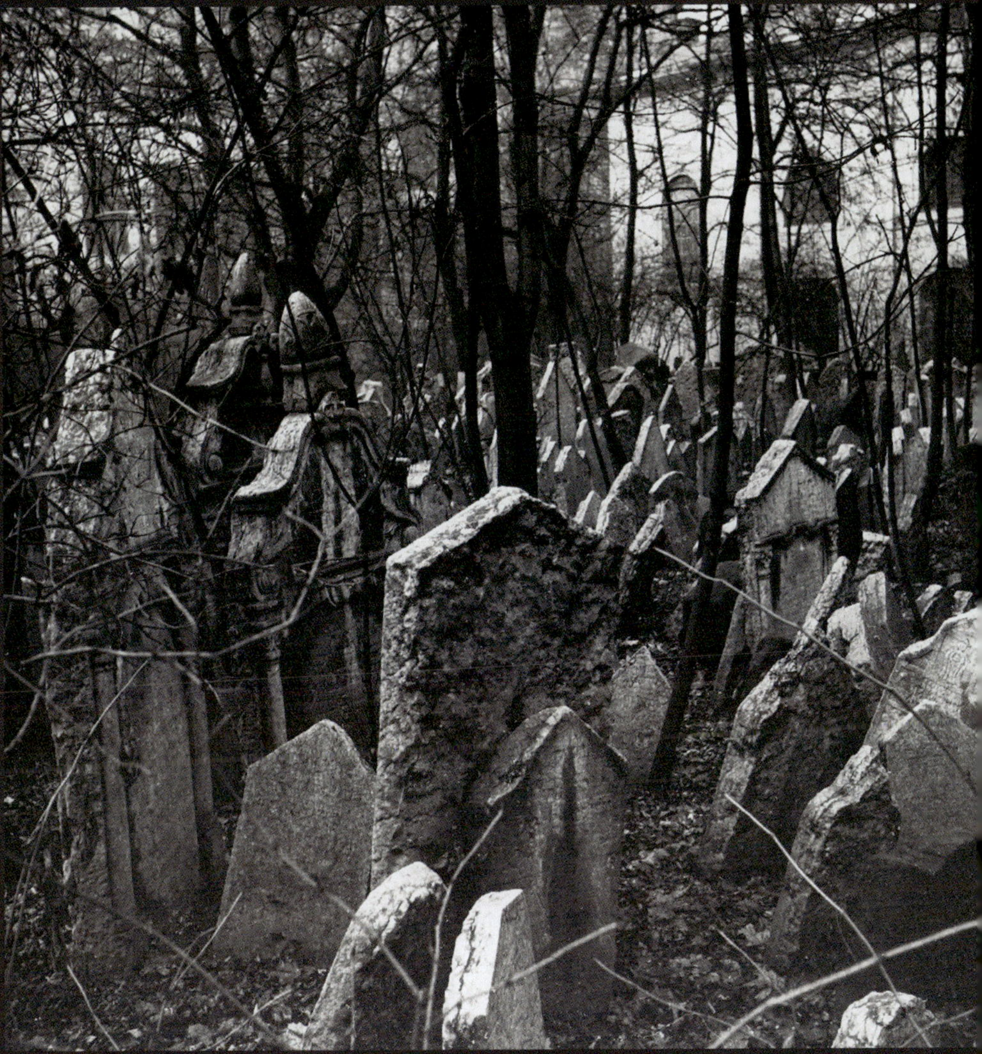

KEN SCICLUNA/JWL/AURORA

Berka believed a false rumor that his fiancée had been unfaithful to him. Furious, he married another woman, and when his fiancée found out she drowned herself. A distraught Berka then killed his wife and hung himself.

Now his wandering spirit gets a shot at salvation only once every 100 years. If he can find a virgin and talk to her for an hour, he will end his ghostly servitude.

Sadly, he seems to have missed his chance in 2009 . . . but he's keeping his spectral fingers crossed for 2109. ■

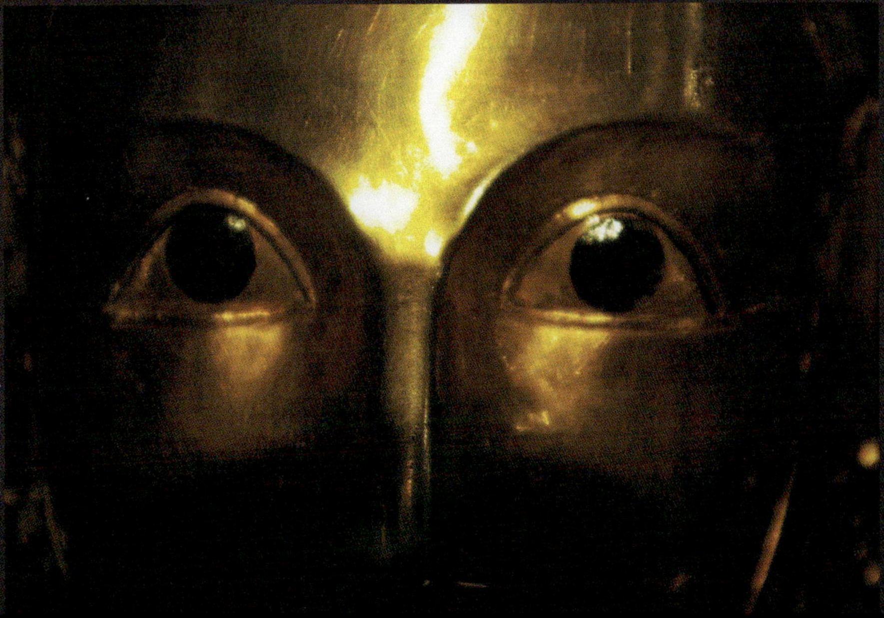

E & S GINSBERG/ALAMY

TOWER OF LONDON

ENGLAND

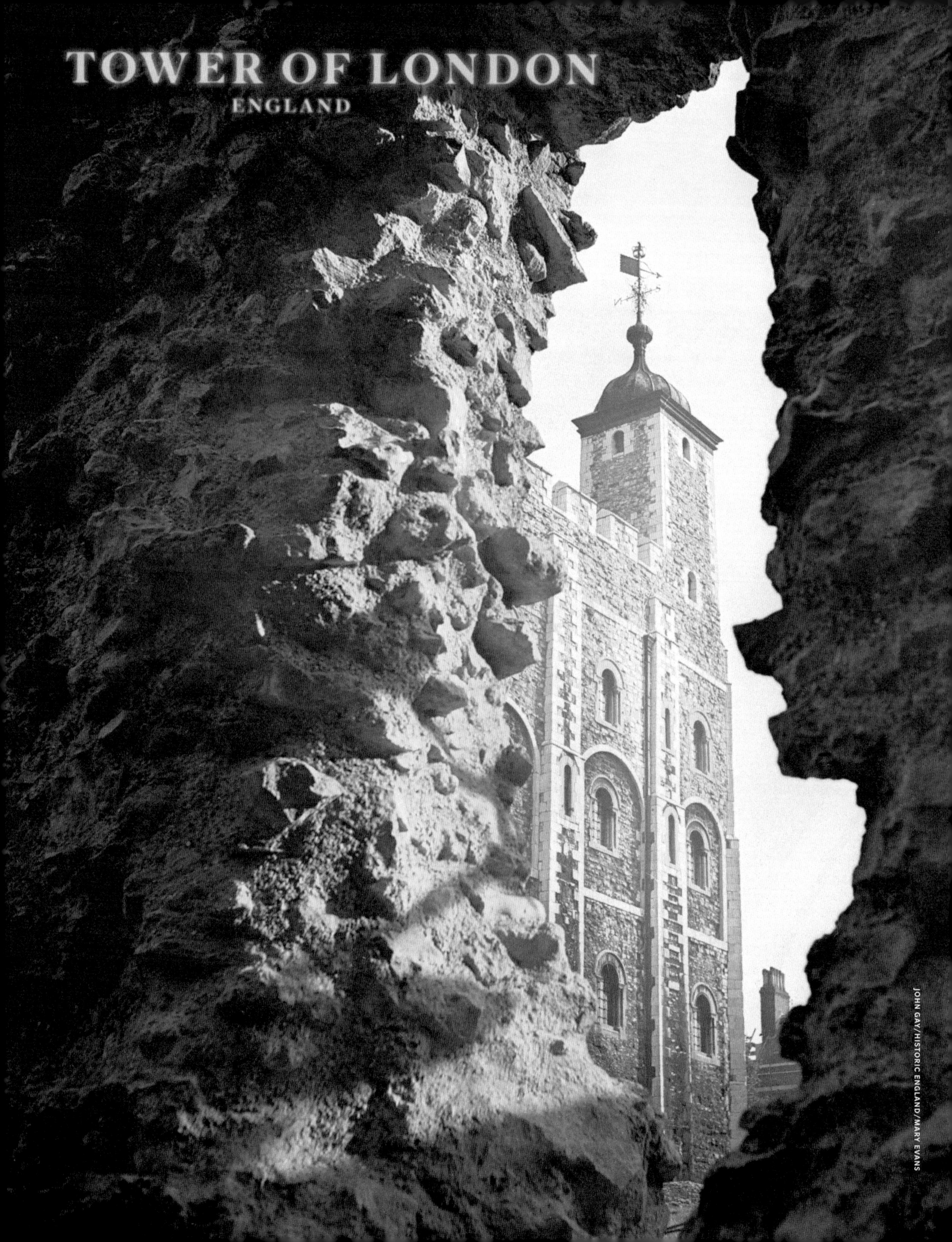

JOHN GAY/HISTORIC ENGLAND/MARY EVANS

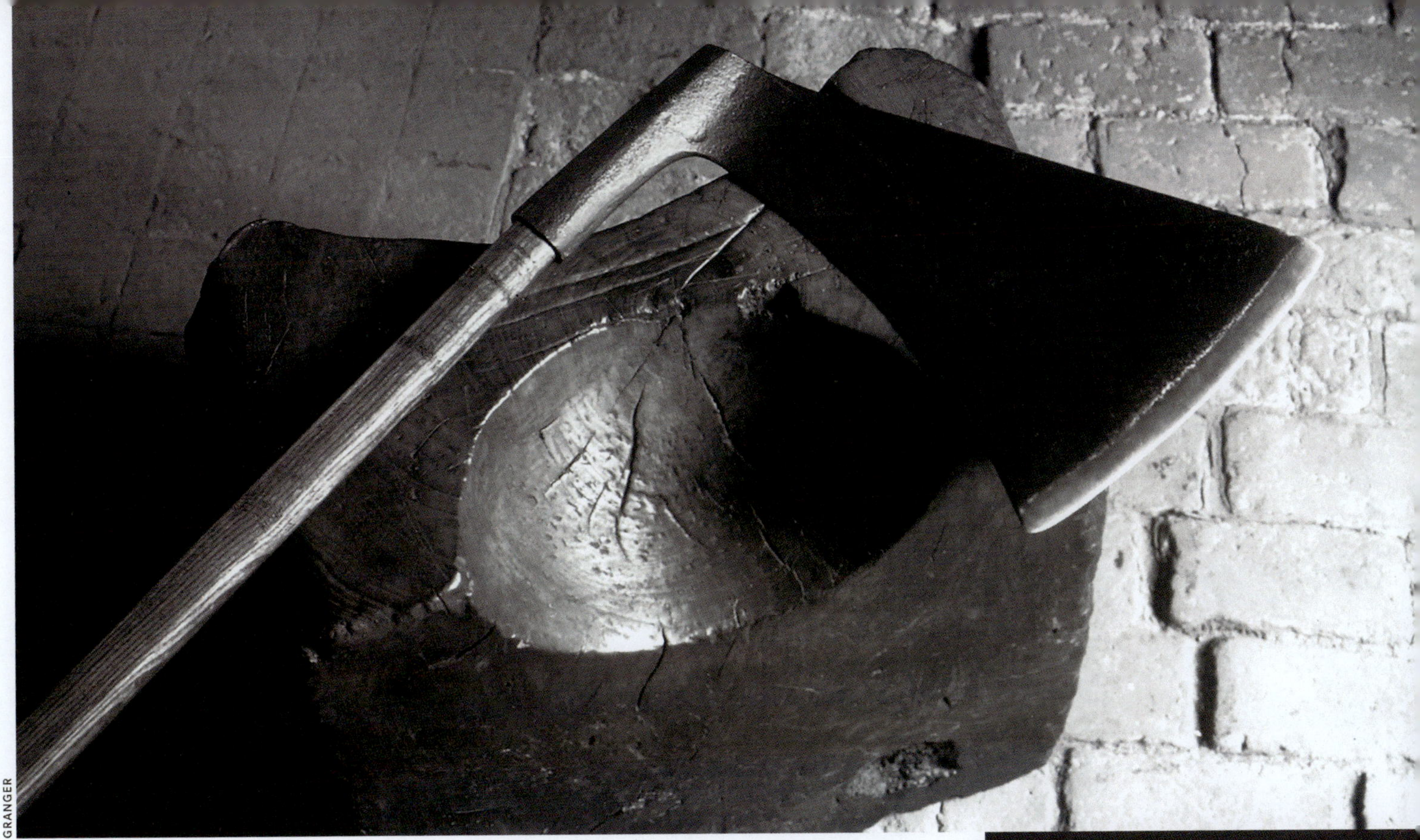

GRANGER

"THERE'S ONLY YOU and I here," a disembodied (and ungrammatical) voice supposedly said to Tower of London night watchman Arthur Crick, who had stopped along his nightly rounds to rest his feet. "Just let me get this bloody shoe on," Crick responded, "and there'll only be *you!*"

Guards aren't the only ones who say they have experienced supernatural phenomenon in England's fearsome, ancient fortress on the River Thames. Started by William the Conqueror in 1066, the complex of towers—now home to everything from the crown jewels to an ax probably used in the last public beheading on Tower Hill—is widely considered the most haunted building in England.

For good reason. Throughout its notorious history, it has seen more than its share of bloodshed and misery. It's supposedly home to the ghost of Henry VI, who was possibly praying here when he was stabbed to death—allegedly in the presence of Richard Plantagenet, the Duke of Gloucester—in 1471. The unhappy Henry is now said to haunt the Wakefield Tower, where tortures often took place.

But the most storied part of the complex is, not surprisingly, the oldest: The White Tower is where the ghost known as the "White Lady" wanders, her perfume often smelled at the entrance to the Chapel of St. John's. A headless ghost said to be that of Anne Boleyn is sometimes seen near the Queen's House, close to where she was executed on Tower Green, and the Nine Day Queen, Lady Jane Grey, was reportedly spotted by guards on February 12, 1957, the 403rd anniversary of her death by execution.

Maybe saddest of all are the wraiths of Edward IV's young sons Edward V and Richard. In 1483, they were sent to the Tower after being declared illegitimate by the their uncle Richard (the Duke of Gloucester again!), who may also have had them murdered (he then became King Richard III). The skeletons of two young boys were discovered beneath a staircase in 1674, but the brothers' spirits continue to be seen in white nightgowns, clutching each other in terror. ■

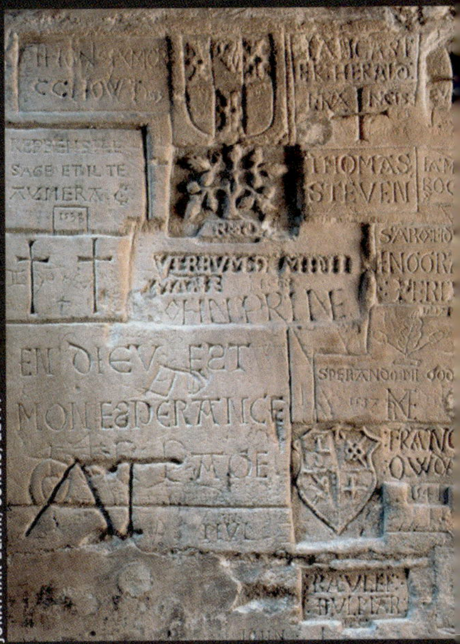

JONATHAN BLAIR/CORBIS/GETTY

OPPOSITE PAGE: The south side of the Tower of London's so-called White Tower, the oldest part of the structure, as seen through a gap in the wall. Top: The execution block on which Catherine Howard, the fifth wife of King Henry VIII, reportedly practiced laying her head the night before her execution in 1542. Just above: Prisoner graffiti in Beauchamp Tower. The walls of this tower—particularly on the first floor—are covered with such writings, most carved during the 16th and 17th centuries.

BELOW: The embalmed body of Vladimir Lenin on display in his tomb in Moscow's Red Square. At right: The Russian capital's famed Kremlin, which bridges medieval Muscovy and the Soviet Union—and may have more than mere mortal occupants.

THE BLOODY KREMLIN

MOSCOW

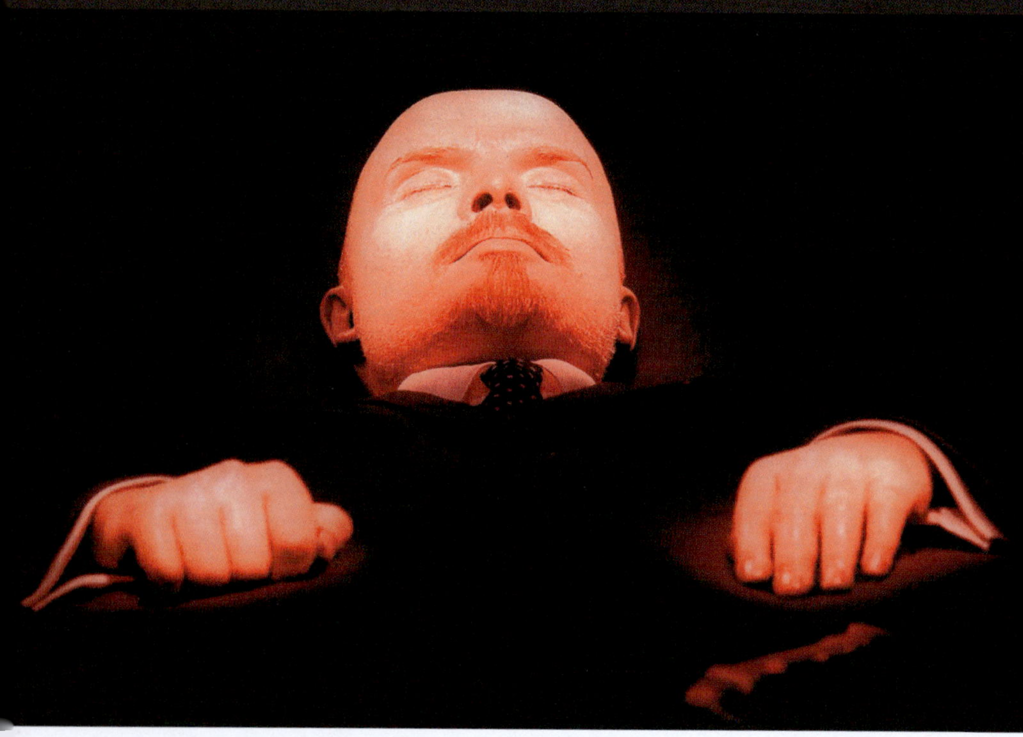

SERGEI KARPUKHIN/AP/SHUTTERSTOCK

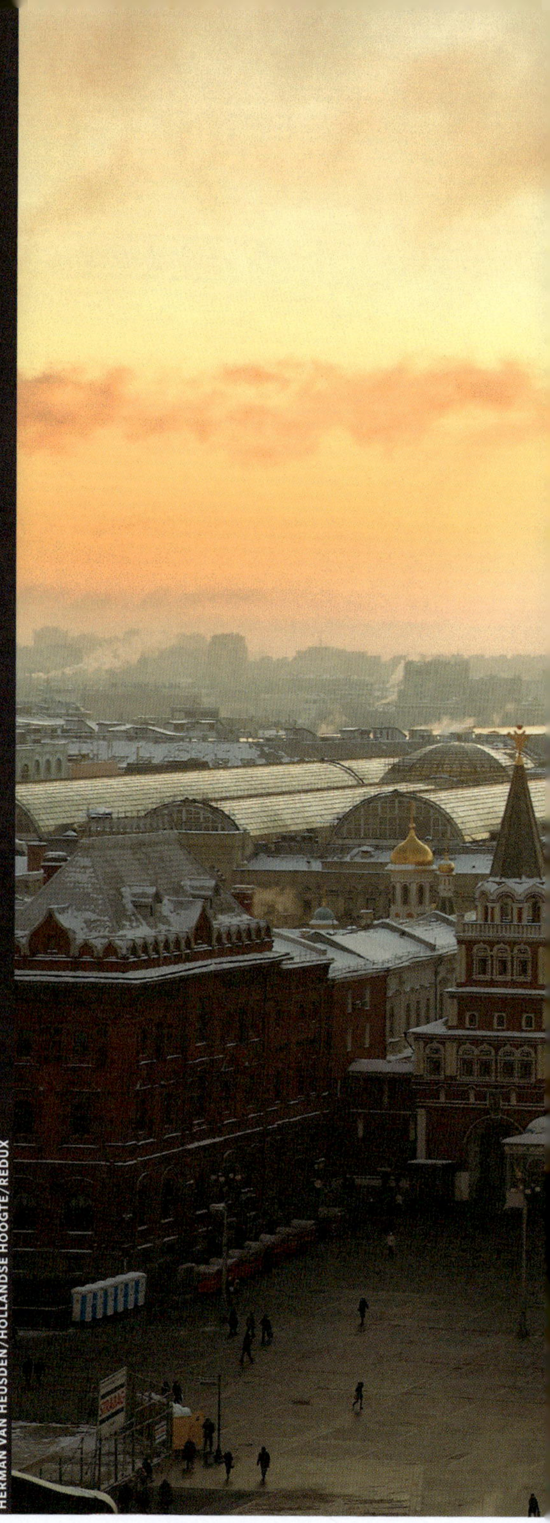

HERMAN VAN HEUSDEN/HOLLANDSE HOOGTE/REDUX

ON AUGUST 30, 1918, Vladimir Lenin was speaking at a Moscow factory named Hammer and Sickle. Afterward, as the founder of the Communist Party and first head of the Soviet state left the building, revolutionary Fanya Kaplan called out to him—and fired three shots. One hit him in his shoulder; the other hit his neck. (That's the official Soviet story, anyway.)

Though the fiery leader survived, he never fully recovered, and the injuries he sustained may have led to the series of strokes that ultimately killed him. He was for years afterward unable to walk without a cane. Which is why in 1923 witnesses—so the legend goes—thought it strange to see him moving quickly and unaided through the building's halls. Even stranger: The corporeal Lenin was away from the complex at the time.

A bad omen? Maybe. Mere months

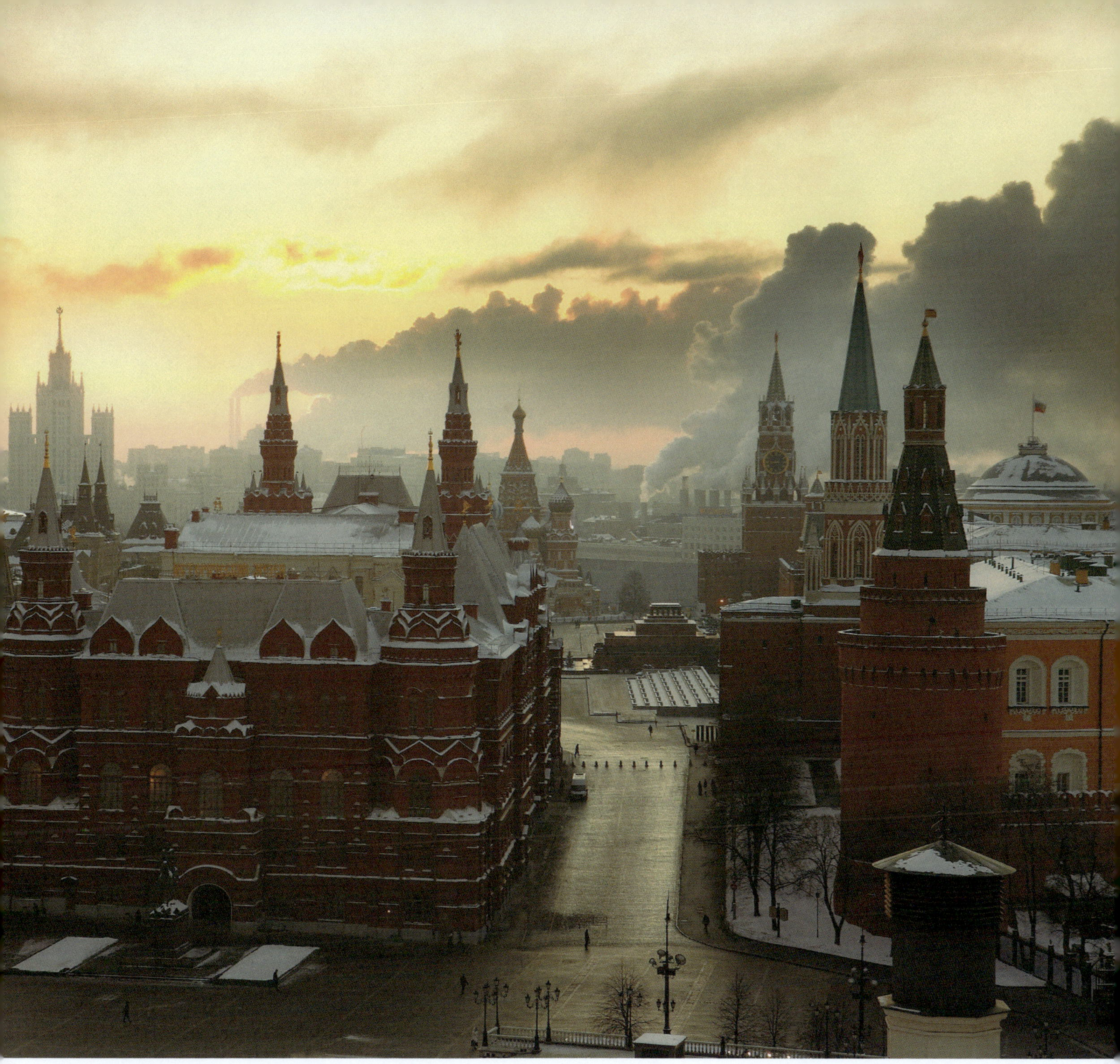

after this sighting, in January 1924, Lenin died. Though his embalmed body is now creepily entombed in Red Square in front of the Kremlin Wall, surrounded by 240 victims of his October Revolution, his ghost prowls the fortress, where he has plenty of company.

Ivan the Terrible, who died of a stroke while playing chess, is sometimes seen in the Ivan the Great bell tower. The ghost of Soviet dictator Joseph Stalin, who also died of a stroke as he slipped into paranoid old age, brings with him a blast of cold air. And the spirit of Kaplan herself, who was executed soon after the assassination attempt, is said to haunt the Komendantskaya bell tower, a pale disheveled woman holding a gun.

Like any other city steeped in history and mystery, Moscow proper has its share of ghosts, its storied sites supposedly haunted by the likes of a spectral cat on Tverskaya Street, a ghost carriage on Kuznetsky Most, and an old man on Myasnitskaya Street. There's even a notorious thoroughfare from Lyubertsy to Lytarkino streets that is the site of so many mysterious accidents it's called Death Road.

Whether any of these events and apparitions are "real" may be beside the point. In the words of the great Russian writer Anton Chekhov: "Man is what he believes."

DECORATED FOR THE traditional Via Crucis Procession on Good Friday, the Colosseum, right, is said to be haunted by the ghosts of gladiators. Below: The bones of thousands of dead monks create an unusual form of interior decoration at the Capuchin Crypt under the Church of Santa Maria della Concezione.

EERIE ROME

ITALY

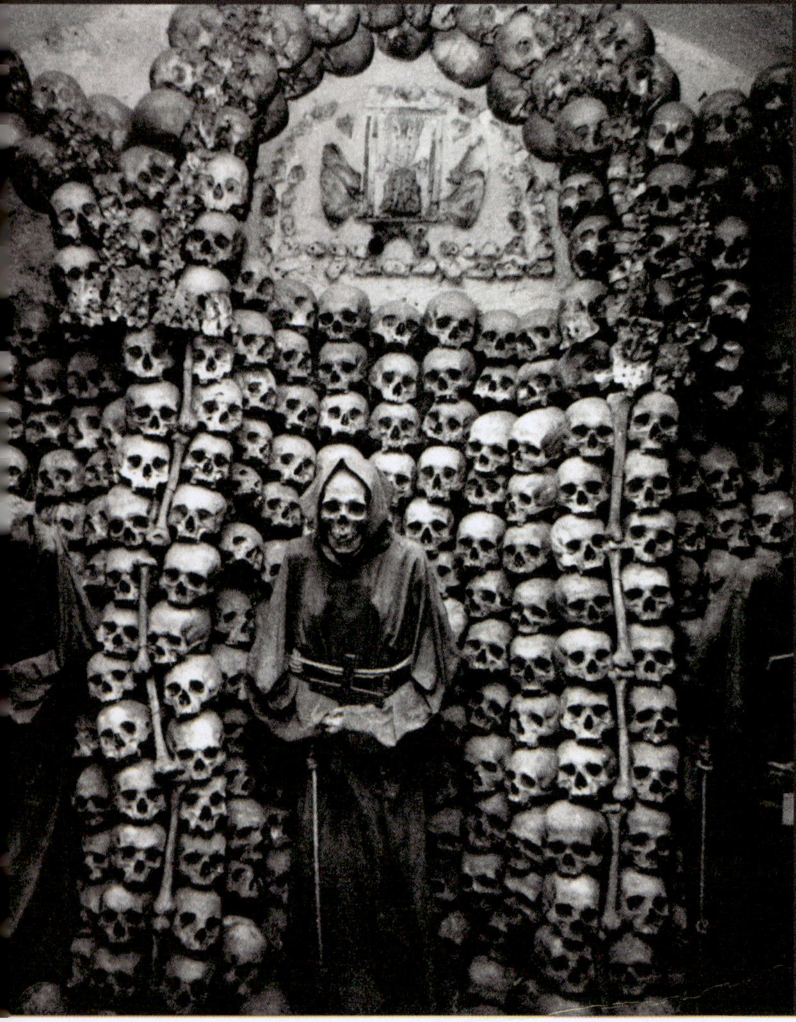

ELLIOTT ERWITT/MAGNUM

GIOVANNI DEL BRENNA

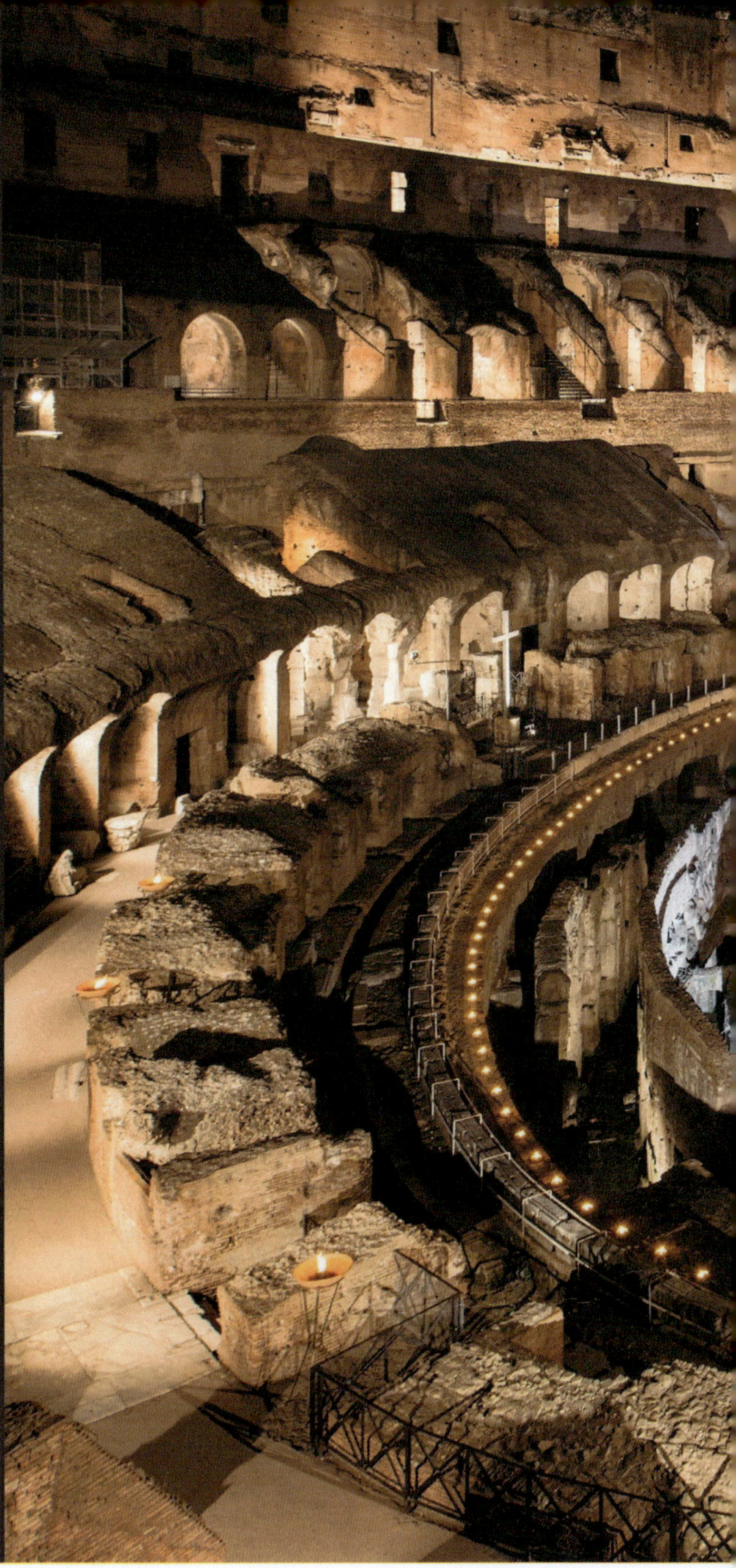

"A VIOLENT thunderstorm suddenly arose and enveloped the king in so dense a cloud that he was quite invisible," the historian Titus Livius wrote of Romulus, the mythical founder of Rome, in one of the writer's 142 books on the great city. "From that hour, Romulus was no longer seen on earth."

This fabled disappearance occurred in what was then the Campus Martius (Field of Mars), one remnant of which remains the Pantheon, the monument built by Emperor Hadrian to honor the pagan gods. The structure is now said to be haunted

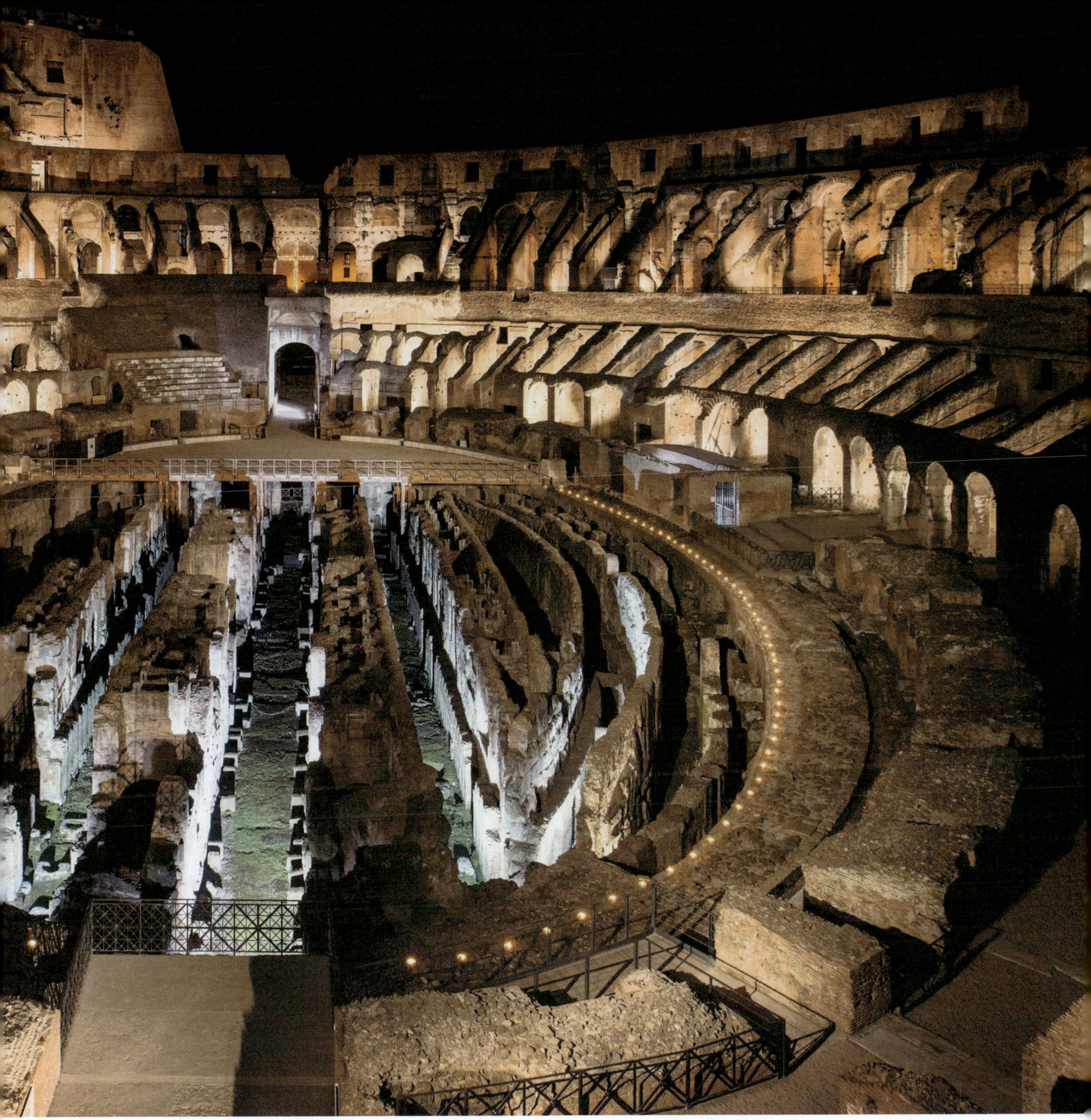

by ancient priests, and eerie blue lights have been seen in its interior.

Other supposedly haunted sites in the Eternal City include the Colosseum, host to the ghosts of dead gladiators; the skeleton-filled Capuchin Crypt; and the church of Santa Maria del Popolo, which is said to be haunted by Emperor Nero, who might have been buried on this spot. According to legend, so many people saw the mad emperor here that in 1099 Pope Paschal II was petitioned to exorcize his ghost, which ultimately led to the building of the church.

Skeptical about all this? So was Titus Livius, who, after relating Romulus's celestial disappearance, wrote that humans want to believe in this sort of phenomenon. "It is marvelous," he wrote, "how the army was soothed by the belief that had been created in [Romulus's] immortality." ■

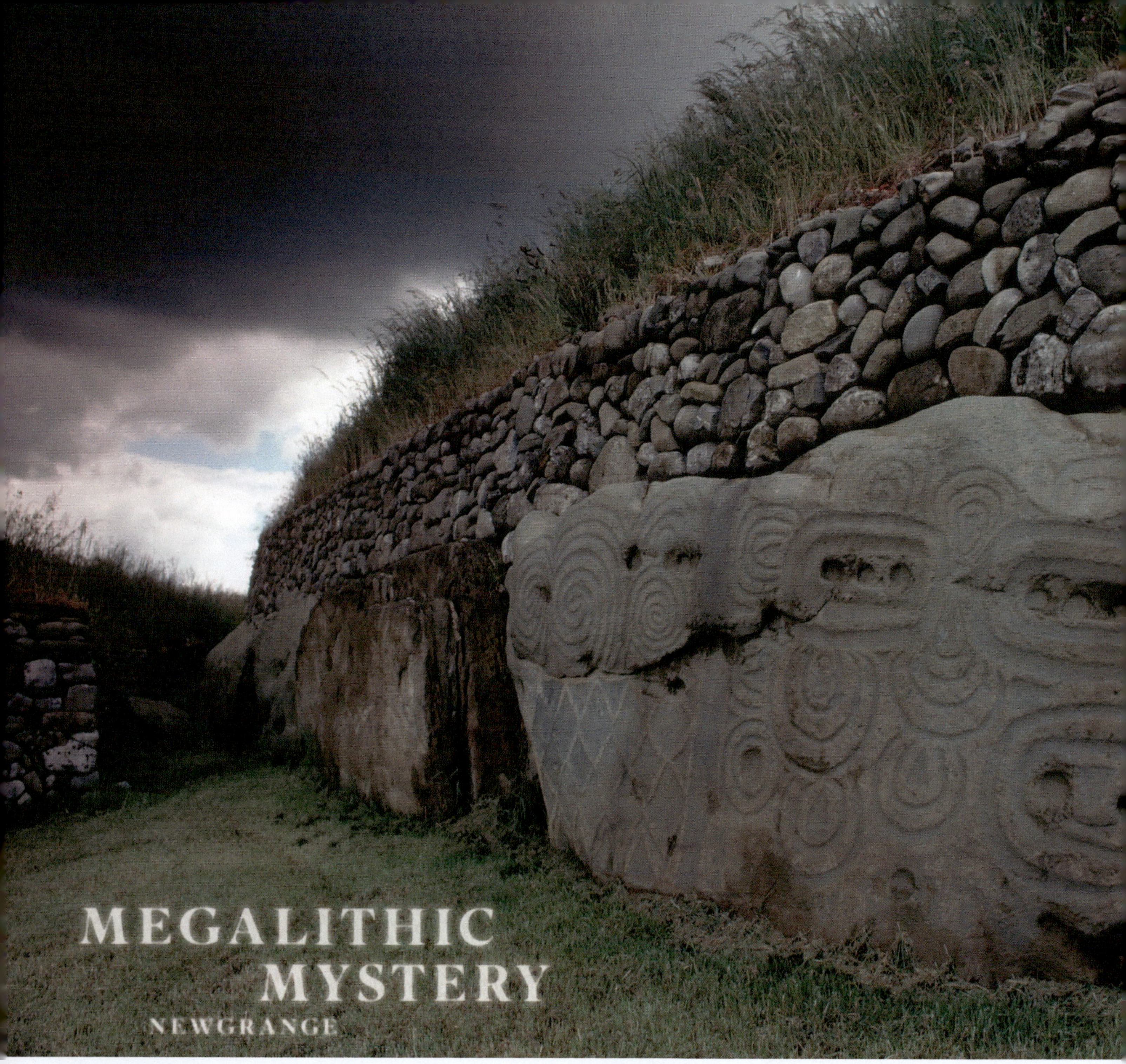

MEGALITHIC MYSTERY

NEWGRANGE

IN 1699, Charles Campbell—a landowner in Boyne Valley, County Meath, Ireland—asked his workers to dig for stone in a seemingly nondescript mound on his land. It wasn't long before the men discovered what they thought was the mouth to a cave, but this was no ordinary cavern.

It turned out to be the entrance to what would eventually be known as Newgrange, an elaborately decorated megalithic structure built in 3200 B.C. Predating Egypt's Great Pyramid of Giza by 700 years and Stonehenge by a few hundred, the World Heritage Site is one of the oldest buildings in the world. (So much for harvesting stones!)

In time, Newgrange was revealed as only one of more than 90 ancient structures (the most significant being Newgrange, Knowth, and Dowth), forming a complex known as Brú na

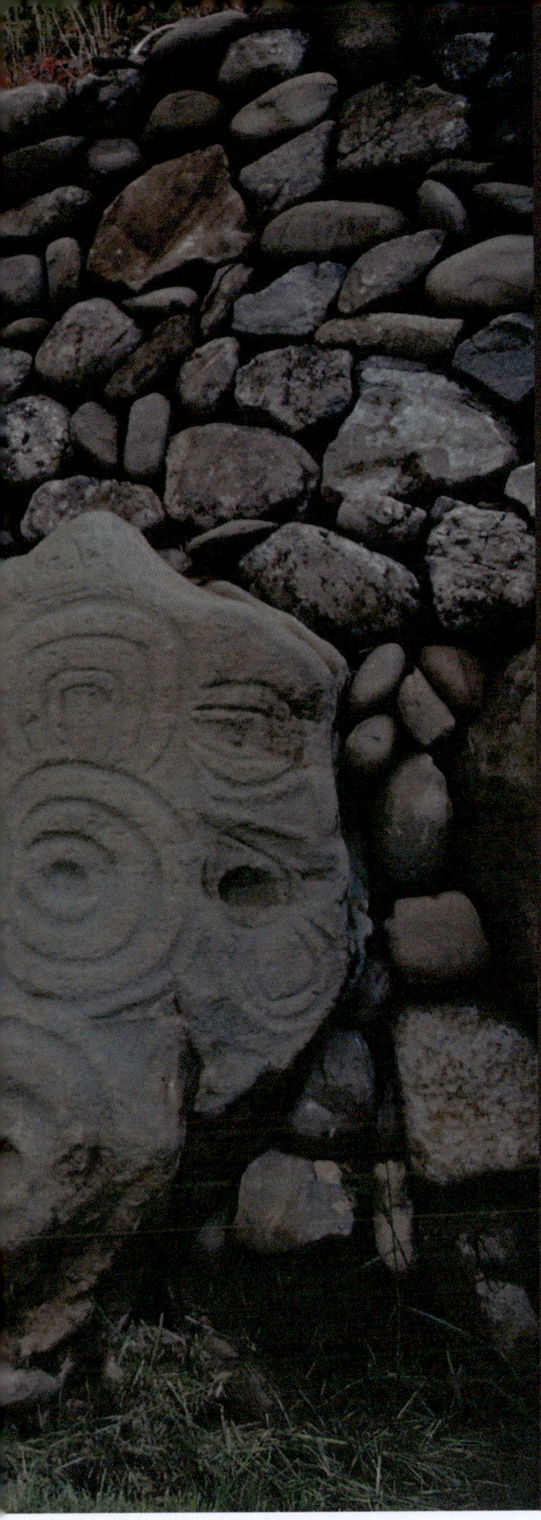

ADAM WOOLFITT

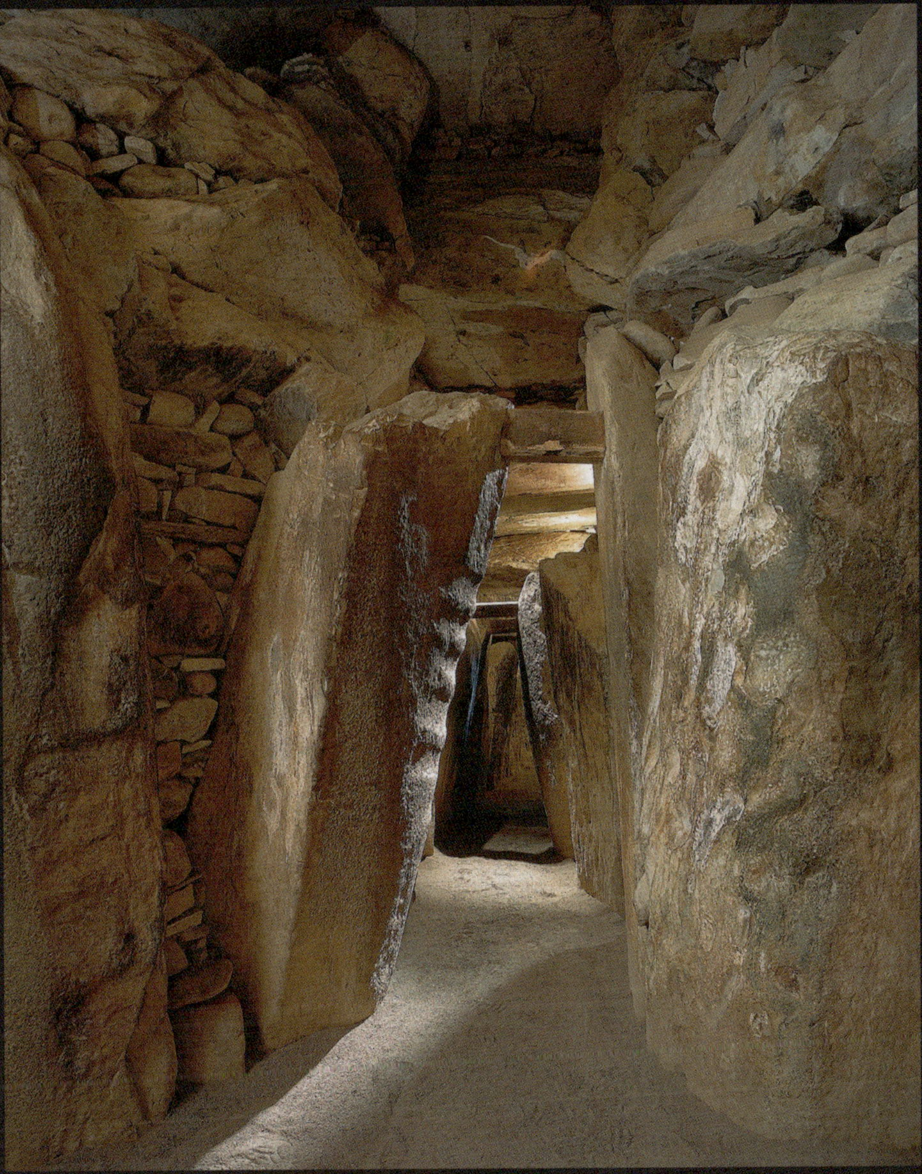

DEA/G. DAGLI ORTI/DE AGOSTINI/GETTY

LEFT: COVERED WITH ART that may have been symbolic or astronomical, Newgrange is synonymous with the folklore and legends of Ireland's mysterious prehistory. Above: A view of the structure's interior corridor, carefully calibrated to come to life with sunlight every winter solstice.

Bóinne, meaning the Palace of the Boyne. At first Newgrange was seen as only a passage tomb, meaning that it led to a funerary chamber where bodies, often cremated, were buried. But some believe it to be a temple, and it has been acknowledged as a place where ancient people encountered different realms of existence, other-dimensional beings, spirits, and dead ancestors.

"The three great Boyne tombs must have been sources of awe, wonder, and superstition from very early times, perhaps even from their very beginning," Michael and Claire O'Kelly wrote in *Newgrange: Archaeology, Art, and Legend.*

They still are. Crowds of people flock here every year during the winter solstice (the beginning of the Neolithic new year) when, every dawn for nearly a week in late December, a beam of sunlight gradually floods Newgrange's inner chamber through a portal precisely designed for that (perhaps astrological) purpose.

"Thin places" is what the Celts called spots where the line between the living and the dead, the mundane and the mystical, is almost permeable. Newgrange is without question one of these places, filled with not just the mysteries of prehistory but the lore and legends of the Emerald Isle. ■

THE MINERAL PALACE

THE WIELICZKA SALT MINES

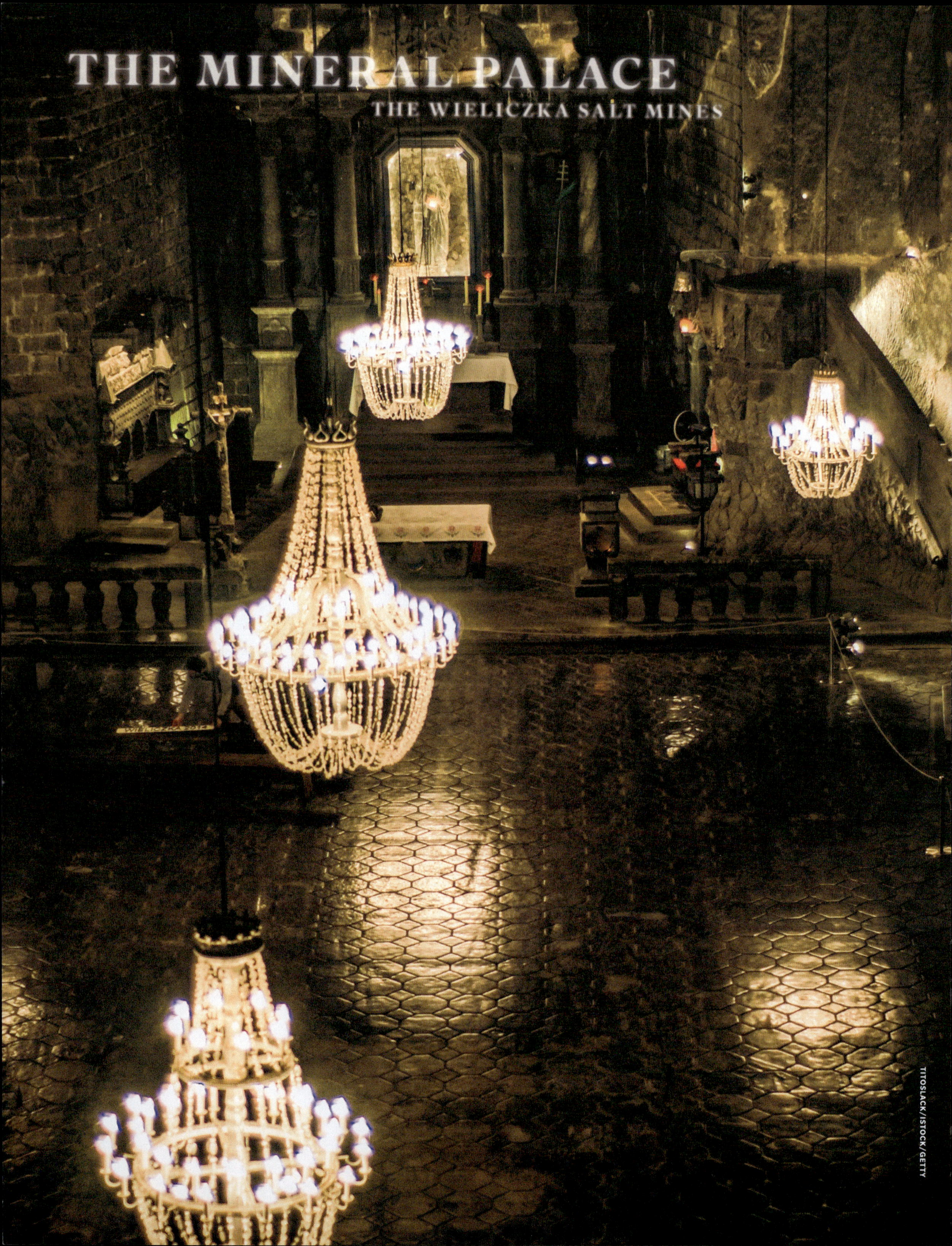

TITOSLACK/ISTOCK/GETTY

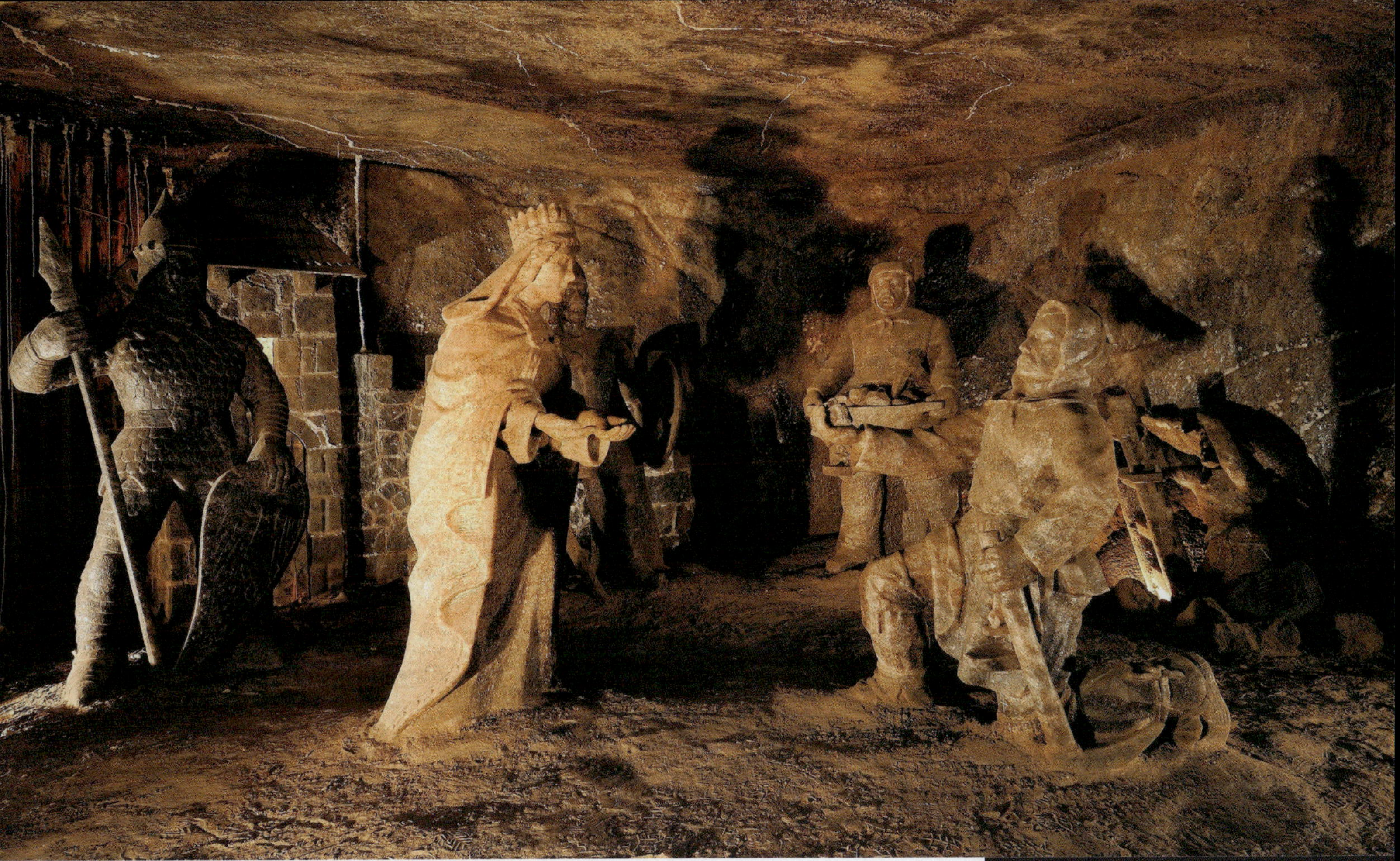

JEAN-BAPTISTE RABOUAN/LAIF/REDUX

BEGINNING in the 13th century and going up until 2007, southern Poland's Wieliczka Salt Mines produced table salt (believe it or not, it was once as valuable as oil is today). Well before Morton's, the miners meticulously and lovingly sculpted subterranean salt art, statues, chandeliers, and even 40 chapels—often at the risk of their own lives. (The most impressive chapel, St. Kinga, is the world's largest underground church.)

"There are many legends and stories about the mine at Wieliczka," according to the *Handbook of World Salt Resources.* One is that of the Hungarian Princess Kinga, the patron saint of Polish salt miners: After she tossed her engagement ring into a Hungarian mine, the story goes, it miraculously reappeared later in Wieliczka.

In the depths of this mineral palace, you'll find statues of the Seven Dwarves and even a "friendly ghost," a sort of sodium Casper. He is said to look out for the miners, warning them of imminent explosions or the presence of lethal methane by saying, "Do not go."

But this underground world has seen its share of tragedy. In the Jozef Pilsudski Chamber, a ferryboat capsized in a lake in 1915, killing a number of Prussian soldiers. These days, a salt statue of St. John of Nepomuk (a Bohemian saint who protects against floods and drowning) stands before the defunct boat.

In 1944, the Nazis forced Polish Jews to work on an assembly line for aircraft machinery in the Staszic Chamber; there the workers carved a Star of David that can still be seen.

These days, the mine has become not only a tourist attraction but an occasional destination spot for thrill-seekers (think bungee jumping, windsurfing, and hot air ballooning). Weddings and even business conferences are held in the depths, and the health resort offers—get this—algae facials . . . but no salt scrubs!

OPPOSITE: WIELICZKA Salt Mines' astonishingly elaborate Chapel of St. Kinga, near Krakow, Poland. Named for Poland's patron saint of miners, the chapel is one of 40 that were carved as spots for devout miners to pray for protection. More than 300 feet below ground, it was created by only three miners over the course of 67 years. The floor was hewn from a single block of salt, and even the chandelier is sodium. Above: A statue of St. Kinga (center).

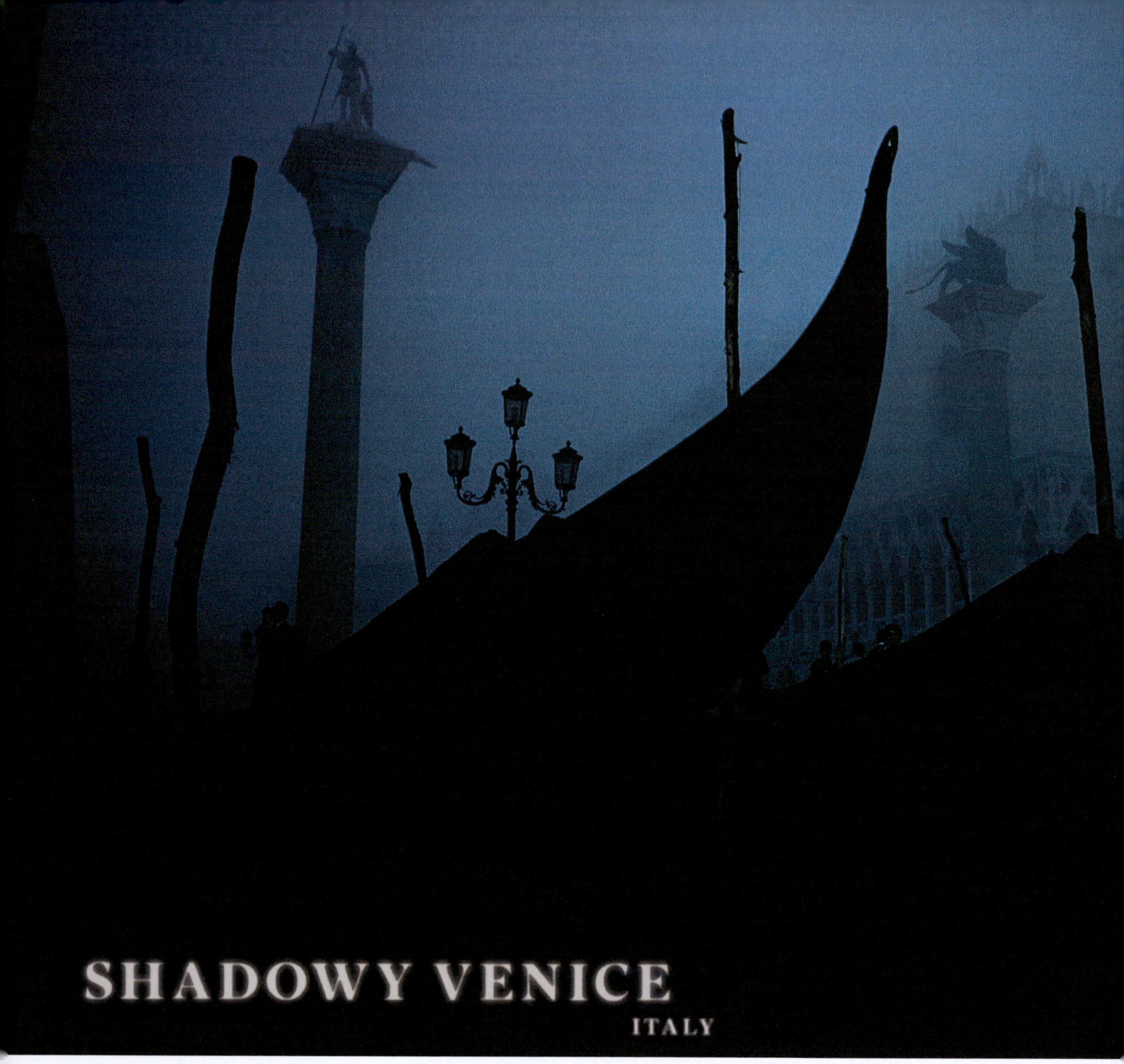

SHADOWY VENICE

ITALY

"WHEN AN EVIL MAN dies, he wakes up in Poveglia"—or so they say in Venice, referring to the deserted 17-acre island in the city's south lagoon that *Time* magazine called the world's most haunted.

Over the centuries, the island has seen mental institutions (unnecessary lobotomies) and thousands of plague victims (reportedly since Roman times), resulting in so many deaths that the soil is said to be 50 percent human ash. And the air is filled, they say, with ghosts, the most famous of which is a plague victim known as Little Maria, said to cry as she stares across the lagoon, pining for her lost home in Malamocco.

The place is so packed with rubble and institutional remains that tourists aren't allowed to set foot on the spot, but that may change

ERNST HAAS/GETTY

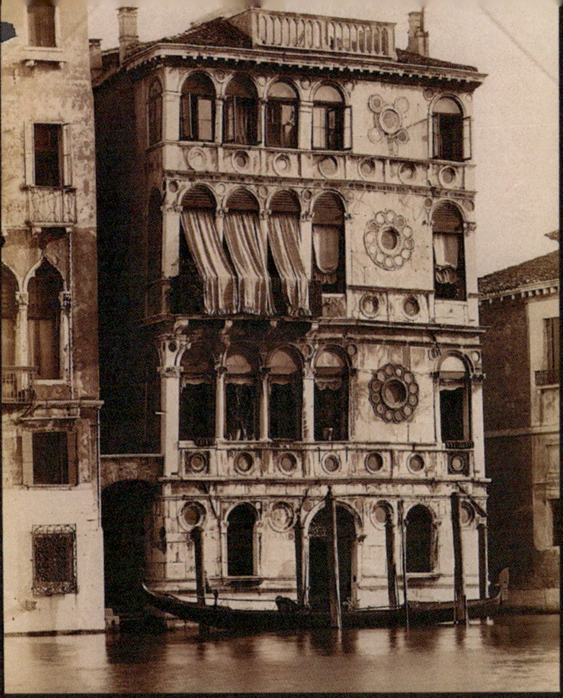

SEAN SEXTON COLLECTION/BRIDGEMAN IMAGES

FAR LEFT: SILHOUETTES of gondolas outlined against the Doge's Palace, one of the most notorious buildings in the city. It had a torture room and also served as a prison before a new one opened across the haunted Bridge of Sighs. At left: Ca'Dario, the 15th-century palazzo known as "The House of No Return," or in B-movie parlance "The House that Kills People." (A disproportionate number of people who have lived there have died in freak accidents, including the man who once managed the rock band the Who.) Below: The notorious Bridge of Sighs.

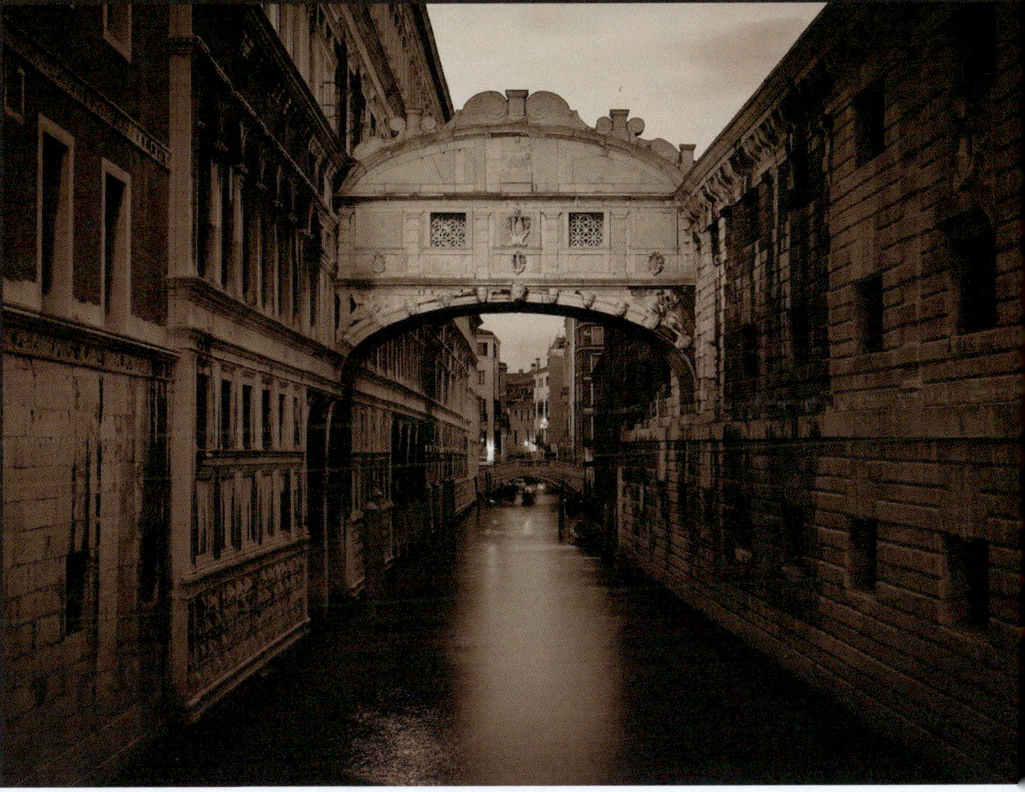

DOUGLAS PEARSON/GETTY

one day. Last year, attempting to pay off its debt, Italy sold the place to an Italian businessman for about $650,000. No word yet on his plans, but officials said they hoped it would become a luxury hotel.

Could the same thing happen with Ca' Dario, the 15th-century palazzo known as the "House of No Return"? An abnormally high percentage of people who have lived within its walls have died unnaturally, they say. Then there's Casa degli Spiriti (House of the Spirits), said to be inhabited by a suicide's ghost. And the aptly named Calle degli Assassini (Street of the Assassins) is haunted by the revenants of many who were murdered there.

Clearly, death in Venice is only the beginning. The many alleged spirits in the twisty, narrow streets of this labyrinthine city seem as present as the tourists who pack the famous Bridge of Sighs, where condemned men once crossed from the Doge's Palace to the prison on the other side of the canal. The bridge's name should be taken literally, since disembodied sighs have been heard here for centuries.

As the artist Arbit Blatas, who worked in Venice, wrote of the Veneto capital, "The play is finished, but the echoes remain." ■

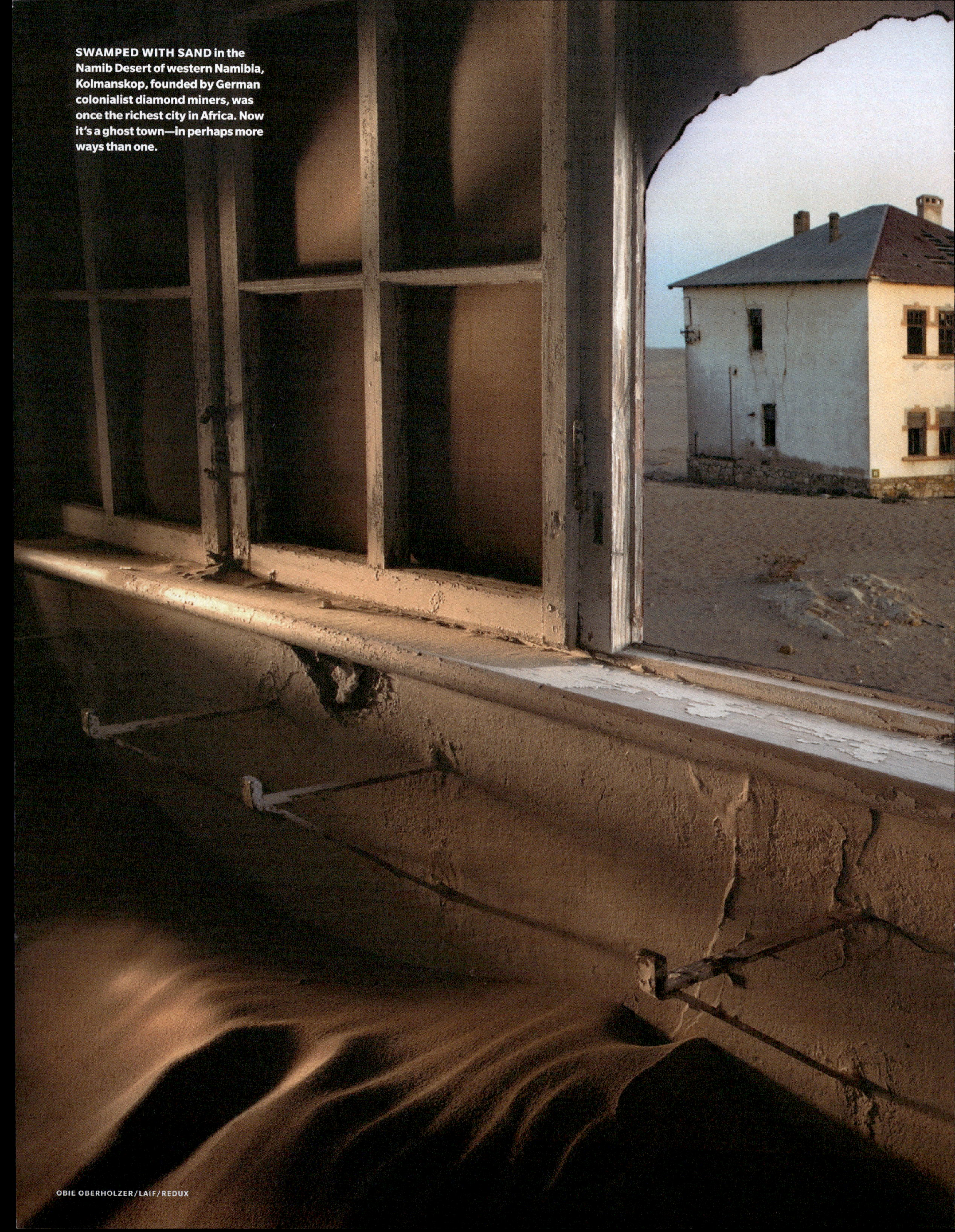

SWAMPED WITH SAND in the Namib Desert of western Namibia, Kolmanskop, founded by German colonialist diamond miners, was once the richest city in Africa. Now it's a ghost town—in perhaps more ways than one.

OBIE OBERHOLZER/LAIF/REDUX

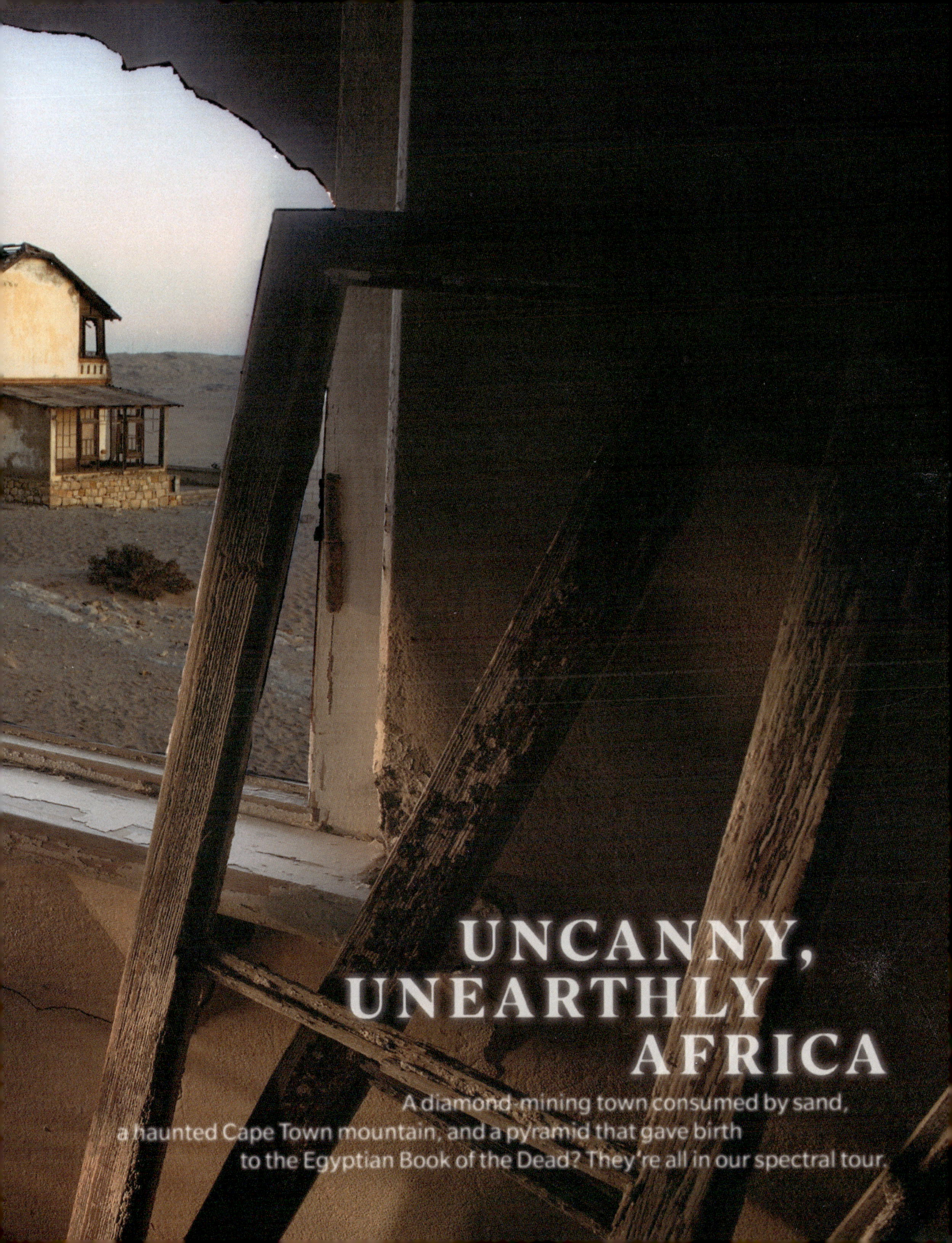

UNCANNY, UNEARTHLY AFRICA

A diamond-mining town consumed by sand, a haunted Cape Town mountain, and a pyramid that gave birth to the Egyptian Book of the Dead? They're all in our spectral tour.

THE GHOSTS OF THE GORGE

TABLE MOUNTAIN

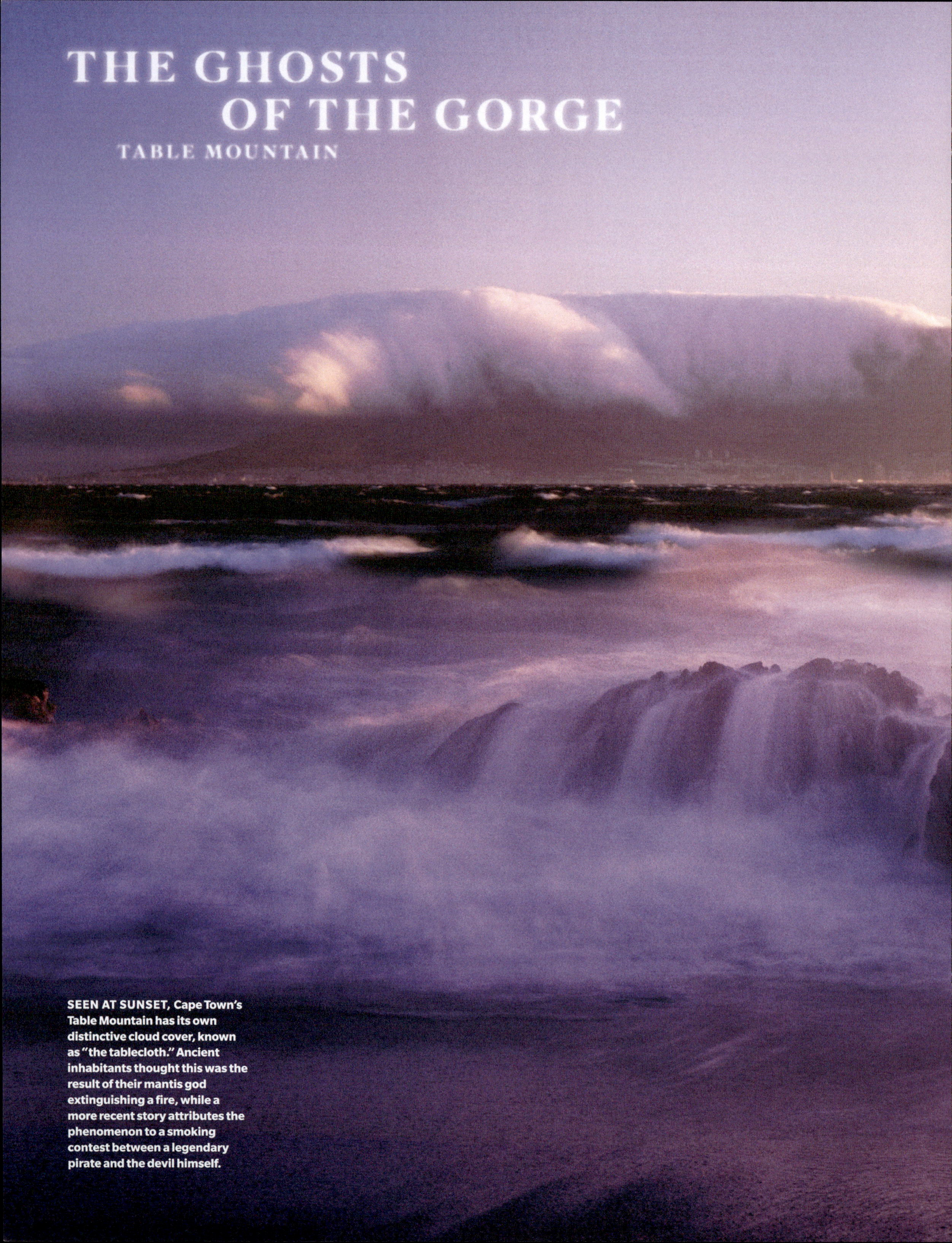

SEEN AT SUNSET, Cape Town's Table Mountain has its own distinctive cloud cover, known as "the tablecloth." Ancient inhabitants thought this was the result of their mantis god extinguishing a fire, while a more recent story attributes the phenomenon to a smoking contest between a legendary pirate and the devil himself.

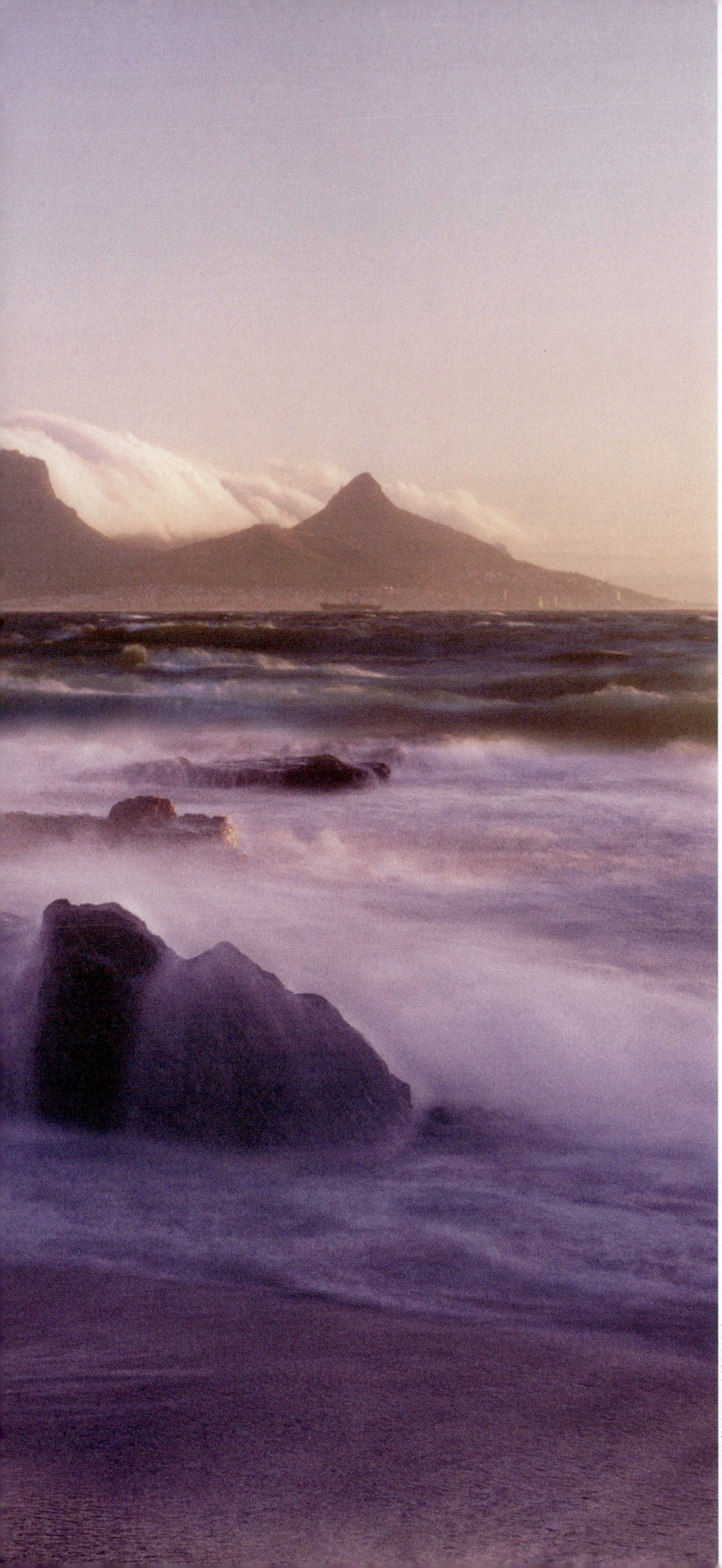
STEVE BLOOM IMAGES/ALAMY

IF YOU CLIMB Platteklip Gorge to the top of Table Mountain—Cape Town's iconic, cloud-shrouded backdrop—you will pass an abandoned house in the woods. Though it once supposedly belonged to a wine merchant, the ruins are now rumored to be the haunt of Aintjie Somers, according to Carrie Hampton's *Table Mountain to Cape Point*.

A slave who died from overwork and who now appears as an often mischievous, sometimes destructive spirit, Aintjie just might pelt you with stones on your way to the summit. Indeed, she is something of a local bogeywoman: Misbehaving children are warned, "Be good or Aintjie Somers will get you."

But she may not be your only companion on the gorge, which is known to be a favored haunt of mountain ghosts. One such spirit is thought to be that of a boy who plays a ghostly flute in Verlatenbosch (the Bush of the Forsaken). According to legend, the name was given when a man who held a grudge against the governor gave the official's son a flute that had been infected by a leper. After contracting the then-incurable disease, the boy spent the rest of his life—and perhaps eternity—playing his flute in the forest.

Though it's also supposedly home to ancient demons, "light beings," and giants, Table Mountain now offers such modern amenities as souvenir shops and a restaurant serving the likes of ostrich-sausage subs. Picnicking is also allowed, but it's a national park and a World Heritage Site, so those who leave their trash behind should watch out for Aintjie Somers. ■

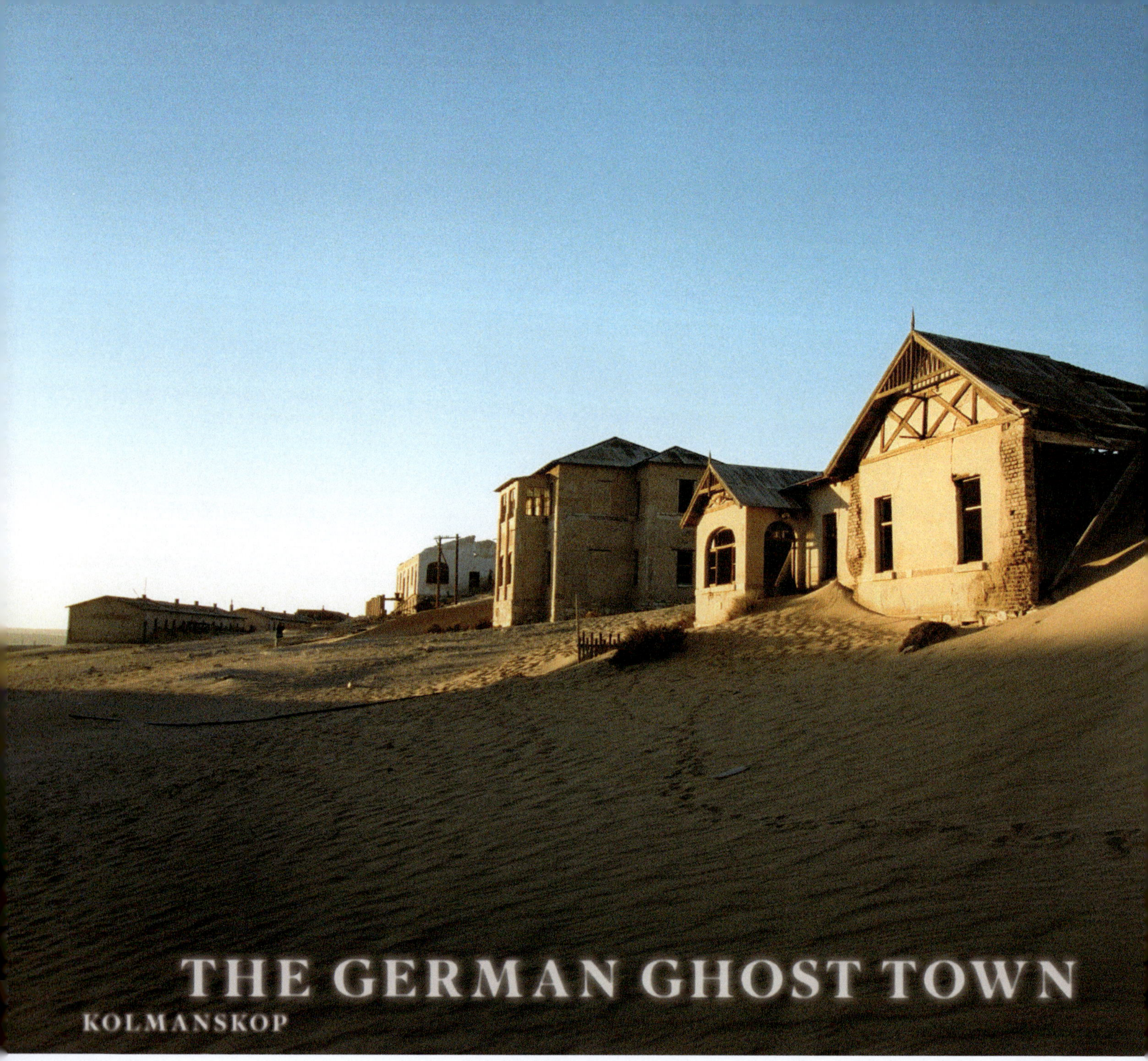

THE GERMAN GHOST TOWN

KOLMANSKOP

IN 1908, A RAILROAD WORKER named Zacharias Lewala found a sparkling stone buried in the sand of Sperrgebiet (the Prohibited Area), not far from the port of Lüderitz in Namibia. He brought it to his German boss, who quickly recognized it as a diamond, sparking a frenzy that quickly led to the construction of the German village of Kolmanskop.

Over the next few years, the diamond-mining enclave became the richest town in Africa, complete with luxurious homes, a bowling alley, a casino, an ice factory, and the first X-ray station in southern Africa. At its peak, the town was home to 300 German adults, 40 children, and 800 Owambo tribal workers.

But, like all boomtowns, it went bust. After reaching its zenith in the 1920s, Kolmanskop lost its edge when diamond deposits were discovered further southeast and local supply dwindled, a ton of the precious gems having been unearthed over the

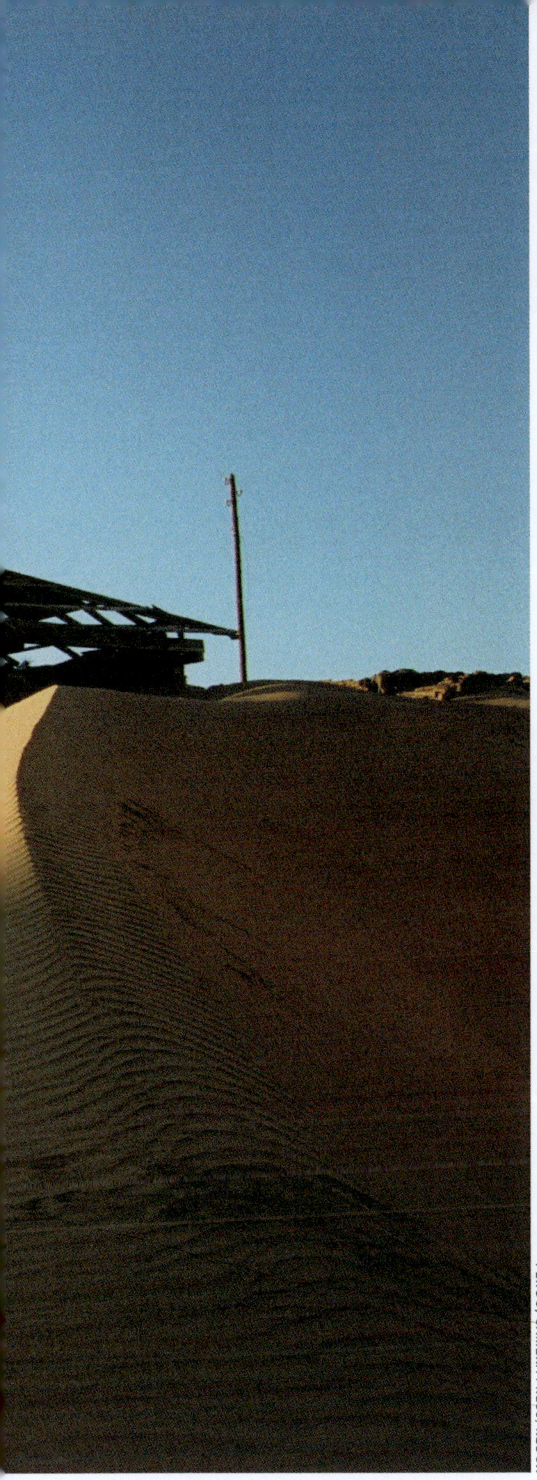

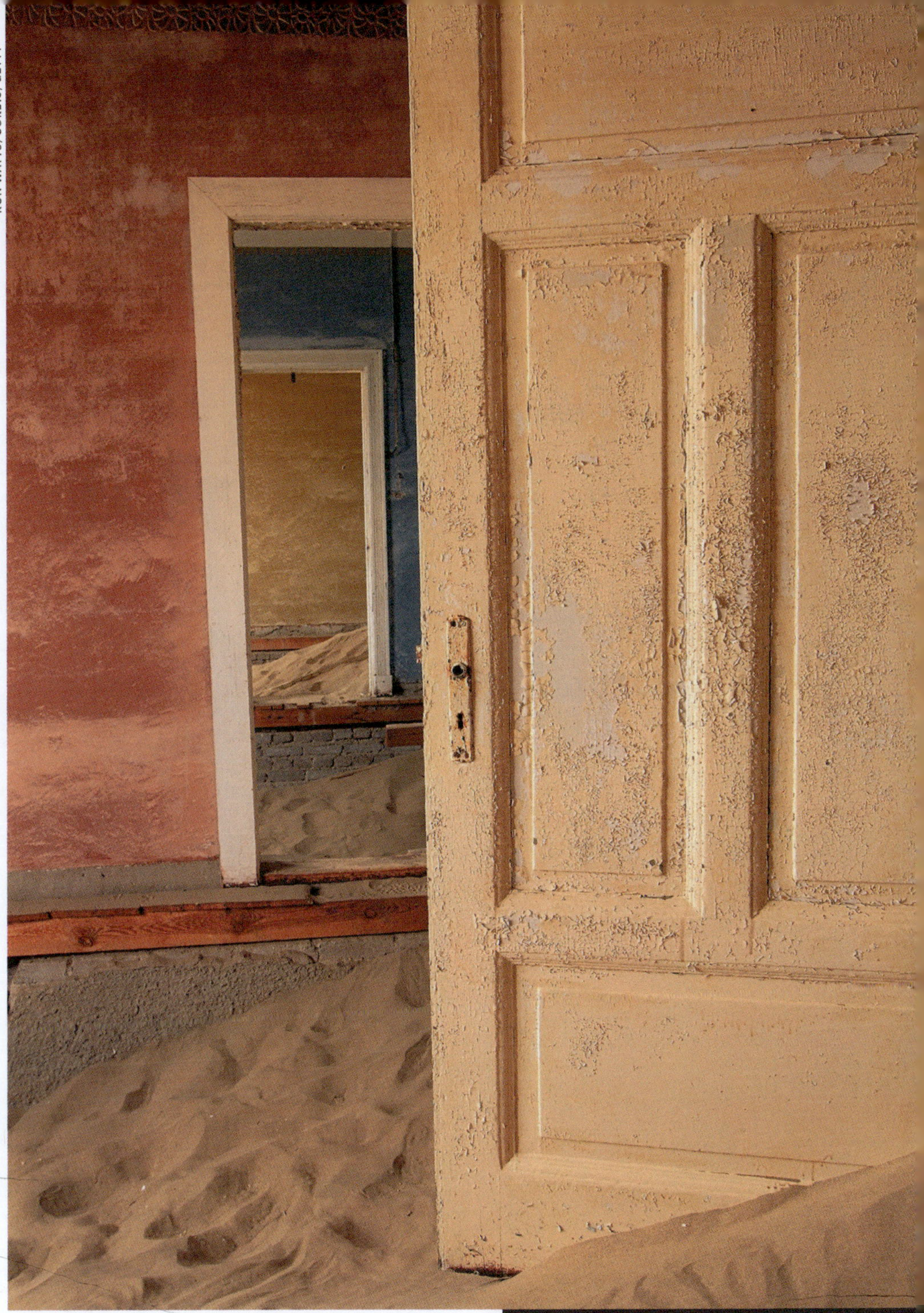

RON WATTS/CORBIS/GETTY

PEROU/CAMERA PRESS/REDUX

decades. The last residents left the town in the 1950s.

Now succumbing to the Namib Desert, Kolmanskop's dune-swamped ruins look like nothing so much as a surreal landscape straight from the brush of Giorgio de Chirico. Though there are other ghost towns in Namibia, this is justifiably the most famous, its otherworldly landscape having been used as a backdrop for many TV shows and movies.

Today, the Ghost Town Tavern (furnished with items from the original watering hole) is a tourist oasis, and the bowling alley appears in remarkably good shape, preserved by the dry climate. The butcher shop still stands, too, and that's where people have felt an eerie presence and have heard footsteps and voices. And tourists have seen "people" who vanish into thin air. The German miners of Kolmanskop are lost to history, of course, but their spirits, like diamonds, are forever. ▪

THE TOWN OF KOLMANSKOP was built on a fortune from diamonds. When the supply dried up after World War I, the town was abandoned. Today off the coast of Namibia, diamonds are also mined by divers using sonar to find them in the bed of the Atlantic Ocean.

BELOW: INSIDE THE TOMB of Idu at Giza, Egypt. At right: Saqqara's Pyramid of Unas, where the magical spells that became the Egyptian Book of the Dead were found. (The damage above the door has since been repaired.) The text was supposed to guide the recently deceased into the afterlife, but if tales of lingering ghosts in Cairo are any indication, it wasn't always successful.

TOMBS OF THE PHARAOHS

PYRAMIDS OF GIZA

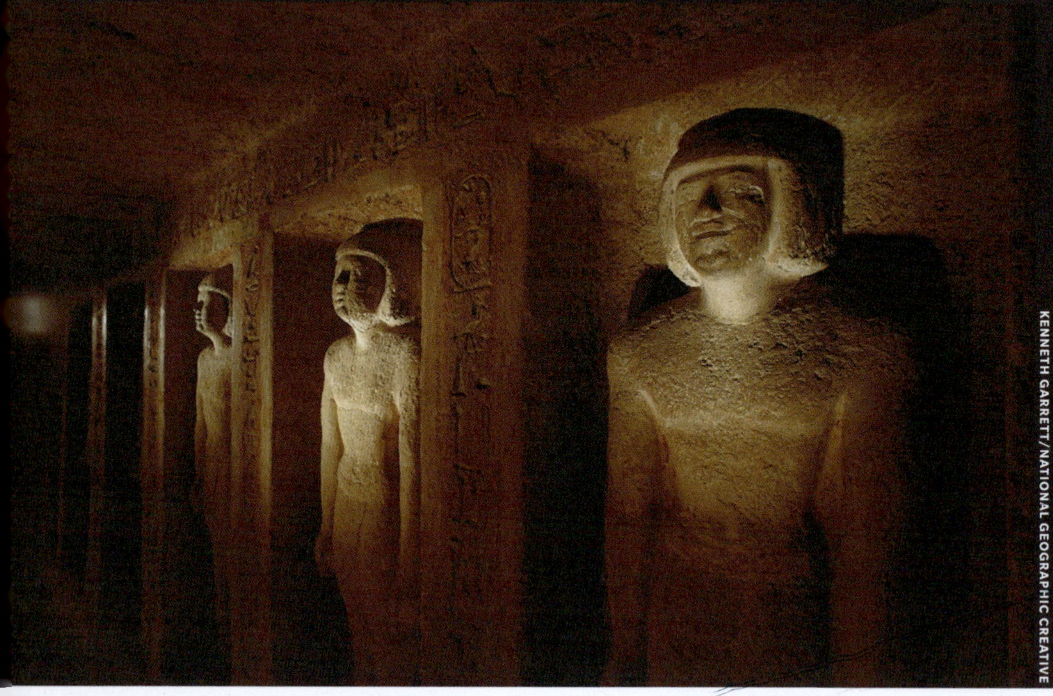

KENNETH GARRETT/NATIONAL GEOGRAPHIC CREATIVE

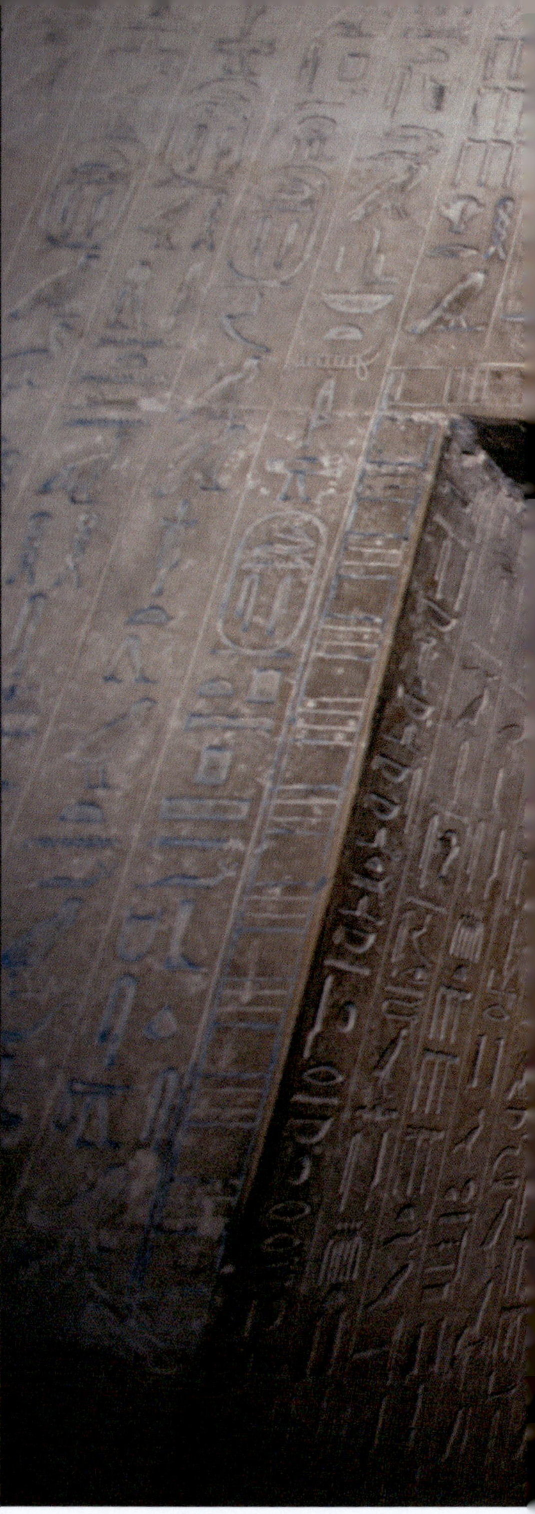

CARVED ON THE WALLS and sarcophagi of the pyramids of Saqqara, about 20 miles outside Cairo, are magic spells designed to help the ancient Egyptian pharaohs navigate the afterlife, and that later became part of the Egyptian Book of the Dead. They're a kind of celestial map, detailing all the ways in which a pharaoh's spirit could travel, and explaining how to reanimate his corpse. "Take your head, collect your bones," one verse reads. "Gather your limbs, shake the earth from your flesh!"

But it seems some pharaohs didn't get the memo: People have claimed that the ghost of Akhenaten, for one, appears in the Egyptian desert. And Khufu, for whom the Great Pyramid of Giza was built, is said to leave his burial place—the largest pyramid in the world—at midnight.

The spooky happenings aren't

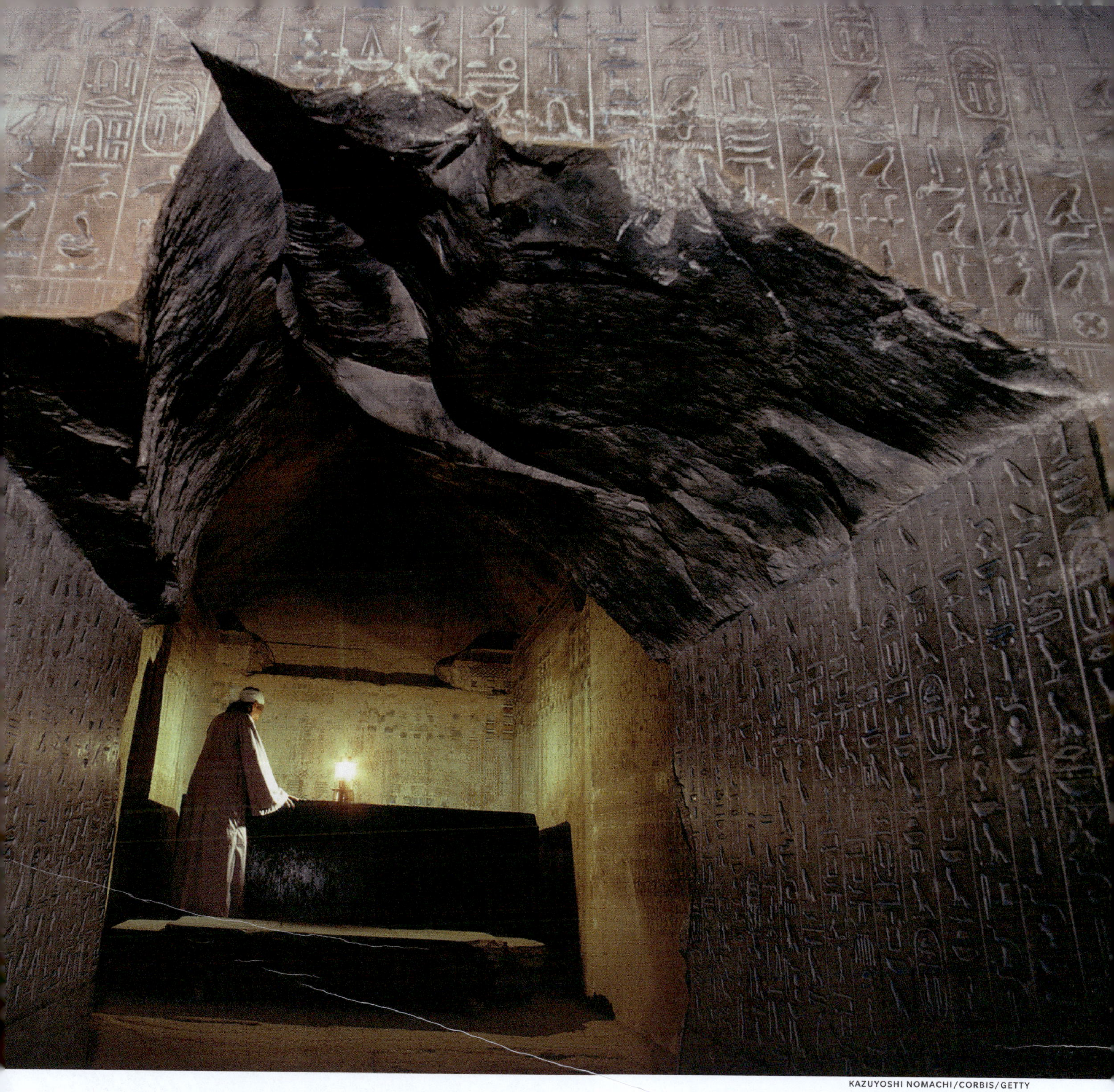

KAZUYOSHI NOMACHI/CORBIS/GETTY

limited to ghosts, though. The so-called Mummy's Curse is, according to legend, not just some Boris Karloff movie. In March 1923, popular British novelist Marie Corelli announced that "the most dire punishment follows any rash intruder into a sealed tomb." The public enthusiastically agreed when George Herbert, the fifth earl of Carnarvon, who had bankrolled the excavation of King Tut's tomb, died of pneumonia a month after the pronouncement. (The cause was most likely an infected mosquito bite, not the actions of an avenging mummy.) A radiologist who supposedly X-rayed the remains of the boy king died of a mysterious illness; a man succumbed to pneumonia after visiting Tut's tomb, and a member of the excavation team allegedly died of arsenic poisoning.

Hokum? Not according to Shirley MacLaine, a star of *Downton Abbey* in its third and fourth seasons, who claimed that Highclere Castle, where the series was filmed, is haunted by Egyptian ghosts. (Carnarvon was master of the estate when he died.) "They had the tomb of King Tut in the basement," she said.

Maybe the ancient Egyptians were right: The spirits of their dead live on. But who knew they'd spend their afterlife among the Crawleys? ■

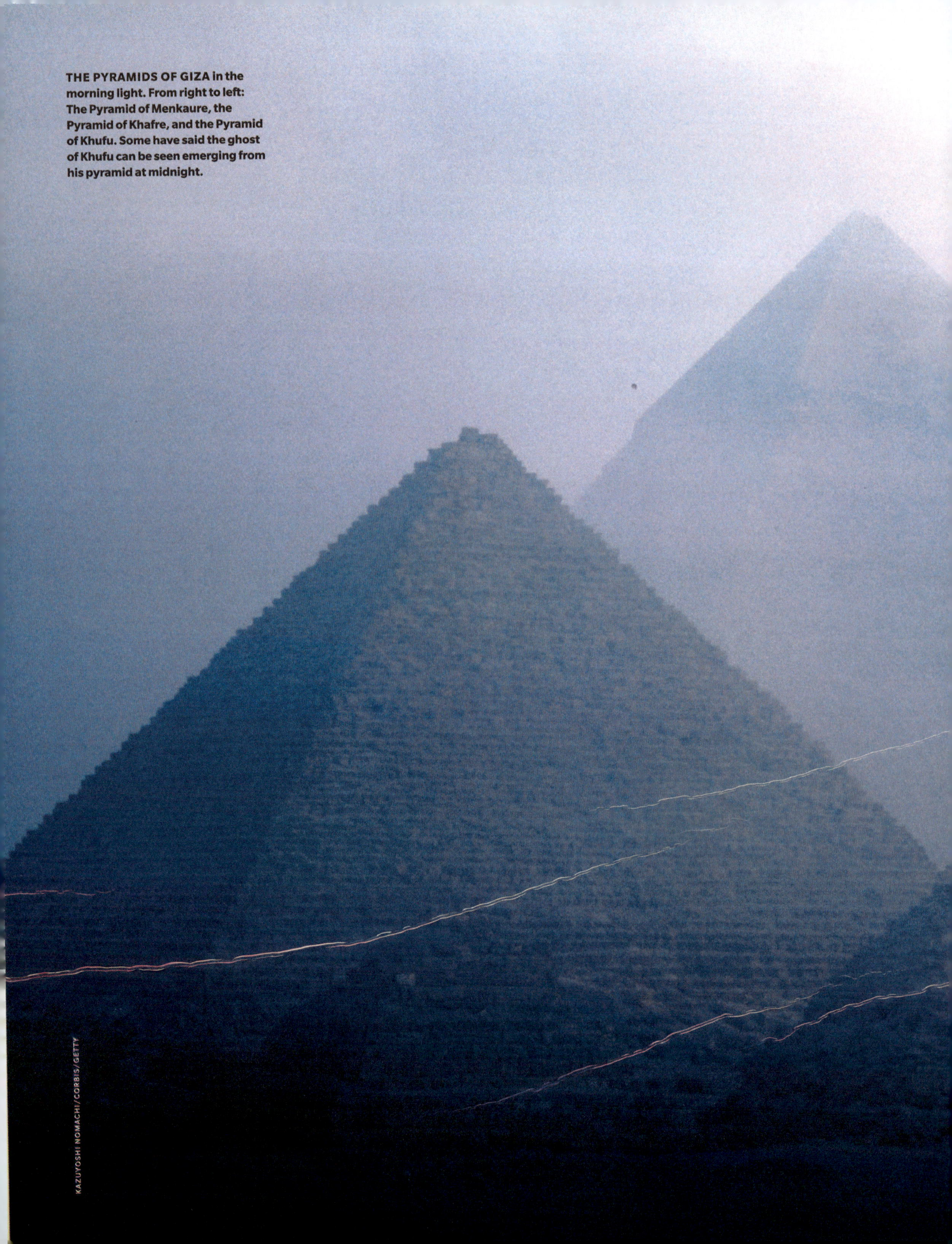

THE PYRAMIDS OF GIZA in the morning light. From right to left: The Pyramid of Menkaure, the Pyramid of Khafre, and the Pyramid of Khufu. Some have said the ghost of Khufu can be seen emerging from his pyramid at midnight.

KAZUYOSHI NOMACHI/CORBIS/GETTY